The Contribution of Family Medicine to Improving Health Systems

A GUIDEBOOK FROM THE
WORLD ORGANIZATION OF FAMILY DOCTORS
Second Edition

Edited by

MICHAEL KIDD

President, World Organization of Family Doctors (WONCA)
Executive Dean, Faculty of Health Sciences, Flinders University, Australia

CHAPTER LEAD AUTHORS

Cynthia Haq, Jan De Maeseneer, Jeffrey Markuns, Hernan Montenegro,
Waris Qidwai, Igor Svab, Wim Van Lerberghe, and Tiago Villanueva

ORIGINAL EDITION AUTHORS

Charles Boelen, Cynthia Haq, Vincent Hunt, Marc Rivo, and Edward Shahady

Foreword by

DR MARGARET CHAN

Director-General
World Health Organization

Radcliffe Publishing
London • New York

Radcliffe Publishing Ltd
33–41 Dallington Street
London
EC1V 0BB
United Kingdom

www.radcliffehealth.com

British Library Cataloguing in Publication Data

A catalogue record for this book is available from the British Library.

ISBN-13: 978 184619 554 9

The paper used for the text pages of this book
is FSC® certified. FSC (The Forest Stewardship
Council®) is an international network to promote
responsible management of the world's forests.

Typeset by Darkriver Design, Auckland, New Zealand
Printed and bound by TJI Digital, Padstow, Cornwall, UK

Contents

List of boxes and tables

Boxes

Tables

Foreword

Human rights and dignity, fairness, participation and inclusion have long been core values of WHO. They underpin our contribution to global welfare and sustainable development. Delivering health services in line with these values remains a major challenge in the health sector globally, despite tremendous gains made over the past few decades. Those who end up suffering the most are vulnerable populations, especially in low-income settings. Investing in health and health systems thus remains essential not only for improving overall health service delivery but also to overcome poverty, build human capital, and promote sustainable development.

Universal health coverage (UHC), based on available, acceptable, accessible and affordable health services of high quality, is of extraordinary significance in delivering better health to all, and is a unifying goal for health system development, as envisioned by Alma Ata and other more recent global declarations. The path to universal health coverage requires considerable investment in improving health services based on primary healthcare principles and values. Health services can be too costly for a population (affordability barrier), too far away (accessibility barrier), poorly staffed with long waiting hours (availability barrier), or do not conform to people's cultural and gender preferences (acceptability barrier). And when people do access services, they are often of poor quality, and in some cases, even harmful. In addition, services tend to be fragmented, curative, hospital-based and disease-oriented, all of which further hampers access to comprehensive and quality care services.

Launching and sustaining primary healthcare as an integral part of a comprehensive health system requires several key elements: among others, good governance, adequate and sustainable financing, and an able and motivated workforce. An important component of the latter is family medicine, within the context of a multidisciplinary team working closely with the family and community, and delivered around people's health needs. These elements must come together to help overcome the barriers of change, draw on the lessons of the past, and identify specific avenues for the future.

This guidebook systematically analyses the contribution of family medicine to high quality primary healthcare in addressing the challenges faced by current health systems, and provides options for moving forward. It serves as a pragmatic guide to potential strategies for putting in place family care teams which effectively contribute to health sector development within a variety of contexts. I believe that the adaptation of family medicine models to the local context is particularly relevant, and thus demands special attention.

I look forward to continued collaboration between WHO and WONCA and encourage more partnerships of this kind to promote the important agenda of high quality, people-centred, and integrated health service delivery for universal health coverage.

Dr Margaret Chan
Director-General
World Health Organization
May 2013

Executive Summary

This guidebook shows how family medicine can help countries throughout the world maintain and improve their citizens' health and well-being by developing a more productive, coordinated, and cost-effective approach to health care. It describes:

➤ the rationale for structuring health systems to be more responsive to the needs of people
➤ a vision of optimal health services delivery based on primary health care
➤ challenges to achieving this vision
➤ family medicine's response to these challenges
➤ strategies for developing and strengthening family practice within countries.

Throughout this book, flexible approaches are advocated for implementing options that are consistent with each country's specific health care needs, resources, and cultural expectations. Even though health systems are confronted with universal challenges, successful implementation involves effective responses at the local level.

In order to develop responsive and sustainable health systems, **Chapter 1** considers the critical importance of balancing complementary viewpoints and conflicting priorities among those who contribute to health care. These divergent perspectives can be resolved by focusing on basic unifying priorities such as the health status of each person within the community, the collective health of the population, and equitable distribution of health care. In this manner, shared solutions can be developed that maximize the strengths and aptitudes of partners whose contributions are indispensable for a coherent approach to health services delivery. These solutions vary according to the socioeconomic and developmental circumstances of a society. Thus a variety of representative scenarios are described along with relevant concerns and critical decisions that leaders will need to make in order to implement family medicine optimally within their specific countries.

The characteristics and functions of health care delivery systems, as described in **Chapter 2**, can also guide decisions that involve competing interests. This chapter delineates a variety of current challenges to health care that add further complexity to the task. When approaching these difficult issues there is mounting evidence that a key determinant for improving people's health is the manner in which a country organizes its available resources. The most cost-effective way to decrease morbidity and mortality in a population is through a well-developed system of primary health care services that ensure accessible, comprehensive, coordinated, and people-centered care – characteristics that are associated with positive health outcomes. The composition of the health care workforce in such a system is critical, not only to deliver high-quality primary care but also to avoid excessive overutilization of scarce personnel and undue reliance on expensive technology, both of which are major determinants of the cost of care.

Chapter 3 explains why family doctors can make a significant contribution to this primary health care infrastructure. It describes the attributes of family doctors, their roles and responsibilities, and the quality and cost-effectiveness of their work. Their competence is developed through participating in rigorous preparation deliberately based on the needs of the population they serve. Their contribution is further enhanced when their education is infused with greater emphasis on public and community health. Specifically trained family doctors are prepared to provide people-centered care in a comprehensive and continuous manner to all patients within the community. They coordinate care among health providers, thus linking the community to the academic medical centers, the village health workers to the consultant medical specialists, and their patients to a wide array of available resources. Their flexibility allows them to adapt to the specific needs of the community they serve as well as to its changing epidemiological patterns and variations in available resources. Because of these qualities, family doctors add value to systems of primary care. They, and similarly oriented health professionals such as nurses and social workers, empower one another in a mutually reinforcing manner.

In order to fulfill the roles described in **Chapter 3**, family doctors need training that will allow them to master the distinct body of knowledge, attitudes, and skills that are necessary for optimal practice in the communities they serve. **Chapter 4** outlines the continuum of this education that begins in medical school, extends through specialty training, is sustained through a process of continuing medical education, and is nourished through professional development of teaching faculty. Emphasis is placed on the importance of educating physicians in ambulatory settings with the same academic rigor that has previously been reserved for the hospital environment. Thus the community becomes the clinical and research laboratory. These settings do not necessarily involve new investments. Existing structures, with moderate modifications, can usually be converted into teaching environments that are relevant to the needs of trainees as well as to the needs of society.

A supportive environment is necessary for optimal practice. **Chapter 5** delineates various components of this environment that need to be fostered in order for family doctors to contribute most effectively to a country's health care system. It calls for unified efforts among policy makers, health managers, health professionals, academic institutions, and community representatives. Family medicine is ideally suited to strengthening health systems by integrating individual and community health activities. However, this requires dedicated leadership, institutional commitment, strategic policy development, and appropriate resources.

One of the major global challenges facing family medicine is its effective implementation in many lower- and upper-middle income countries. Building on the experiences of Brazil, China, the Eastern Mediterranean Region, and Thailand, **Chapter 6** outlines lessons learned from the development of family medicine in these countries and builds the case for the need and feasibility of introducing family medicine even in medium- and low-resource settings.

Compared with the rest of the world, health care in Africa is characterized by a huge discrepancy between the high burden of disease and the scarcity of health care workers to carry this burden. Family medicine offers opportunities to address these challenges and **Chapter 7** provides an overview of the development of family medicine in Africa including examples from South Africa and nations in East Africa and West Africa, and ways to overcome challenges in the implementation of family medicine and see improvements in primary care delivery to people in some of the most resource-poor nations of the world.

In spite of the formidable challenges involved in achieving the expectations described in this guidebook, the quest to maintain and improve the health and well-being of people throughout the world is enriching. It adds substantial meaning to the lives of those who contribute to a process that joins the human family in a common undertaking based on intrinsic respect for the dignity of each individual. The roots of this process run as deep as humanity's oldest efforts to alleviate suffering, yet they are nourished by the approaches described in the following pages that draw on current developments in education and patient care, recent epidemiological research, and ongoing examples of successful implementation among diverse communities throughout the world.

Glossary

appropriate care: (i) care that meets the health needs of the entire population; (ii) care that is effective and based on the best available scientific evidence; (iii) interventions that are safe and that do not cause any harm or suffering; and priorities for the allocation and organization of resources that are based on equity and economic efficiency.[1]

burden of disease: a measurement of the gap between current health status and an ideal situation where everyone lives into old age, free of disease and disability.[2]

community medicine: specialty of medicine concerned with the health of specific populations or groups; focuses on health of the community as a whole rather than individuals; includes epidemiology, screening, and environmental health and is concerned with promotion of health, prevention of disease and disability, and rehabilitation, through collective social actions, often provided by state or local health authorities.

comprehensiveness of care: the extent to which the spectrum of care and range of resources made available responds to the full range of health problems in a given community. Comprehensive care encompasses health promotion and prevention interventions as well as diagnosis and treatment or referral and palliation. It includes chronic or long-term home care, and, in some models, social services.[3]

continuity of care: a term used to indicate one or more of the following attributes of care: (i) the provision of services that are coordinated across levels of care – primary care and referral facilities, across settings and providers; (ii) the provision of care throughout the life cycle; (iii) care that continues uninterrupted until the resolution of an episode of disease or risk; (iv) the degree to which a series of discrete health care events are experienced by people as coherent and interconnected over time, and are consistent with their health needs and preferences.[4]

disease management: coordinated information and intervention system for populations that suffer from diseases that share the value of self-care in their treatment and control. They focus on patients with specific diagnoses; they target diseases that are highly prevalent, that require intensive or high-cost care, or that represent high drug costs; and they focus on interventions whose results can be measured and for which significant variations in clinical practice have been described.[5]

family doctor: a medical practitioner who is a specialist trained to provide health care services for all individuals regardless of age, sex, or type of health problem; provides primary and continuing care for entire families within their communities; addresses physical, psychological, and social problems; coordinates comprehensive health care services with other specialists as needed; may also be known as a family physician or a general practitioner in some countries.

family medicine: specialty of medicine concerned with providing comprehensive care to individuals and families and integrating biomedical, behavioral, and social sciences; an academic medical discipline that includes comprehensive health care services, education, and research; known as general practice in some countries.

family physician: see *family doctor.*

family practice: health care services provided by family doctors; characterized by comprehensive, continuous, coordinated, collaborative, personal, family and community-oriented services; comprehensive medical care with a particular emphasis on the family unit; known as general practice in some countries.

first level of care: the entry point into the health care system, at the interface between services and community. Where the first level of care satisfies a number of quality criteria it is called primary care. See *primary care.*

general practice: see *family practice.*

general practitioner: see *family doctor.*

health: the state of complete physical, mental and social well-being and not merely the absence of disease or infirmity.[11]

health inequality: is the generic term used to designate differences, variations, and disparities in the health achievements of individuals and groups. Health inequality is a descriptive term that need not imply moral judgment. It is a dimensional concept, simply referring to measurable quantities,[6] differences in health status or in the distribution of health determinants between different population groups. Some health inequalities are attributable to biological variations or free choice and others are attributable to the external environment and conditions mainly outside the control of individuals concerned.[7]

health inequity: refers to those inequalities in health that are deemed to be unfair or stemming from some form of injustice. The identification of health inequities entails normative judgment premised upon (i) one's theories of justice; (ii) one's theories of society; and (iii) one's reasoning underlying the genesis of health inequalities. It is a political concept, expressing a moral commitment to social justice.[6]

health service: any service (i.e., not limited to medical or clinical services) aimed at contributing to improved health or to the diagnosis, treatment, and rehabilitation of sick people.[8]

health system: (i) all the activities whose primary purpose is to promote, restore, and/or maintain health;[3] (ii) the people, institutions, and resources, arranged together in accordance with established policies, to improve the health of the population they service, while responding to people's legitimate expectations and protecting them against the cost of ill-health through a variety of activities whose primary intent is to improve health;[9] (iii) the ensemble of all public and private organizations, institutions, and resources mandated to improve, maintain, or restore health. Health systems encompass both personal and population services, as well as activities to influence the policies and actions of other sectors to address the social, environmental, and economic determinants of health.[10]

levels of the health system: functional subsets of the health system that focus on delivering care to specific groups; the primary or community level delivers essential services on the local level; the secondary level delivers selected services, usually by consultants or specialty physicians; the tertiary level delivers services needed by a smaller subset of the population, usually in hospitals and often requiring sophisticated technology; the quaternary level is also used sometimes as an extension of tertiary care in reference to medicine of advanced levels which are highly specialized and not widely accessed.

people-centered care: care that is focused and organized around the health needs and expectations of people and communities rather than on diseases. People-centered care extends the concept of patient-centered care to individuals, families, communities, and society. Whereas patient-centered care is commonly understood as focusing on the individual seeking care – the patient – people-centered care encompasses these clinical encounters and also includes attention to the health of people in their communities and their crucial role in shaping health policy and health services.[12]

personal health services: Health services targeted at the individual. These include, among others, health promotion, timely disease prevention, diagnosis and treatment, rehabilitation, palliative care, acute care and long-term care services.[13]

primary care: often used interchangeably with first level of care. (i) The part of a health services system that assures person focused care over time to a defined population, accessibility to facilitate receipt of care when it is first needed, comprehensiveness of care in the sense that only rare or unusual manifestations of ill health are referred elsewhere, and coordination of care such that all facets of care (wherever received) are integrated. Quality features of primary care include effectiveness, safety, people-centeredness, comprehensiveness, continuity, and integration.[3,14] (ii) The provision of integrated, accessible health care services by clinicians who are accountable for addressing a large majority of personal health care needs, developing a sustained partnership with patients, and practicing in the context of family and community.[15] Family medicine/general practice is a component of primary care.

primary health care: a health reform movement launched at Alma-Ata in 1978 to move toward health for all. (i) The year 1978: essential health care based on practical, scientifically sound, and socially acceptable methods and technology made universally accessible to individuals and families in the community through their full participation and at a cost that the community and country can afford to maintain at every stage of their development in the spirit of self-reliance and self-determination. It forms an integral part of both the country's health system, of which it is the central function and the main focus, and of the overall social and economic development of the community.[16] (ii) The 1980s: the set of activities outlined in the Declaration of Alma-Ata: education concerning prevailing health problems and the methods of preventing and controlling them; promotion of food supply and proper nutrition; an adequate supply of safe water and basic sanitation; maternal and child health care, including family planning; immunization against the major infectious diseases; prevention and control of locally endemic diseases; appropriate treatment of common diseases and injuries; and provision of essential drugs. (iii) The 1990s: a level of care, that is the point of entry to the health services system (see *primary care*). (iv) 2008: a set of policy orientations and reforms needed to move toward health for all: moving toward universal coverage; shifting service delivery to people-centered primary care; ensuring health in all policies; promoting inclusive leadership and governance.[3] See *Primary health care reforms*.

primary health care-based health system: health system organized and operated so as to make the right to the highest attainable level of health the main goal while maximizing the equity and solidarity. A primary health care-based health system comprises a core set of structural and functional elements that guarantee universal coverage and access to services that are acceptable to the population and that enhance equity. It provides comprehensive integrated and appropriate care over time, emphasizes prevention, promotion, and first-contact primary care as well as intersectoral actions to address other determinants of health and equity.[1]

primary health care reforms: policy reforms need to move toward health for all: moving toward universal coverage in order to contribute to health equity, social justice, and the end of exclusion; shifting service delivery to people-centered primary care, to make health services more socially relevant and responsive to the changing world, while producing better outcomes; ensuring health in all policies to secure healthier communities by integrating public health actions with primary care and by pursing healthy public policies across sectors; promoting inclusive leadership and governance, to replace disproportionate reliance on command and control or on laissez-faire disengagement of the state by participatory negotiation-based leadership.[3]

public health: an organized effort by society, primarily through its public institutions, to improve, promote, protect, and restore the health of the population through collective action. It includes services such as a health situation analysis, health surveillance, health promotion, prevention, infectious disease control, environmental protection and sanitation, disaster and health emergency preparedness and response, and occupational health, among others.[17]

public health services: health services targeted at the population as a whole. These include, among others, health situation analysis, health surveillance, health promotion, prevention services, infectious disease control, environmental protection and sanitation, disaster preparedness and response, and occupational health.[17]

social determinants of health: the conditions in which people are born, grow, live, work, and age, including the health system. These circumstances are shaped by the distribution of money, power, and resources at global, national, and local levels. The social determinants of health are mostly responsible for health inequities – the unfair and avoidable differences in health status seen within and between countries.[18]

universal coverage, or universal health coverage: ensuring that all people can use the promotive, preventive, curative, and rehabilitative health services they need, of sufficient quality to be effective, while also ensuring that the use of these services does not expose the user to financial hardship.[19]

REFERENCES

1. *La renovación de la atención primaria de salud en las Américas: documento de posición de la OPS/OMS.* Washington DC: La Organizacion Panamericana de la Salud, 2007.
2. *The Global Burden of Disease: 2004 update.* Geneva: World Health Organization, 2008.

Available at: www.who.int/healthinfo/global_burden_disease/2004_report_update/en/index.html

3. *The World Health Report 2008: primary health care – now more than ever.* Geneva: World Health Organization, 2008. Available at: www.who.int/whr/2008/whr08_en.pdf

4. Modified from Haggerty JL, Reid RJ, Freeman GK, et al. Continuity of care: a multidisciplinary review. *British Medical Journal.* 2003; **327**: 1219–21.

5. Modified from Pilnick A, Dingwall R, Starkey K. Disease management: definitions, difficulties and future directions. *Bulletin of the World Health Organization.* 2001; **79**: 755–63.

6. Kawachi I, Subramanian SV, Almeida-Filho N. A glossary for health inequalities. *Journal of Epidemiology and Community Health.* 2002; **56**: 647–52. Available at: jech.bmj.com/content/56/9/647.full.pdf

7. Reference – Health Impact Assessment. World Health Organization [online glossary]. www.who.int/hia/about/glos/en/index1.html

8. A glossary of technical terms on the economics and finance of health services. World Health Organization, Regional Office for Europe, 1998. Available at: www.euro.who.int/__data/assets/pdf_file/0014/102173/E69927.pdf

9. WHO Terminology Informational System [online glossary]. Available at: www.who.int/health-systems-performance/docs/glossary.htm

10. The Tallinn Charter: Health Systems for Health and Wealth. WHO European Ministerial Conference on Health Systems: "Health Systems, Health and Wealth", Tallinn, Estonia, June 25–27, 2008. Available at: www.euro.who.int/__data/assets/pdf_file/0008/88613/E91438.pdf

11. World Health Organization (1946): Preamble to the Constitution of the World Health Organization as adopted by the International Health Conference, New York, 19 June–2 July 1946; signed on July 22, 1946 by the representatives of 61 States (Official Records of the World Health Organization, no.2, p. 100) and entered into force on April 7, 1948.

12. *People Centred Care in Low- and Middle-Income Countries – meeting report.* Geneva: World Health Organization, 2010.

13. *Análisis del sector salud, una herramienta para viabilizar la formulación de políticas, lineamientos metodológicos.* Edición especial No. 9. Washington DC: La Organización Panamericana de la Salud, 2006.

14. Starfield B. Basic concepts in population health and health care. *Journal of Epidemiology and Community Health.* 2001; **55**: 452–4.

15. Institute of Medicine. *Primary Care: America's health in a new era.* Washington DC: National Academy Press, 1996.

16. Declaration of Alma-Ata. Available at: www.who.int/publications/almaata_declaration_en.pdf

17. *La salud pública en las Américas: nuevos conceptos, análisis del desempeño y bases para la acción.* Publicación científica y técnic No. 589. Washington DC: Organización Panamericana de la Salud, 2002.

18. World Health Organization. *Social Determinants of Health.* Geneva: World Health Organization, 2013. Available at: www.who.int/social_determinants/en/

19. World Health Organization. *Health Financing for Universal Coverage.* Geneva: World Health Organization, 2013. Available at: www.who.int/health_financing

List of contributors

Editor

Michael Kidd is a family doctor, president of the World Organization of Family Doctors (WONCA) and past president of the Royal Australian College of General Practitioners. He was previously professor of general practice at The University of Sydney and is now executive dean of the Faculty of Health Sciences at Flinders University in Australia.

Chapter lead authors

Jan De Maeseneer is head of the Department of Family Medicine and Primary Health Care and Vice-Dean for Strategic Planning at the Faculty of Medicine and Health Sciences of Ghent University in Belgium. He is chairman of the European Forum for Primary Care and secretary-general of The Network: Towards Unity for Health. Since 1997 he has been promoter of different projects in relation to the development of family medicine in Africa.

Cynthia Haq is a family doctor, founding director of the University of Wisconsin–Madison Center for Global Health in the United States, and director of Training in Urban Medicine and Public Health. She has focused her career on education for primary health care and has promoted family medicine programs in Pakistan, Uganda, and Ethiopia.

Jeff Markuns is executive director of the Boston University Family Medicine Global Health Collaborative. He is a former family medicine assistant residency director at Boston University in the United States, completed a fellowship in medical education and now leads international technical consultations in family medicine development, primarily focused on Southeast Asia.

Hernan Montenegro is a senior health systems adviser at the World Health Organization in Geneva, Switzerland. He is a medical doctor from the University of Chile and holds a master degree in public health from the Johns Hopkins University. He has also worked for the Chilean Ministry of Health and for the World Bank.

Waris Qidwai is professor and chair of the Department of Family Medicine at Aga Khan University in Karachi, Pakistan. He has played an important role in the development and promotion of family medicine in the South Asia region and is the current chair of the WONCA Working Party on Research.

Igor Svab is a family doctor, primary care researcher, and professor of family medicine at the University Medical School in Ljubljana, Slovenia. He is a past president of the WONCA Europe region.

Wim Van Lerberghe is a past director of the Department for Health Systems Policies and Workforce at the World Health Organization headquarters. He is a medical doctor with master and doctoral degrees in public health and has worked in Mozambique, Zaire (now the Democratic Republic of the Congo), Djibouti, Morocco, Tanzania, and Thailand. Previously he was professor of health policy at the Institute of Tropical Medicine in Antwerp, Belgium.

Tiago Villanueva works as a locum general practitioner in the Greater Lisbon area in Portugal and as a freelance news writer for the specialist medical press. He is a former British Medical Journal Clegg Scholar and editor of *Student BMJ* and senior editor of the Harvard Medical School – Portugal Health Information Program.

Contributing authors

Guo Aimin is the vice dean of the School of Public Health and Family Medicine of the Capital Medical University in China. She is vice director of the Training Centre of General Practice with the Ministry of Health, China. She has been involved in education and research on general practice since 2000.

Samia Almusallam is a trainer in family medicine and director of the family medicine residency program at Kuwait Institute for Medical Specialization. She has and continues to play a leadership role in the development and promotion of family medicine in Kuwait and the Middle East region.

Liliana Arias-Castillo is a family doctor and professor and chair of the Department of Family Medicine at the Universidad del Valle in Cali in Colombia. She is a past president of the WONCA Iberoamericana region.

Bruce Arroll is a graduate from The University of Auckland, New Zealand and worked at McMaster University in Canada. He has been involved in Cochrane reviews and is part of the Cochrane Primary Care Field that developed the PEARLs (Practical Evidence About Real Life Situations). He also works in clinical practice in South Auckland.

Mohammad Assai is a regional adviser on Primary and Community Health Care at the Eastern Mediterranean Regional Office of the World Health Organization. He previously worked as director general for primary health care at the Ministry of Health in Iran and as a medical officer with the World Health Organization in Pakistan.

Olayinka O Ayankogbe is senior lecturer in family medicine and head of the Family Medicine Unit at the Department of Community Health and Primary Care of the College of Medicine at the University of Lagos in Nigeria. He is also consultant in charge of the Family Medicine Unit at the Lagos University Teaching Hospital.

Charles Boelen is an international consultant in health systems and personnel. He worked for 30 years in the World Health Organization and served as coordinator of the program of human resources for health. He cochairs the Global Consensus for Social Accountability of Medical Schools.

Chen Bowen is the vice president of the Capital Institute of Paediatrics, Beijing, and vice Chairman and general secretary of the Community Health Association of China. He has been committed to promoting the establishment of China's community health service since 1997. In 2012, he won the United Arab Emirates health fund award.

Luís Filipe Cavadas is a general practitioner at Lagoa Family Health Unit in Matosinhos in Portugal. He is also a trainer of medical students and foundation year and general practice trainees, a researcher at the Senhora da Hora Research group, and a past editor of the *Portuguese Journal of General Practice*.

William E Cayley Jr is a professor in the University Of Wisconsin Department of Family Medicine. He is a member of WONCA, the Society of Teachers of Family Medicine, and the Christian Medical and Dental Association. He is the book reviews editor for the journal *Family Medicine* and is an editor for the Cochrane Heart Group.

Yin Delu is an assistant professor at the Capital Institute of Pediatrics. He is the director of the Management Consultancy Department of the Community Health Association of China. Much of his work focuses on conducting research on community health service in China.

Marcelo Marcos Piva Demarzo is a family doctor and assistant professor at the Family Medicine Unit of the Department of Preventive Medicine in the Escola Paulista de Medicina of the Universidade Federal de São Paulo, Brazil. He is a Fellow of the International Primary Care Research Leadership Program of the University of Oxford.

Nandani de Silva is Emeritus Professor of Family Medicine at the University of Kelaniya, and chair of the board of study of the College of General Practitioners of Sri Lanka. She is a WONCA Council member and member of the Nominations and Awards Committee, Working Party on Education, and Working Party on Women and Family Medicine.

Akye Essuman is a lecturer and acting head of the Family Medicine Unit of the Department of Community Health at the University of Ghana Medical School. He is the first graduate of family medicine in Ghana and he works as a senior specialist family physician at the Korle-Bu Teaching Hospital in Accra.

Maaike Flinkenflögel is a Dutch medical doctor who has been working in medical education and development of family medicine training in Africa for several years. She supported the establishment of the Primafamed Network from Ghent University in Belgium and is now working as associate professor at the Department of Family Medicine and Community Health at the National University of Rwanda.

Juan Gérvas is a retired general practitioner who has worked in the Spanish health system in urban and rural areas. He is a researcher in primary care and leader of the multi-professional research, study and teaching in primary care and general medicine group (CESCA). He is professor of public health with the Autonomous University Madrid and professor of international health with the National School of Public Health, Madrid.

Felicity Goodyear-Smith is professor in general practice and primary health care at the University of Auckland in New Zealand and has a strong research track record involving interdisciplinary and intersector collaboration on a variety of primary health care issues. She is founding editor of the *Royal New Zealand College of General Practitioners Journal of Primary Health Care.*

Kim Griswold is a faculty member in the Department of Family Medicine at the University at Buffalo, The State University of New York, and is responsible for teaching medical and nursing students, as well as family practice residents. She provides clinical care for an underserved population in urban Buffalo, including many refugees and immigrants.

Gustavo Gusso is past president of the Brazilian Society of Family and Community Medicine and professor of general practice at the University of São Paulo. He is a member of the WONCA Working Party on Research and contributes toward extensive development and promotion of family medicine in South America in general and Brazil in particular.

Iona Heath is an internationally renowned leader in family medicine and worked as a general practitioner in Kentish Town in London. She is a past president of the Royal College of General Practitioners in the United Kingdom and has served as a member of the WONCA executive and as WONCA's liaison person with the World Health Organization.

Ilse Hellemann-Geschwinder is a family physician involved in group lecturing at the Medical University of Graz, Austria. She was a member of the WONCA World Executive Committee responsible for WONCA/World Health Organization liaison and now is on the council of the European Society of General Practice/Family Medicine and the European Academy of Teachers in General Practice/Family Medicine.

Mary K Hunt has had a 30-year career in community-based research at schools of public health in Minnesota, Boston, and the United States Centers for Disease Control and

Prevention. In her international work in Bahrain and Uganda she has focused on nutrition and the integration of primary health care and family medicine with public health.

Vincent Hunt is a former rural family physician, residency director, and chair of the Department of Family Medicine at Brown University in the United States. He has provided consultation to family medicine programs in the United States and in many countries throughout the world, most recently serving as project manager of WONCA's East Africa Initiative.

Victor Inem is associate professor of community health and primary care at the College of Medicine at the University of Lagos in Nigeria. He is an active member of International Federation of Primary Care Research Networks and contributes toward the development and promotion of family medicine in Africa in general and Nigeria in particular.

Janko Kersnik is a rural family doctor, head of the Family Medicine Department at University Maribor and head of research at the Family Medicine Department of the University Ljubljana in Slovenia. He is president of the Slovenian Family Medicine Society and president of the European Academy of Teachers in General/Family Practice (EURACT).

Tawfik Khoja is a Saudi Arabia-based consultant family physician and current director general of the executive board of the Health Ministers Council for Cooperation. He plays a pivotal role as a researcher and author in this field and in the development and promotion of family medicine in the Eastern Mediterranean Region.

Meng-Chih Lee is superintendent of the Taichung Hospital in Taiwan and is a visiting principal investigator of the Institute of Population Health Sciences with the National Health Research Institutes in Taiwan. He is the president of Taiwan Medical Alliance for Control of Tobacco.

Mart Leys is a technical officer at the World Health Organization in Geneva, Switzerland. She is a political scientist from the University of Ghent and holds a European master degree in international humanitarian action. She previously worked at the Fund for Development Cooperation in Brussels, Belgium, and the University of Antwerp.

Donald Li is a specialist in family medicine in private practice and a past president of the WONCA Asia Pacific Region. He is a president of the Hong Kong Academy of Medicine, censor of the Hong Kong College of Family Physicians, and advisor to the Chinese Society of General Practice of the Chinese Medical Association.

Lawrence Loh is a family and public health physician working as a medical specialist at the Public Health Agency of Canada. He completed medical school at the University of Western Ontario, residency training at the University of Toronto, and a master degree in public health at the Johns Hopkins Bloomberg School of Public Health.

Inderjit Singh Ludher is a family medicine physician, past president of the Academy of Family Physicians of Malaysia and past chair of the academic programs of the Academy. He has been involved in primary health care education in Cambodia and with the Baha'i Community in Social Action, building capacity in populations in need in developing nations.

Roar Maagaard is a specialist in general practice/family medicine near Aarhus, Denmark, and is associate professor at the University of Aarhus responsible for general practitioner specialist training. He was president of the Danish College of General Practitioners and is honorary secretary of the European Academy of Teachers in General Practice/Family Medicine.

Bob Mash is Head of the Division of Family Medicine and Primary Care at Stellenbosch University in South Africa and is editor of the *African Journal of Primary Health Care and Family Medicine*. He has been involved in supporting the development of family medicine in South Africa, Botswana, Zimbabwe, Namibia, Malawi, Tanzania, Kenya, Uganda, and Ghana.

Claunara Schilling Mendonça is professor of family medicine at the Federal University of Rio Grande do Sul, Brazil, and is manager of a community health service in Porto Alegre. She holds a master degree in epidemiology and previously worked for the Brazilian Ministry of Health as a family doctor and director of the Primary Health Care Department.

Khaya Mfenyana is a family physician, past president of WONCA Africa Region and a past vice-president of the South African Academy of Family Practice/Primary Care. He is the executive dean of the Faculty of Health Sciences at Walter Sisulu University in South Africa and chair of the South African Committee of Medical Deans.

Daniel Ostergaard is a family physician and a past president of the WONCA North America Region. He has been a vice president of the American Academy of Family Physicians with responsibility for international and interprofessional activities as well as education and health of the public.

Luisa Pettigrew is a family doctor with an interest in health systems and education in global health. She has helped develop international exchange programs for medical students and general practice trainees across Europe. She has a master degree in health policy, planning and financing, has worked in the World Health Organization's department of Health Systems Financing, and is a member of the international committee of the Royal College of General Practitioners.

Lesley Pocock is a postgraduate global medical education strategist, working with nongovernmental organizations and individual nations. She is an accredited provider of continuing professional development for family doctors and is the publisher of a range of international and regional medical journals, including the *Middle East Journal of Family Medicine*.

Yongyuth Pongsupap is a senior expert at the National Health Security Office in Thailand. He works on the dissemination of family practice models throughout the country and previously worked as a family doctor in the first demonstration health center for a new approach to quality primary health care in Thailand.

Dheepa Rajan is a technical officer at the World Health Organization in Geneva, Switzerland. She earned her medical degree from the University of Göttingen in Germany and has worked previously at the Swiss Tropical and Public Health Institute in Basel, Switzerland, and Real Medicine Foundation in Jhabua and Bangalore, India.

Steve Reid is a family physician with extensive experience in clinical practice, education and research in the field of rural health in South Africa. He has a background in rural clinical practice, management and research, and is the Glaxo-Wellcome Chair of Primary Health Care at the University of Cape Town in South Africa.

Marc Rivo is a family doctor, senior vice president for managed care and population health at Health Choice Network, and chief medical officer of Prestige Health Choice. He is a former director of the Division of Medicine in the United States Department of Health and Human Services, and a past editor of *WONCA News*.

Edward Shahady is a clinical professor of family medicine and past president of the Society of Teachers of Family Medicine in the United States. He has visited and taught in several countries and now heads a Diabetes Collaborative in Florida.

Hassan Salah is a technical officer in Health Policy and Planning at the Eastern Mediterranean Regional Office of the World Health Organization. He has over 20 years of senior international experience in governance, private sector, health policies and strategic planning, and integrated district systems based on family practice.

Sameen Siddiqi is director at the Department of Health Systems Development at the Eastern Mediterranean Regional Office of the World Health Organization. He is a medical doctor with master and doctoral degrees in public health and has worked on health policy, governance, and service delivery with the World Bank, the German Agency for Technical Development, and the Ministry of Health in Pakistan.

Jinan Usta is associate professor of clinical medicine at the Family Medicine Department of the American University of Beirut, Lebanon. She is a past president of the Lebanese Society of Family Medicine and also works as a consultant for the World Health Organization, OXFAM, and rescue organizations.

Allyn Walsh is professor in the Department of Family Medicine at McMaster University,

Canada and chair of the WONCA Working Party on Education. She has held several educational portfolios at McMaster, including family medicine postgraduate program director, assistant dean faculty development, and most recently chair of student affairs.

Alex Warner is a family doctor in London and a National Institute for Health research in-practice fellow in the Department of Primary Care and Population Health at University College London. He is interested in primary care mental health, health inequalities, and in primary care organization and delivery.

Preethi Wijegoonewardene is a family doctor, past president of the College of General Practitioners of Sri Lanka, past president of the Sri Lanka Medical Association and a past president of the WONCA South Asia region. He is a visiting lecturer in family medicine with the Postgraduate Institute of Medicine at Colombo University in Sri Lanka.

Dong Yanmin is chairman of the Community Health Association of Tianjin City, China, and previously worked as director of the Tianjin Health Bureau. She has been involved in general practice and community health management for many years and now works as a consultant for the Chinese Association of General Practice and as a family doctor.

Yun Yu is a technical officer at the World Health Organization in Geneva, Switzerland. She is a medical doctor and has a master degree in public health from the University of Cambridge. She previously worked in the areas of primary health care and health promotion at the Shanghai Municipal Health Bureau.

CHAPTER 1

Meeting people's health needs

In spite of remarkable advances in medical science and technology, over one billion people throughout the world do not have access to basic health services.[1-4] Thus, more than one out of seven persons lives daily with the threat of premature morbidity and mortality from diseases that could be treated or prevented. This immeasurable human suffering overwhelms our comprehension, raises serious humanitarian and ethical issues, and evokes a profound desire for more effective approaches to providing quality health care for the world's population.

The challenges of ensuring consistent access to high-quality health care for the entire population are not limited to low-income countries. Middle- and high-income countries are dealing with unsustainable costs, fueled by aging populations, rapid increases in the prevalence of noncommunicable diseases, and fragmentation, duplication, and maldistribution of health services with consequent lack of access especially in rural and low-income communities. The potent forces propelling medicine toward specialization and reductionism accentuate the corresponding need to complement and integrate more narrowly focused, specialty-oriented endeavors with an approach that concentrates on the whole patient within a comprehensive health care system. Primary health care, strengthened by family medicine provides the necessary framework for achieving this synthesis.[5]

Family medicine also serves to link those concerned with population health and those who are at the forefront of delivering health care to individuals. The convergence of public health and person-centered care expands opportunities to deliver better-quality health care that is more cost-effective, relevant, equitable, and sustainable. Consequently, this approach is likely to address the needs of patients, health care providers, and decision makers, regardless of their country's state of economic development.

This chapter identifies peoples' current and evolving health care needs, introduces the role of family physicians in health systems, delineates challenges involved in implementing primary health care and family medicine, and provides country-specific scenarios to clarify and facilitate health policy decisions by national leaders.

1.1 IDENTIFYING PEOPLE'S CURRENT AND EVOLVING HEALTH NEEDS

The health status of individuals and populations is influenced by a variety of biological, social, and economic determinants. Key variables include a country's stage of socioeconomic development, availability and distribution of resources, the number and distribution of physicians and other key health workers, and the epidemiology of diseases.

Stages of economic development, resources, and physician numbers and distribution

There is wide variation among countries in their stages of economic development and available resources. Access and quality are strongly influenced by the amount and distribution of funding that individuals and countries allocate to health services. Average per capita expenditures range from US$25 in low-income countries to US$4692 in high-income countries.[6] Many sub-Saharan African countries lack adequate facilities, diagnostic equipment, drugs, and human resources to care for their populations. While many health professionals are needed for the delivery of health services, the availability of doctors often determines access to life-saving care. Malawi and Ethiopia have doctor-population ratios of 1:50 000.[6] In contrast, many European countries have more than three doctors per 1000 people and a relatively abundant supply of health care facilities.[7] Social and economic factors such as poverty, lack of clean water, poor sanitation, inadequate roads, low levels of education, limited access to information, and political instability further accentuate health disparities.[8,9]

Epidemiology challenges

There are also major discrepancies in disease burdens among countries. For instance, in sub-Saharan countries over 60% of this burden is due to communicable diseases and maternal, perinatal, and nutritional conditions. The leading causes of death in children between 0 and 4 years are diarrhea, respiratory illnesses, and those associated with the perinatal period such as birth asphyxia, premature birth, and low birth weight. Communicable diseases and maternal conditions are the leading causes of death in adults. Trauma, violence, and noncommunicable diseases are also major causes of premature morbidity and mortality.[7] Although more challenging to document, mental illnesses such as depression, schizophrenia, and alcoholism are also substantial contributors to the disease burden in low- and middle-income countries.[10]

Noncommunicable diseases are the leading causes of death in all regions except Africa.[11] Diabetes, hypertension, cancer, and chronic lung disease predominate in the European countries, with only 5% of mortality ascribed to infectious diseases. A similar spectrum is encountered in the United States where there has been a significant increase in prevalence of diagnosed diabetes in adults over the 15-year period from 1995 to 2010.

In spite of their predominance in high-income countries, noncommunicable diseases disproportionately affect low- and medium-income countries, accounting for nearly 80% of the 36 million noncommunicable disease-related deaths worldwide. Furthermore, the World Health Organization (WHO) projects that noncommunicable disease-related deaths will increase by 17% over the next 10 years, with the greatest increases in the African (27%) and the Eastern Mediterranean (25%) regions.

This dramatic rise is a major concern throughout the world. In addition to their impact on individuals, noncommunicable diseases are closely linked with global social and economic development. Thus, the WHO calls for overall health system strengthening so that both the public and the private sectors have the elements necessary for the management and care of chronic conditions. Elements specified include appropriate policies, trained human resources, adequate access to essential medicines and basic technologies, well-functioning referral mechanisms, and quality standards for primary health care.[12]

1.2 RESPONDING TO PEOPLE'S HEALTH NEEDS

The discrepancy between our capacity to improve health and actual health outcomes has triggered responses from communities and world health leaders regarding the fundamental importance of primary health care.

Primary health care and primary care: universal needs, local solutions

In 1978 the Declaration of Alma-Ata identified primary health care as the most cost-effective way to deliver essential health services.[13]

There has been some confusion since that time about the terms primary health care and primary care. We need to differentiate primary health care, as a strategy to attain health for all, from primary care, as first-contact care. Primary health care as a strategy encompasses high-quality primary care services.

There have been variations and refinements of the concept of primary health care throughout the past 3 decades, with committees and individuals stressing the importance of the following attributes of high-quality primary care services:[5,14–19]

➤ personal – patients treated with dignity and efficiency
➤ first contact – provides accessible entry into the health system
➤ continuous – establishes longitudinal and sustained relationship with patients over time
➤ comprehensive – addresses all health care needs, common problems, and comorbidities, including physical, psychological, social, and cultural determinants of health and disease
➤ coordinated with other health professionals
➤ cost-effective
➤ high quality
➤ equitable distribution of health services
➤ community oriented, including local involvement and partnerships
➤ accountable.

The unique features of primary care include first contact, longitudinality (continuity), comprehensiveness, and coordination.[18] The way in which these characteristics are organized and incorporated into a systematic approach within successful primary health systems is distinctive and thus provides a template for countries seeking to improve the efficacy of the care they provide to their citizens.

The contribution of family medicine

While a variety of health professionals are essential for the delivery of health services, family doctors are particularly well suited to this function because they are trained to care for individuals of all ages. They also serve as integral, complementary members of the primary health care team, providing supervision for other health workers and ensuring comprehensive, continuous, and coordinated health care for individuals, families, and communities.

Family medicine is a component of primary care and is defined as a specialty of medicine concerned with providing comprehensive care to individuals and families and integrating biomedical, behavioral, and social sciences; it is known as general practice in some countries. Family doctors are medical specialists trained to provide health care services for all individuals regardless of age, sex, or type of health problem. They provide primary and continuing care for entire families within their communities, address physical, psychological and social problems, and coordinate comprehensive health care services with other specialists as needed. Family doctors may also be known as family physicians or general practitioners. They differ from general doctors who may work in the community without further specialist training following medical school.

The scope of each family doctor's training and practice varies according to the contexts of their work, their roles, and the organization and resources of the health systems in each country. A wide spectrum of skills is necessary for family doctors to adapt to the health care needs of their individual countries. In those countries with few medical practitioners, such as in some countries in sub-Saharan Africa, family doctors may be employed in the public sector and serve as the backbone of district hospitals, performing surgical procedures including caesarean sections, managing trauma, and caring for adults and children. In some countries in Europe they may concentrate on ambulatory primary care and serve as the gateway to hospital and specialised services. Increasingly, as members of multidisciplinary primary care teams, around the world their scope of practice is expanding to include public health activities such as teaching and consulting with village health workers and midwives; working with schools, churches, and other groups within the community; and providing care in homes, clinics, and community health centers.[20] Also, the worldwide increase in noncommunicable diseases (NCDs) accentuates the need for well-trained family doctors to manage and care for people with chronic diseases and their associated comorbidities.

The wide range of contexts in which family doctors function is summarized in Box 1.1.

BOX 1.1 Range of contexts where family doctors may work

- Low- to middle- and high-income countries
- Homes, communities, clinics, and hospitals
- Rural, suburban, and urban environments
- Solo, medium, and large group practices
- Public, nongovernmental, and private health systems

Likewise, their scope of practice, which can be tailored to fit the needs of the populations they serve, is described in Box 1.2.

BOX 1.2 Scope of practice of family doctors

- Care for patients of all ages, from "womb to tomb"
- Ensure access to comprehensive primary and secondary services
- Manage infectious and chronic diseases
- Provide emergency, acute, and long-term care
- Serve as clinicians, teachers, advocates, and leaders
- Coordinate individual clinical, community, and public health services

---

The ability of well-trained generalist doctors to adapt to the unique circumstances and specific health care needs within each country is reflected in the rapid growth of the World Organization of Family Doctors (WONCA) from 18 founding member organizations in 1972 to 126 member organizations representing over 130 countries by 2012.[21]

This diversity requires a flexible, yet deliberate, educational approach to ensure that competencies are aligned with local needs. Doctors are best prepared for these multifaceted roles when their training is concentrated on the specific problems and diseases they are likely to encounter in their future practices. Thus, the knowledge base necessary to manage the majority of these recurring events can be mastered. This focus provides the expertise and confidence that is necessary for family doctors to provide quality care to their patients without unrealistic expectations upon themselves or from patients, other providers or decision makers. Subsequent chapters will describe the rationale for considering family medicine as an essential component of primary health care, evidence of its efficacy, and practical consideration of its implementation with examples from various countries.

1.3 MEETING THE CHALLENGES AND CONVINCING THE LEADERSHIP

The health of the population and the social and economic capacity of a nation are interdependent.[1] Therefore, each nation has a fundamental interest in promoting and improving the health of its people. Government authorities, educational institutions, health care organizations, financial systems, and civil society play distinct and complementary roles in the oversight, production, and maintenance of complex health systems. These groups influence the policies, organization, staffing, financing, and delivery of health care services that in turn affect economic as well as individual and population health outcomes. This reciprocal relationship makes it even more important for governments to employ their finite budgets and available resources efficiently as they strive to achieve maximal health outcomes that require the active participation of all sectors of the population.

Primary health care challenges

All countries face formidable challenges as they strive to provide high-quality health care that is cost-effective, relevant, equitable, and sustainable.[5] These challenges, as described in the World Health Report 2008, can be summarized as follows.

➤ **Inverse care**: people with the most means consume the most care, whereas those with the least means and greatest problems consume the least, often because of a lack of access to affordable, acceptable services.

➤ **Impoverishing care**: when people lack social protection and health payments are out-of-pocket, health problems may lead to catastrophic expenses.

➤ **Fragmented care**: excessive specialization and a focus on specific diseases discourage a holistic and continuing approach to health services.

➤ **Misdirected care**: resources are mostly allocated to curative, acute services, often neglecting primary prevention and health promotion.

➤ **Unsafe care**: poorly designed systems and unsafe practices lead to high rates of hospital-acquired infections, errors, and adverse effects.

Health policies that address these inequities and ensure adequate resources and incentives are required to support robust primary health systems and human resources for health.

Insights gained from experiences throughout the world indicate that solutions must be specific, based on sound evidence, and sensitive to local contexts. The World Health Report 2008 delineates four interdependent reforms that are necessary for robust primary health systems.[5]

1. **Universal coverage reforms**: to ensure that health systems contribute to equity and end exclusion on the basis of such variables as income and ethnicity; and to invest adequate resources for maintenance of a robust primary health system with universal access.

2. **Public policy reforms**: to integrate public health with primary care and to promote public health policies across sectors; to promote collaboration between family doctors, communities, government and private sectors, and academic institutions to address the evolving health needs of societies; and to ensure the recruitment, training, deployment, and retention of health professionals according to the needs of the population.

3. **Leadership and research reforms**: to promote inclusive, participatory, negotiation-based decision making based on the values of solidarity, social justice, and accountability; to conduct research to assess quality, satisfaction, and outcomes and to revise services based on sound evidence; and to promote global solidarity and shared learning.

4. **Service delivery and educational reforms**: to reorganize health services with teams of health workers delivering people-centered, culturally appropriate, community-based health promotion, preventive services and primary care; and to train family doctors and other health workers to manage the most common problems at the community level and to support and/or refer patients to other specialists as needed.

Family medicine challenges

Family doctors face unique challenges related to their identity, roles, and financial support. When family medicine is a new concept, the public and other health professionals often do not understand or appreciate the unique skills of family doctors. In some cases, family doctors may experience role conflicts with other health professionals. This confusion may be exacerbated by inconsistent standards, policies, and communications within and between health professional groups.

Adequate resources, incentives, and salaries are also required. If family doctors are remunerated at much lower rates than other medical specialists, it will be difficult to recruit and retain sufficient numbers especially in rural areas, in district hospitals, and in areas with high concentrations of people living in poverty. Inadequate preparation and working conditions will promote the migration of health professionals to more attractive working environments and exacerbate the burden of work for those left behind.

Additional challenges include medicine's expanding knowledge base, increasing reliance on expensive technology, and the complexity of managing patients with comorbidities. Flexible models of training and continuing education address these factors through focusing on the needs of the populations to be served and promoting primary health care teams, protocols that maintain high quality and use of low-cost information technology to remain current and communicate with other specialists. The latter will include mastery of such tools as online learning and curricula, telemedicine consulting, and computer population mapping.

Those working in rural areas may also require advanced obstetric, surgical, and trauma skills. Furthermore, they may feel isolated and be concerned about access to educational, cultural, and employment opportunities for family members. These challenges can be addressed in part through the support provided by group practices and the congregation of several practitioners in centrally located community health settings or in district hospitals. Doctors can thus share the workload and have time for recreation and family activities. They can still serve a network of surrounding villages through consultation, teaching, and supervision of other primary health care workers based in those communities.

Convincing the leadership

Exemplary leadership and advocacy by political, community, and medical leaders will be required to steer a wide range of interventions toward meeting these challenges. Successful implementation often involves balancing competing values in a manner that is complementary and mutually reinforcing. For example, health systems that ensure equitable access to comprehensive services need to integrate the care of individuals with public health measures. Both components of health care are essential and more effective when working in synergy. Furthermore, quality needs to be balanced with cost-effectiveness in order to provide care at a cost that each society can afford and sustain. The dichotomy between comprehensive, integrated approaches and specialized, reductionist approaches to health care presents additional challenges.

The realignment of health systems to best meet people's needs also involves important societal changes. Flexibility on the part of each stakeholder will be necessary in order to manage competing priorities in the context of finite resources. When addressing these challenges, leaders may achieve consensus among key stakeholders by focusing on shared goals and values such as health promotion, the prevention and alleviation of suffering, and the importance of equity and cost-effectiveness.

The implementation of family medicine will vary according to the circumstances in each country, as reflected by internationally recognized classifications such as per capita income levels, indebtedness, and economies in transition or emergency status. Each category requires a specific, flexible approach to the development of family medicine in each country. Identification of the stage of development of a nation will facilitate understanding of the particular contribution family medicine can make and of the critical decisions that have to be made in order for the discipline to succeed. The following scenarios describe this spectrum of developmental stages within nations.

Amplification

In many low- and middle-income countries family medicine is considered synonymous with primary health care, and components of this discipline are, therefore, practiced by a variety of health professionals, the majority of whom are nonphysicians – that is, medical assistants, nurse practitioners, and community health workers. This workforce, often identified as primary health care workers, provides essential health services to a large proportion of the population, particularly in rural and remote areas. The WHO has described how primary care requires

> teams of health professionals: physicians, nurse practitioners and assistants with specific and sophisticated biomedical and social skills – it is not acceptable that, in low-income countries, primary care would be synonymous with low-tech, nonprofessional care for the rural poor who cannot afford any better.[5]

Because of limitations in numbers and the scarce resources available to these countries, the most effective contributions of family doctors under these circumstances may be to provide training and supervision for primary health care workers throughout a region, to complement care for those patients with complex problems, and to facilitate appropriate referrals. In these situations, decisions need to be made about the roles, responsibilities, distribution, and compensation of family doctors, and how they can strengthen the delivery of primary health care at the community level.

Substitution

In some countries the discipline of family medicine is not yet established or recognised, and therefore does not attract medical school graduates to enter family medicine specialty training. In these cases, medical schools may tailor their basic educational programs to train doctors to address the most relevant health needs, with the assumption that all doctors should be competent in delivering primary care services. Decisions need to be made about whether this approach is an effective substitute for deliberately trained family doctors, and whether establishing formal specialty training would improve outcomes.

Recognition

In many countries the discipline of family medicine is formally recognized and taught as a specialty, but there are few incentives or opportunities for the career advancement of family doctors. In these scenarios, the general public often favors direct access to subspecialists in the belief that they provide the best service. There have been initiatives from many governments and health service organizations to reverse this trend and promote family medicine through appropriate legislation, public education, and professional incentives. Where these initiatives do not already exist, decisions need to be made about whether increased recognition and support for family medicine would improve access, quality, comprehensiveness, or cost-effectiveness of health care.

Reconstruction

Countries may be reconstructing their health systems after major political changes or armed conflicts. In these cases, the introduction of family medicine is an important contribution to health system reforms: supporting decentralization, improving access to health care at the community level, and providing private practice options. However, a multiplicity of interventions and a relative lack of coordination may lead to confusion and uncertainty, with distraction from the goal of efficiency and equity. In these situations, the most important contribution of family medicine is as an integral component of a comprehensive, coordinated plan for overall health system improvement.

Productivity

Some countries are using family medicine to improve patient satisfaction and to control rising costs in health service organizations. In such situations, while the privileged have ready access to high-quality care, the health needs of disadvantaged individuals and groups may be neglected. These nations face the challenge of developing universal access to high-quality, cost-effective health care in environments where market forces and individual freedom to choose one's personal physician are publicly recognised virtues. In these cases, decision makers need to consider whether educating the public and training and supporting sufficient numbers of family doctors will enhance the delivery of comprehensive, cost-effective, community-based health services and ultimately contribute to the improvement of population health.

Humanism

In countries with a tradition of social solidarity supported by government policies, primary health care is recognised and nurtured as a fundamental human right. Equal opportunities for personal development, respect for differences, social justice, and enhancement of the public interest underlie the foundations of these societies. Decisions to invest in family medicine may represent tangible contributions to a renaissance of humanistic values, improving the quality of life by building a more socially responsive health system.

Strategies for change

These scenarios are not an exhaustive taxonomy of situations that leaders of family medicine will encounter, nor does any scenario completely describe a specific country. The majority of nations share the features of several scenarios. Health system leaders are more likely to consider investments in family medicine, however, if recommendations are based on careful needs assessments that take into account their country's cultural and societal context, demographic circumstances, epidemiology, stage of development, and available resources.

There is an urgent need to link family medicine, and the implementation of high-quality primary care, with the global movement to achieve universal health care coverage. This approach provides the most efficacious means for guaranteeing first-contact quality health care to all people.

The confidence of health service leaders in making this link may be further enhanced by the following measures.

➤ **Present the evidence**: factual information and arguments emphasizing the benefits of family medicine are necessary to convince national leaders, and for use by these leaders to convince other concerned parties. When evidence is insufficient for a specific context, it may be necessary to develop pilot projects to gather additional information.

➤ **Show living examples**: successful family medicine programs, documentation of practical experiences, site visits, and case studies serve to build confidence in the feasibility and impact of family medicine development projects.

➤ **Develop international collaboration**: partnership arrangements among countries provide opportunities for mutually beneficial international exchanges of information and experts. These exchanges facilitate comparisons and adaptation of projects to fit local needs and enhance visibility, and may generate additional resources.

These strategies will clarify the contributions that family doctors can make to people's health. In so doing they will provide perspectives that help to reconcile health care dilemmas and create synergies throughout the full range of developmental scenarios.

Conclusions

The Universal Declaration of Human Rights states that, "Everyone has the right to a standard of living adequate for the health and well-being of oneself and one's family."[22] Family doctors have the potential to make vital contributions to this laudable goal through the provision of comprehensive primary health care services. The following chapters describe the rationale for considering family medicine as an essential component of health systems, evidence of its efficacy, and practical considerations for its implementation.

Further details about the current state of family medicine in each region of the world are available on the WONCA website (www.globalfamilydoctor.com).[21]

REFERENCES

1. World Bank. *World Development Report 1993: Investing in Health*. Available at: wdronline. worldbank.org/worldbank/a/c.html/world_development_report_1993/abstract/WB. 0-1952-0890-0.abstract1
2. Crisp N. *Turning the World Upside Down: the search for global health in the twenty-first century*. Royal Society of Medicine Press, 2010.
3. Collier P. *The Bottom Billion*. Oxford University Press, 2007.
4. Sen A. *Development as Freedom*. Alfred A Knopf, 2001.
5. World Health Organization. *World Health Report 2008: primary health care (now more than ever)*. Available at: www.who.int/whr/2008/en/

6. World Health Organization. *World Health Statistics 2012*. Available at: www.who.int/gho/publications/world_health_statistics/2012/en/index.html

7. World Health Organization. *Global Health Observatory Data Repository 2012*. Available at: apps.who.int/gho/data/?vid=10015#

8. World Health Organization. *Commission on Social Determinants of Health Final Report: Closing the gap in a generation: health equity through action on the social determinants of health, 2008*. Available at: www.who.int/social_determinants/thecommission/finalreport/en/index.html

9. Marmot M, Friel S, Bell R, et al.; on behalf of the Commission on Social Determinants of Health. Closing the gap in a generation: health equity through action on the social determinants of health. *Lancet*. 2008; **372**: 1661–9.

10. Patel V, Araya R, Chatterjee S, et al. Treatment and prevention of mental disorders in low-income and middle-income countries. *Lancet*. 2007; **370**: 991–1005.

11. World Health Organization Media Centre. Noncommunicable diseases fact sheet, September 2011: 1–4. Available at: www.who.int/mediacentre/factsheets/fs355/en/index.html

12. World Health Organization. *Action Plan for the Global Strategy for the Prevention and Control of Noncommunicable Diseases, 2008*. Available at: www.who.int/nmh/publications/9789241597418/en/

13. World Health Organization/UNICEF. *Primary Health Care: report of the International Conference on Primary Health Care, Alma-Ata, USSR, 6–12 September 1978*. Geneva: World Health Organization, 1978 (Health for All Series, No.1).

14. Alpert JJ, Charney E. *The Education of Physicians for Primary Care*. Washington DC: US Department of Health, Education and Welfare, 1973.

15. Donaldson MS, Yordy KD, Lohr KN, et al. (eds). *Primary Care: America's health in a new era*. Washington DC: Institute of Medicine, National Academy Press, 1996.

16. Ljubljana Charter on Reforming Health Care. *Bulletin of the World Health Organization*. 1999; **77**: 48–9.

17. Vienonen M, Jankauskiene D, Vask A. Towards evidence-based health care reform. *Bulletin of the World Health Organization*. 1999, **77**: 44–7.

18. Starfield B. *Primary Care: balancing health needs, services and technology*. New York: Oxford University Press, 1998.

19. Boelen C. *Towards Unity for Health: challenges and opportunities for partnership in health development. A working paper*. Geneva: World Health Organization, 2000.

20. Roberts RG, Hunt VR, Kulie TI, et al. Family medicine training: the international experience. *Medical Journal of Australia*. 2011; **194**(11): 84.

21. World Organization of Family Doctors (WONCA). Available at: www.globalfamilydoctor.com/

22. United Nations. Universal Declaration of Human Rights, 1948. Available at: www.un.org/en/documents/udhr/

CHAPTER 2

Improving health systems

This chapter reviews the values, goals, and functions of health systems, describes common challenges that undermine their successful implementation, and outlines strategies to respond to these challenges. It provides the context for assessing the contributions that family medicine can make to people's health as an integral component of health systems.

2.1 VALUES OF HEALTH SYSTEMS

A variety of initiatives sponsored by the World Health Organization (WHO) around the world have emphasized the importance of quality, equity, relevance, and cost-effectiveness in achieving optimal health outcomes.[1-3]

Quality

Quality of care can be viewed from a clinical as well as a population perspective. The clinical perspective focuses on how care provided by individual practitioners or groups of practitioners affects the health of their patients. The population perspective focuses on how health systems affect the health of populations and reduce disparities in health across population subgroups.

Clinical indicators of the quality of care encompass four components:
1. adequacy of resources
2. delivery of services
3. clinical performance
4. health outcomes.

A variety of resources is necessary for delivering high-quality care. Health systems need appropriately trained personnel, sufficient numbers of suitable facilities in which to provide services, adequate financing for primary care services, accessibility of these services to the population, adequate information systems, and effective mechanisms of governance.[4]

Because effectiveness and equity of health services are dependent on a strong primary health care system, delivery of services can be assessed by evaluating both the capacity of a health system to deliver primary health care and its performance in providing key characteristics of primary health care such as longitudinality, comprehensiveness, coordination, and cost-effectiveness. The subject of enhancing the quality of clinical performance and outcomes is considered more thoroughly in Chapter 5, Section 5.4, on improving access to primary care.

Equity

Social justice includes equal health care opportunities for all. This implies that equivalent health services are consistently available throughout each country. In spite of positive examples of improved equity in health services and health status, marked disparities in health care access, quality, and outcomes are common between and among national populations.[5]

Inequalities in health are very frequently socially determined and are not inevitable. Disparities can be associated with income and social class and relate to race, sex, age, educational level, occupation, disabilities, and geographical location. Health care equity can be assured by developing a primary health care system that is truly comprehensive. To achieve such a system requires the needs of the population to be explicitly recognized in the planning and delivery of services. It also means empowering and educating people to assume an active role in promoting and protecting their own health.

While equity and quality may be viewed as competing goals, achieving a balance between them is a mark of excellence in health services. High-quality health care for a few, without attention to equity, may even reduce the quality of life for all. In today's global community, where populations are increasingly interdependent, health risks are rapidly transmitted among and between populations. Furthermore, health status is an important determinant of the economic vitality and well-being of a community. Poor health among subgroups reduces the population's overall productivity. On the other hand, the goal of equity must not sacrifice quality. Substandard, poor-quality health services can do more harm than good. Thus, quality and equity are distinctive but interrelated attributes of a strong health system.

Relevance

Relevance implies providing care that is consistent with the most important health care priorities of a country. Priorities will vary according to local epidemiology, available resources, and the needs of specific populations.

Optimal primary health systems provide a comprehensive range of health services that consist of core services relevant to every population and additional services for groups with common special needs. By applying the principle of relevance to health care, resources can be focused on the most important health concerns and on those in greatest need, making it possible to attain both quality and equity.

A similar approach can increase the relevance of education for health professionals. It will include creating links with partners in the community, developing curricula and strategies that reflect the society's health needs, and measuring the effects of these educational interactions.[6] Furthermore, efforts by countries to decentralize their delivery of health services can increase the likelihood of relevance as well as local control and community involvement.[7,8]

Cost-effectiveness

The values of quality of care, equity, and relevance need to be considered within the context of cost-effectiveness. An intervention is cost-effective when it achieves the intended health outcomes at the lowest possible cost.

Cost-effectiveness can be accomplished without sacrificing quality. For instance, assigning tasks appropriately can reduce costs of services. Reviews can be conducted at national or local levels to allocate or reallocate responsibilities of various health personnel so that the least costly personnel are delivering the highest quality services. Health professionals and policy makers need to have access to objective, regularly updated information on cost-effectiveness to inform the decisions they make. Perhaps the most critical factor in achieving cost-effective health care is the organization of a well-functioning infrastructure for the delivery of health services.

Balancing interrelated values

While each of the values of quality, equity, relevance, and cost-effectiveness is important for health systems, it is the harmonious integration and balance of these values that allow health systems to be most effective. Some systems may deliver sophisticated technical care but only to certain segments of the population, siphoning off a substantial proportion of resources while a large percentage of the population lacks access to basic health care. Other systems may deliver essential care such as immunizations at low cost, but fail to cope with common chronic conditions such as hypertension. Progress in promoting any of these values independently may affect the others negatively or positively. The goal of an optimally functioning health system is to achieve equilibrium among these values in order to meet the health needs of each community (*see* Box 2.1).[2]

BOX 2.1 Compass of interrelated values

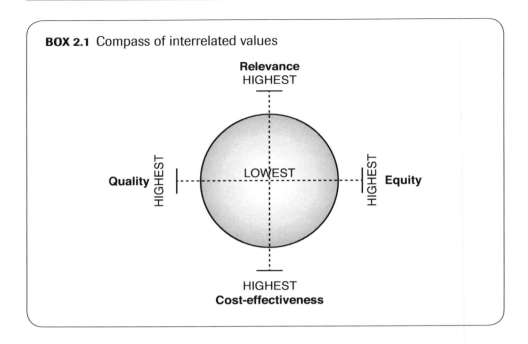

The right to the highest attainable level of health, equity, and solidarity

In 2007 the Pan American Health Organization released a position paper on renewing primary health care in the Americas. This paper identifies three core values for a primary health care-based health system as being the right to the highest attainable level of health, equity, and solidarity. Solidarity is the extent to which people in a society work together to define and achieve the common good.[9]

2.2 GOALS OF HEALTH SYSTEMS

Although resources and health needs vary, the basic goals of health systems are to achieve optimal levels of health and the smallest possible differences in health status among individuals and groups. According to the Constitution of the World Health Organization, health is a state of physical, mental, and social well-being. The WHO promoted this as a universal good through the Declaration of Alma-Ata (*see* Annex A). Over the past decades, this aspiration has guided decisions and priorities for health systems while affirming the essential importance of primary health care in achieving this vision.

The WHO and its Member States agree that health systems should provide high-quality essential care for all, defined by criteria of effectiveness, afford-able costs, and social acceptability; and that each country needs to measure its progress regularly in these areas. These objectives can be accomplished by employing the most advanced state of knowledge about the cause of diseases, management of illnesses, and use of health resources. All nations have mechanisms for delivering health services; however, the quantity of resources devoted to health care, the degree of coordination of activities, and the health outcomes achieved by these systems vary considerably.

2.3 FUNCTIONS OF HEALTH SYSTEMS

Health systems can be described as consisting of several core functions: providing essential health services, generating human and physical resources, financing these services and resources, and collecting data to inform planning and policy development. Furthermore, responsible leadership is necessary to guide and coordinate these interdependent functions toward the best possible outcomes.

Providing essential health care services

Numerous studies confirm large variations of health outcomes even among countries with similar spending, income, educational levels, and socioeconomic conditions.[10–12] Additional input of revenues may not translate into corresponding health gains. Often the costs of interventions do not correlate well with positive results, resources are not fully exploited and often money is wasted. Some health services are very cost-effective, with low costs per unit of health gained, while others are less effective with small gains at very high costs. The way in which health services are organized makes a critical difference and requires careful consideration in order for countries to maximize their resources and achieve optimal health outcomes.

Effective health care services, according to the WHO World Health Report on improving the performance of health systems[13] are characterized by:

➤ prioritization of essential services
➤ adequate organization and financing
➤ consistent service delivery
➤ incentives that reinforce priorities
➤ proper equipment and facilities
➤ appropriate training and support of health care providers.

The priorities, organization, and equitable delivery of health care services have a direct impact on the health of populations. In addition, when allocating resources for health care services, other important competing determinants of health have to be considered, such as education, employment policies, and poverty reduction. Since costs of potential interventions exceed resources allocated for health care in all countries, each health care system must make the best use of available resources in responding to prioritized needs.

Fortunately, it is possible for most countries, even those with limited budgets, to provide high-quality and affordable essential clinical and public health services to the entire population. A minimum level of spending can provide a basic set of essential clinical and public health services that could have a remarkable effect on the health of a population. For instance, in 1993 the World Bank estimated that an expenditure of US$12 per person per year in low-income countries could reduce the burden of disease by one-third.[11,12,14] While more recent estimates give higher values, many low-income countries continue to struggle to provide high-quality essential services to their populations. Better allocation of resources could improve the situation but many low-income countries lack the financial means and the political will to carry out such reforms.

WHO World Health Reports after 2000 have also stressed the importance of adequate delivery of health services, especially the reports in 2008 *Primary Health Care: Now More Than Ever*[15] and in 2010 *Health systems financing: the path to universal coverage*.[10] In order to achieve this outcome, however, a functional infrastructure needs to be in place to deliver these services, sharing costs, personnel, and resources. A well-functioning referral system linking health centers and district hospitals is also necessary.

Achieving sustained, substantial improvements in people's health requires long-term partnerships and collaboration across programs that are well integrated vertically and horizontally. Vertical programs focus on a specific goal, such as immunizing children. This would involve effective production, delivery, and administration of vaccines. Horizontal programs coordinate multiple tasks to achieve broader goals. For instance, child survival is enhanced through provision of immunizations, but more substantially improved through integrated programs that address nutrition, sanitation, immunization, and the diagnosis and treatment of infectious diseases. Core packages, or other forms of "selective" approaches to primary care, are not likely to lead to sustainable improvements in health status unless embedded in a more comprehensive system of health service delivery. This is especially clear when dealing with complex health problems, such as HIV/AIDS and tuberculosis, which require a multifaceted, integrated, and sustainable response. Health systems that provide a balance of preventive and curative therapies, address health problems that are prevalent within specific localities, and provide the most cost-effective therapies are more likely to reduce inequalities in health outcomes.[4]

Generating human and physical resources

Effective health systems require a mixture of providers and facilities designed to deliver essential preventive and clinical services based on local needs, available resources, and affordable costs. This includes adequate numbers of health professionals who have been adequately trained. They need to have an adequate mix of skills and should be provided with the necessary facilities for accurate diagnosis and therapy. They have to be geographically distributed to meet the needs of the population. Investments in the health workforce, which may consume up to two-thirds of a nation's health budget, need to ensure the correct number, type, and distribution of health professionals necessary to provide the desired spectrum of individual and public health services. In order to allocate appropriate funding to educate the right balance of health professionals, it is necessary to consider the health needs and priorities of the population to be served, the resources available, and how all the members of the health system will work together to provide comprehensive services. At present, the skill mix of small numbers of expensive professionals is often not matched to the health needs of populations.[16]

Determining the appropriate match of physician supply and specialty mix is more likely to be successful when done in conjunction with an analysis of the expectations for each medical discipline as well as for other categories of health workers. There is no single approach and effective workforce strategies will differ for each country, taking into account local factors and historical context.[15]

For instance, the shortage of physicians working in remote areas is more realistically assessed by taking into account the availability of allied health staff that are able and authorized to deliver specific medical services under the supervision of doctors, as well as the existence of adequate referral systems. Likewise, a response to the widely recognized shortage of nurses is much more effective if the planning process identifies disincentives that deter health workers from assuming nursing functions and remedies that involve collaborative approaches among health personnel.

A comprehensive approach to human resources development is essential to ensure that health systems are being staffed with the right number and types of health personnel. This requires active planning, strong institutions, and quality regulation. Optimal results are more likely to be achieved when the educational institutions, professional associations and health service organizations share a common vision regarding the job profile for each health care professional, including basic educational requirements, working conditions, rewards, and career development pathways. This type of collaboration will ensure consistency, mutual support, and synergetic actions.[15]

In 1995 the World Health Assembly formally recognized this need for a better-coordinated approach in human resources development in its resolution WHA 48.8 on reorientation of medical education and medical practice for health for all[17] (*see* Annex B), which urged Member States:

➤ to collaborate with all bodies concerned, including professional associations, in defining the desired profile of the future medical practitioner and, where appropriate, the respective and complementary roles of generalists and specialists and their relations with other primary health care providers, in order to respond better to people's needs and improve health status;

➤ to promote and support health systems research to define optimal numbers, mix, deployment, infrastructure and working conditions to improve the medical practitioner's relevance and cost-effectiveness in health care delivery.

The WHO has described strategies for implementing this resolution and for concomitant reform of health care, medical practice, and medical education – all of which involve developing a more responsive and effective workforce.[18]
    World Health Assembly Resolution 57.19 in 2004[19] urged Member States:

➤ to develop strategies to mitigate the adverse effects of migration of health personnel and minimize its negative impact on health systems;

➤ to establish mechanisms to mitigate the adverse impact on developing countries of the loss of health personnel through migration, including means for the receiving countries to support the strengthening of health systems, in particular human resources development, in the countries of origin.

An important resolution for family medicine, was the World Health Assembly Resolution 62.12, in 2009,[20] where the Member States were urged:

➤ to train and retain adequate numbers of health workers, with appropriate skill-mix, including primary health care nurses, midwives, allied health professionals, and **family physicians**, able to work in a multidisciplinary context, in cooperation with nonprofessional community health workers in order to respond effectively to people's health needs.

The approach to providing physical resources is similar to that of generating human resources. It is most effective when priorities are guided by the health needs of the population to be served, coordinated with the resources that are available, and consistent with an ongoing, accurate inventory. In this way available funding will be maximized and health personnel will have the facilities to utilize their skills in an optimal and cost-effective manner. There are many instances, however, in which these guidelines are not followed, despite their intuitive logic. For example, countries may invest in expensive tertiary care facilities while failing to meet the basic primary health care needs of their populations. The recent Global Consensus for Social Accountability of Medical Schools provides an interesting array of strategic directions to assist medical schools as well as other health professionals' schools to better respond to people's priority health needs and to health system challenges in countries.[21]

In the *Lancet* report "Health professionals for a new century: transforming education to strengthen health systems in an interdependent world,"[22] the authors emphasized the need to scale up human resources for health care in different continents. Moreover, the report invites institutions for health professionals' education to engage in a process of "transformative learning," with an emphasis on interprofessional learning, and to create providers who are not only good "scientists" and not only good "health care providers," but who can also act as "change agents" in order to continuously improve health care delivery.

Financing health systems and remunerating health services

The context of financing health services delivery reflects the values, heritage, and culture of each country. Most nations use a combination of public and private funds for health care services. Whatever the starting point, financing systems need to adapt over time as the demands on them also change.

The 2010 World Health Report[10] identified the role of health system financing in moving toward universal health coverage. In this report, the WHO outlined how countries can modify their financing systems to move more quickly toward universal coverage and to sustain those achievements.

Health system revenues may be collected through taxation, mandatory or voluntary private insurance, or out-of-pocket expenditures. Out-of-pocket payment for health services has been shown to restrict access to health care, excluding the poorest members of society. Financial pooling combines revenues so that the costs of health care are spread among a group, rather than having each individual purchase services independently, and allocation may be adjusted to promote equity of access. Strategic purchasing uses a variety of mechanisms to create incentives and to distribute effective services equitably, based on socially responsive and cost-effective priorities, while balancing local responsibility and authority with more centralized guidelines.[10,13,52]

Because financial resources for health care are finite, health systems must limit available care. Some systems use price controls to restrict overall budgets or coverage for expensive therapies. Others use strategies to control referrals to specialist services, such as requiring the patient to first see a primary care physician· or obtain prior approval of payment for specialty services. With any system, however, if priorities are not selected and funded, it is unlikely that cost-effective therapies will be included consistently in the services covered, or that maximal results will be achieved with the resources available.

Regardless of the mechanism adopted, it is important to assure that funding policies are consistent with a country's health care priorities and that remuneration systems are sufficient to recruit, train, and motivate a competent workforce consistent with the needs of the population being served. The implications of systems of payment for remunerating the complex tasks performed by family doctors are considered in Chapter 5, Section 5.3.

A joint report of WONCA, the WHO, and the Royal College of General Practitioners in the United Kingdom on physician funding makes a useful overview of funding mechanisms with particular reference to family physicians and their roles as primary health care providers.[23]

Collecting data

A systematic collection of accurate information is necessary in order to make appropriate decisions about services, resources, and finances on the basis of identifying problems, determining priorities, and assessing outcomes.

Traditional statistics on mortality, morbidity, and childbirth can be amplified by standardized data sets for ambulatory care that routinely report problems and diagnoses made in office-based practice. In order to achieve maximal effectiveness and consistent responses from busy practitioners, it is necessary to develop simple and efficient data collection systems that integrate both individual health and public health functions. These data are then also a valuable resource for health research. Surveys of populations outside of health facilities provide further ways to understand the health needs of a population.

Often, information systems in countries are planned and managed without sufficient input at the district and health unit level where the main health interventions are implemented. The key strategy is to decentralize the information system so that it can be used more effectively to implement both individual and community interventions. Examples of relevant community data include notification of cases of infectious disease outbreaks; identification of high-risk children, women, and families; and coverage of disadvantaged populations with health and social services.

Leadership

Although each government has the ultimate responsibility for overseeing the performance of their health system, all those involved in health services delivery contribute to leading the system toward better outcomes. Functions of leadership include defining a vision, establishing an orientation, developing health policy, setting standards and regulations, and collecting and responding to information. Effective leaders teach by their example, involve participants, and steer the health system toward providing the best quality of health care for all people at a cost the system can afford.

Stewardship, an aspect of leadership, implies the careful supervision of available resources to maintain and strengthen the system for the benefit of all. It also implies responsibility for mobilizing and convincing influential partners on the health scene to join forces and agree on collaborative actions.[13]

International aid should be aligned and harmonized around national health policies in those countries that have high dependency on external financing. The Organisation for Economic Co-operation and Development (OECD) Paris Declarations and Accra Agenda for Action on effective delivery of aid are useful resources.[24]

2.4 TRENDS AFFECTING HEALTH SERVICE DELIVERY

Advances in education, economic development, health-related behaviors, public policy, science, technology, and public health have dramatically improved health status for many over the past 50 years. Quality and length of life have been enhanced by sanitation, a cleaner environment, healthier lifestyles, nutrition, antimicrobials, immunizations, family planning, and progress in diagnoses, therapies, and surgical procedures. In large part, as a result of these measures, life expectancy in low-income countries increased from 40 years in 1950 to over 65 years in 1997.[25] People throughout the world live almost 25 years longer today than their counterparts at similar income levels in 1900.

Good health contributes both to improvements in the overall quality of life and to gains in economic productivity. These accomplishments, however, are not shared by a large segment of the world's population. Over one billion people live in poverty, lacking access to basic health and education, safe drinking water, and adequate nutrition. Thus, as pointed out by the 1996 Human Development Report, human development over the past 30 years is a "mixed picture of unprecedented human progress and unspeakable human misery."[26]

The WHO 2008 report on social determinants of health[49] highlighted the importance of improving daily living conditions and tackling the inequitable distribution of power, money and resources, and the need to measure and understand the problem of health inequity. Moreover, the report states that

> health-care systems have better health outcomes when built on Primary
> Health Care – that is, both the primary health care-model that emphasizes
> locally appropriate action across the range of social determinants, where

prevention and promotion are in balance with investment in curative interventions, and an emphasis on the primary level of care with adequate referral to higher levels of care.

In order to achieve optimal results for both rich and poor countries, health planners must address the following major trends affecting society: the burden of disease, changing patterns of disease, population growth, aging of the population, and globalization.

Burden of disease

Although the world has witnessed unprecedented improvements in overall health status, the WHO has documented enormous global health problems that remain.[27,28]

Between 1990 and 2002 average overall incomes increased by approximately 21%. During this time the number of people living in extreme poverty declined by an estimated 130 million; child mortality rates fell from 103 deaths per 1000 live births a year to 88; life expectancy rose from 63 years to nearly 65 years; an additional 8% of the developing world's people received access to water; and an additional 15% acquired access to improved sanitation services.

Yet between 1975 and 1995, a total of 16 countries actually experienced a decrease in life expectancy. While some populations have achieved low fertility and low mortality, premature mortality still remains unacceptably high in many regions. Around 10 million children under 5 years of age die each year, mainly from preventable causes; in 30% of cases the underlying cause is undernutrition. Over half a million women die from the direct complications of pregnancy and childbirth.[27]

These statistics represent immense suffering that is avoidable.

Even in affluent countries, the burden of disease is considerable. Just as in low-income countries, income inequalities have detrimental effects on the health of those in lower socioeconomic positions. The overuse of diagnostic technology may contribute to false positive diagnoses, expensive follow-up evaluations, and unnecessary treatment. Iatrogenic problems related to errors, adverse effects of treatment, and contraindicated care appear to be considerable, adding to the burden of disease in both low- and high-income populations.[29]

In the "Global Burden of Disease Study 2010," the changing pattern of disease, injury, and risk worldwide have been depicted.[28] The study puts an important spotlight on disability – from, for example, mental health disorders, substance use, musculoskeletal disease, diabetes, chronic respiratory disease, anemia, and loss of vision and hearing. More people will be spending more years of their lives with more illnesses – this is multi-morbidity. This will be a new challenge for family medicine and primary health care.

Changing patterns of disease

Disease patterns vary widely among countries, resulting in differing effects on health systems. Although mortality from communicable diseases has decreased over the past forty years in most countries, the rates of these largely preventable or inexpensively curable diseases are still high in low-income countries. For instance, in sub-Saharan Africa, approximately 70% of the disease burden is due to communicable diseases whereas these diseases account for only about 10% of the burden in industrialized countries. More than 36 million people are now living with HIV/AIDS, and more than 70% of HIV-positive individuals live in Africa.[30] In high-income countries, noncommunicable diseases, such as cardiovascular problems, cancer, and diabetes, predominate.[11]

Furthermore, all countries face new health challenges. The growing toll from AIDS, drug-resistant malaria and tuberculosis, and tobacco-related deaths from cancer and heart and lung disease, may erase recent gains in longevity. Ensuring adequate and safe supplies of food and water, uncontaminated blood, and clean air will continue to be important priorities for the global community.

Population growth

The annual growth rate of the world population peaked at 2% per year during 1965–1970, had fallen to 1.16% during 2005–2010, and is projected to decline to 0.44% per year by 2045–2050. The average number of children born per woman has fallen from 4.45 in 1970–1975 to 2.52 in 2005–2010, although this global average still includes considerable variation between countries.[31] Some low- and middle-income countries have already reached stable population levels of around 2.1 children per family, and it is anticipated that 132 countries will achieve total fertility rates of 2.1 or less by 2045–2050.[31]

Nevertheless, the world population will continue to increase by approximately 80 million people per year until 2010, after which the increment is anticipated to decline gradually to 40 million by 2050. The current population is thus projected to increase from seven billion in 2013 to nine billion by 2050, this increase being in developing countries. It is anticipated that this growth will be accompanied by substantial increases in the number of individuals living at or below subsistence levels, which will create additional pressures on health service delivery systems.

Aging of the population

The aging of the population is another social phenomenon that will have profound health consequences in all countries. By 2011, the proportion of older persons in more developed countries had exceeded the proportion of children, and by 2050 is projected to be around double the proportion of children. In less-developed countries, a period of rapid population aging is also now forecast, with the proportion of older persons predicted to reach 20% by 2050.[31] The declining workforce under the age of 30 years of age and the increasing numbers of people over 65 years of age will strain pension funds and increase the proportion of the gross domestic product being expended on health care, since older adults consume a greater amount and percentage of health care resources.

Chronic diseases are the largest cause of death in the world.[51] In 2002, the leading chronic diseases (cardiovascular disease, cancer, chronic respiratory disease, and diabetes) caused 29 million deaths worldwide. Despite growing evidence of epidemiological and economic impact,[32] and the United Nations convening its first ever high-level meeting on noncommunicable disease prevention and control in 2011,[33] the global response to the problem remains inadequate.

The classical approach to chronic conditions, based on mono-disease guidelines, will be problematic with increasing multi-morbidity. This will invite health care providers, to shift the paradigm from "problem-oriented" care toward "goal-oriented" care.[34]

Globalization

Global economic and political forces also influence the population's health, the allocation of resources, and the delivery of services. Political and economic changes have contributed to cross-border travel, increasing the likelihood of the spread of diseases. Emigration resulting from economic deprivation places major health care demands on the receiving country. Ethnic and political struggles within and between nations have resulted in millions of refugees living in unsanitary conditions, providing fertile ground for emerging and opportunistic diseases.

Global forces also affect the movement of health professionals. For instance, more than half of all migrating doctors and nurses come from developing countries. Health systems in a number of high-income countries depend heavily on doctors and nurses who have been trained abroad. Over the last 30 years, the number of migrant health workers increased by more than 5% per year in many European countries. In OECD countries around 20% of doctors come from abroad. Earning differentials and poor working conditions often lead to the decision to emigrate, resulting in a lack of qualified personnel in the immigrants' home countries.[35]

Computer-based information provides rapid access to evidence and to management systems that have the potential to improve quality of care throughout the world. Globalization influences medical education as well, with increasing exchanges of students and faculty among medical schools throughout the world, attendance at international conferences, and use of similar textbooks. Furthermore, ministries of health and education, international nongovernmental organizations, and the WHO are exploring standards of accreditation for medical schools that take into account uniform criteria while retaining flexibility to respond to diverse local needs and circumstances.[21,36-38]

A small but increasing percentage of health care services is delivered within a global marketplace. Many pharmaceutical companies, hospital chains, large health insurers, and health maintenance organizations are becoming multinational health care corporations. Although these corporations might standardize expectations for health services financing and delivery across countries, they are more likely to respond to international market forces and shareholder interests than to the needs of local populations. Thus, without attention to equity, their focus on profits may fail to provide care for the poor or other disadvantaged populations.

Additional global forces include movements to privatize, commercialize, and decentralize the delivery of health services. Even among countries where both health care policy and health services are public sector driven, governments are promoting the potential of private sector involvement as a means of increasing cost-effectiveness and, at times, of shifting costs. Commercial interests, however, can overshadow humane ethical considerations and a sense of social responsibility among caregivers and academic organizations.[39]

2.5 CHALLENGES TO OPTIMAL HEALTH SERVICE DELIVERY

In addition to responding to the aforementioned societal trends, health systems obtain more value for their investments if they address four major challenges that impair delivery of health care throughout the world: (1) misallocation of resources, (2) inequitable distribution of services, (3) inefficiency, and (4) rapidly rising costs.[11]

Misallocation of resources

Misallocation of public resources is one of the most serious problems preventing rich and poor countries from adequately responding to priority health needs. Often funds are spent on interventions with low cost-effectiveness, while more cost-effective interventions are underfunded. Public funds may be expended on high cost hospital services that disproportionately serve the more affluent urban sector. For instance, in some countries, a single tertiary care hospital may absorb 20% or more of the ministry of health budget, at the expense of failing to deliver more effective clinical care through small health facilities decentralized throughout urban and rural communities.[11] Scarce resources may be expended on training too many doctors, a mix of specialists that does not coincide with the needs of society, or doctors who are not likely to practice where they are most needed, particularly in rural communities or among the poor.

Inequitable distribution of services

Once priorities have been selected, it is then important to deliver care consistently and equitably. Inequalities in health care are common even in the most affluent countries, and are strongly associated with social class. Some less affluent nations have reduced inequities in outcomes by providing essential services to all, though there is still a significant gap to address before the goal of universal health coverage is reached. Some affluent nations continue to spend a great deal but achieve less desirable outcomes because of inequities in the delivery of essential services. The poor often receive lower quality of care as a result of insufficient resources and uneven implementation of programs intended to meet their needs. Providing consistent, high-quality health services is a particular challenge in rural areas where low population density and fewer amenities make it difficult to attract the necessary range of health professionals (*see* Chapter 5, Section 5.4).

Inefficiency

The organization of health services has a significant effect on health outcomes.

These services may be highly centralized and coordinated, or fragmented with many overlapping systems operating simultaneously. Central coordination can improve efficiency but may stifle autonomy and innovation. Multiple systems of health care may stimulate creativity, but might also result in fragmentation, redundancy and inefficient use of limited resources. Health workers may not be appropriately deployed or adequately supervised. The frequent separation and lack of coordination of public preventive services and individual clinical services creates additional inefficiencies. The 2010 WHO World Health Report highlighted how inefficiencies may account for 20%–40% of total health expenditure.[10]

It has been demonstrated that in tackling global health problems in the twenty-first century, services needed to be integrated and that vertically organized services are not as efficient. This additionally stresses the importance of the comprehensive primary care services provided through family medicine.[50]

Rapidly rising costs

All countries face similar challenges in choosing how to achieve the best health outcomes in the context of increasing costs and expectations. Rising health care costs are fueled by several factors, such as disproportionate growth of specialist physicians, readily available expensive medical technology, and insurance schemes with fee-for-service reimbursement that generate a growing demand for costly tests, procedures, and treatments, some of which may not be associated with scientific evidence of positive health outcomes.[29]

Implications for the physician workforce

These four challenges to optimal delivery are often interdependent. For instance, in many countries, misallocation of resources has resulted in an oversupply of physicians that contributes to competition and excessive medical expenses without a corresponding improvement in health outcomes. Often there are too many insufficiently trained generalists, combined with a rapidly growing population of specialists whose training has emphasized the use of sophisticated technology for hospitalized patients with advanced diseases rather than the primary health care of communities. Decisions by physicians are responsible for consuming a major portion of a country's health budget. Costs are increased by the choice of medications and treatments that are not of scientifically proven value or by undue reliance on expensive high-technology solutions to health problems. These countries could achieve better outcomes with the same allocation of resources by educating fewer physicians, emphasizing the training of generalists, and realigning the focus of specialists to serve as consultants rather than as primary health care providers.

2.6 MEETING THE CHALLENGES THROUGH PRIMARY HEALTH CARE

The discrepancy between the capacity to improve health and actual health outcomes has triggered a number of responses from communities and world health leaders centered on the fundamental importance of primary health care.

The Declaration of Alma-Ata[40] identified primary health care as the most cost-effective way to deliver essential health services. All countries were called upon to prioritize the provision of these services for their entire population. Primary health care was selected because it has the capacity to respond comprehensively to the health needs of individuals and communities even when resources are limited. The Declaration of Alma-Ata was revisited in 2008 by the WHO and a new document, restating the importance of primary health care "Now More Than Ever" was issued.[15]

The unique features of primary health care include first contact, longitudinality, comprehensiveness, and coordination.[4] Furthermore, the way in which the characteristics are organized and incorporated into a systematic approach within primary health systems is distinctive and recognizable (*see* Box 2.2).

BOX 2.2 Example of a patient presenting for primary care

A patient with undifferentiated chest pain may be suffering from a musculoskeletal, cardiac, pulmonary, gastrointestinal, or psychological ailment. Rather than visiting a series of orthopedic, cardiac, pulmonary, gastrointestinal, and mental health specialists, patients with such concerns can usually be managed effectively by a generalist in a primary care setting.

People often present with multiple health problems. In primary care settings, such problems as hypertension, diabetes, and health maintenance can be covered in a single visit. If people have problems that cannot be dealt with in the primary care setting, they are referred to the most appropriate level of specialty care. Primary care thus serves an important coordinating function.

The effectiveness and equity of health systems correlate with their orientation toward primary health care. This correlation was demonstrated in a study by Barbara Starfield that measured the health outcomes of 12 Western industrialized nations in relation to the characteristics of their health system policies and practices that reflect primary health care. Lower mortality rates, longer life expectancy, lower expenditures for health care, and the population's satisfaction with its health system were all associated with a country's orientation to primary health care. Countries that appropriately supported and delivered primary health care achieved better health outcomes at lower costs.[4,29] Further research demonstrated that a greater emphasis on primary care can be expected to lower the costs of care, improve health through access to more appropriate services, and reduce the inequities in the population's health.[41]

2.7 STRATEGIES FOR IMPLEMENTING PRIMARY HEALTH CARE

In 1998, 20 years after the conference in Alma-Ata, the WHO sponsored a follow-up meeting in Almaty, Kazakhstan, to explore new strategies to achieve health for all in the twenty-first century. Participants described substantial health gains resulting from the implementation of primary health care in many regions, but inadequate progress in other areas where there had been deterioration in health status. They concluded that the primary health care approach had resulted in considerable improvements in health outcomes. They recognized inconsistent implementation as a key challenge, and identified the following prerequisites[40] for effective primary health care:

➤ supportive national health policies with long-term commitments
➤ decentralized responsibility and accountability
➤ capacity development at local levels
➤ acceptable conditions for health workers
➤ financing to assure access for the poor
➤ continuous efforts to improve quality
➤ community empowerment and participation
➤ sustainable partnerships.

These elements, when combined in a continuous cycle of planning, implementation and monitoring, can be used to steer a health system toward better performance. A variety of additional strategies will enhance the delivery of primary health care. They include community-oriented primary health care and improving collaboration among stakeholders.

Community-oriented primary health care

Community-oriented primary health care (COPC) is a systematic approach to improving primary health care services through integrating clinical medicine with public health at the community level.[42,43,53]

This involves a sequence of related activities that include:

➤ defining a community by geographical, demographic or other characteristics
➤ determining the health needs of the community in a systematic manner
➤ identifying and prioritizing health problems
➤ developing programs to address priorities within the context of primary health care
➤ assessing outcomes.

In this manner, COPC integrates individual and population-based care, blending the clinical skills of the practitioner with epidemiology, preventive medicine and health promotion. This sequence is a dynamic process that may not be linear. Some components may be better developed than others, some may be developed concomitantly and others may need to be readdressed over time. The main point, however, is that this process is designed to improve the health of a population through systematic application of principles that have been shown to have health benefits for communities.

COPC teams design specific interventions to address priority health problems.

A team, consisting of primary health care staff and community members, assesses resources and develops strategic plans to deal with the problems that have been identified. Interventions that involve community participants and take into account the perspectives and concerns of the target population are more likely to be successful. Specific health indicators are monitored throughout and are measured over time to evaluate the effectiveness of interventions. The cycle of COPC is renewed when teams use results from prior efforts to improve subsequent programs. As teams become more experienced and gather additional resources, they are able to anticipate challenges and increase their effectiveness and scope of activities.

A review of COPC experience, from its origins in South Africa in the 1940s up to 1984, provided data about the effectiveness of COPC programs for various health problems in different countries in the world.[42] In a more recent review of COPC, the authors concluded "COPC has been shown to have a striking impact on the communities where it is practiced."[44]

Others have cautioned that the development of COPC has been hampered by lack of a supportive policy environment, piecemeal approaches that impede comprehensive care, and implementation difficulties including additional costs and problems associated with reallocating resources.[45–47]

The strategies developed by proponents of COPC, however, provide positive approaches toward resolving the separation that has all too frequently developed between public health and individual health care.

Uniting stakeholders through partnership

Primary health care is also enhanced by sector-wide approaches that unite key players, such as development banks, donor organizations, and government agencies, around shared goals and collective responsibilities. The assumption underlying this approach is that better use of available funds is likely to occur when health service delivery policies are developed jointly by involved parties and when those policies are then reflected in consistent resource allocations and institutional frameworks.[48] International aid should also be aligned and harmonized around national health policies in those countries that have high dependency on external financing.[24]

In addition to the need for coordinated sector-wide approaches, a major impediment to providing optimal primary health care is a lack of cohesive and collaborative relationships among those involved in delivering health services. Towards Unity for Health is a WHO-sponsored project designed to unite people and organizations in coordinated approaches to health care through partnerships among principal stakeholders. These stakeholders are those who participate in or benefit from the health system. They include individuals, communities and programs, both within and outside traditional health sectors. While many groups contribute to the optimal functioning of health systems, the key stakeholders include health professionals, academic institutions, health managers, policy makers, and communities. Collaboration among these stakeholders is most likely to improve the overall functioning of health systems (*see* Box 2.3). International development agencies can also be important partners, especially for countries with high dependency on external financing. The fragmentation that exists between these groups can be overcome through shared goals that incorporate the values of quality, equity, relevance, and cost-effectiveness.[2] The WHO and WONCA have collaborated in a variety of initiatives to improve the coordination and delivery of health services (*see* Annex D).

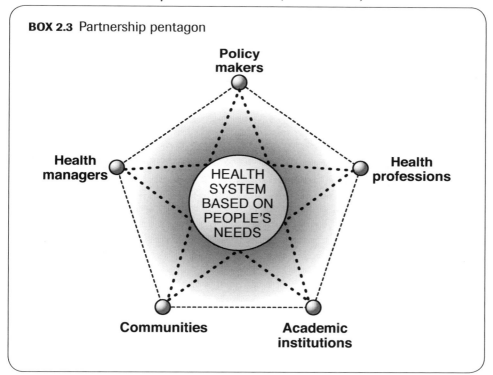

BOX 2.3 Partnership pentagon

The most critical components of a well-functioning health care system are the people who provide health care. They include health care teams and the physicians who participate in them.

Health professionals do not work in a vacuum. They require a system that encourages and supports their efforts and provides adequate facilities with good working conditions. Given the complexity of health systems, substantial progress is more likely when health personnel share common goals and values with other key stakeholders. If teams are well composed, each member understands and depends on the skills of others to create a functional whole and accomplish the best outcomes. The achievement of optimally functioning primary health care teams is considered more extensively in Chapter 3.

Primary care doctors are of particular importance to well-functioning primary care teams. They are called upon to treat a wide range of patients at the community level, including those with complex disorders. In some countries, primary care functions are distributed among a group of doctors, with pediatricians caring for children, internal medicine physicians caring for adults, and obstetricians caring for pregnant women. Other countries have recognized the value of generalist physicians who are deliberately trained to provide care for the entire community. These generalist physicians are referred to as general practitioners or family doctors.

Family doctors are a critical link in the infrastructure of a well-functioning, coordinated, cost-effective health system that responds to the powerful trends and challenges affecting health services delivery with care that represents a judicious balance of quality, equity, and relevance. Family doctors are prepared to bridge the gaps between patients and health resources, individual health and public health, communities and academic medical centers, and primary health care workers and specialists, while working in collegial harmony with similarly oriented health professionals and stakeholders. The functions, education, and support of family doctors for these roles are addressed in the following chapters.

REFERENCES

1. Boelen C, Neufeld V (eds). *Towards Unity for Health: case studies.* Geneva: World Health Organization, 2001.
2. Boelen C. *Towards Unity for Health: challenges and opportunities for partnership in health development. A working paper.* Geneva: World Health Organization, 2000.
3. Boelen C. Building synergies. *Towards Unity For Health.* 2000; **2**: 3.
4. Starfield B. *Primary Care: balancing health needs, services and technology.* Oxford: Oxford University Press, 1998.
5. Marmot M. Social determinants of health inequalities. *Lancet.* 2005; **365**: 1099–104.
6. World Health Organization. *Increasing the Relevance of Education for Health Professionals. Report of a WHO Study Group on Problem-Solving Education for the Health Professions.* Geneva: World Health Organization, 1993 (WHO Technical Report Series, No. 838).
7. Kahssay HM, Taylor ME, Berman PA. *Community Health Workers: the way forward.* Geneva: World Health Organization, 1998 (Public Health in Action, No.4).
8. Tarimo E. *Towards a Health District. Organizing and managing district health systems based on primary health care.* Geneva: World Health Organization, 1991.
9. Pan American Health Organization (PAHO). Renewing primary health care in the Americas: a position paper of the Pan American Health Organization/World Health

Organization, 2007. Available at: www2.paho.org/hq/dmdocuments/2010/Renewing_ Primary_Health_Care_Americas-PAHO.pdf

10. World Health Organization. *World Health Report 2010 – Health systems financing: the path to universal coverage.* Available at: www.who.int/whr/2010/en/index.html

11. World Bank. *World Development Report 1993. Investing in Health.* Available at: wdronline. worldbank.org/worldbank/a/c.html/world_development_report_1993/abstract/WB. 0-1952-0890-0.abstract1

12. Murray CJL, Lopez AD (eds). *Global Comparative Assessments in the Health Sector: disease burden, expenditures and intervention packages.* Geneva: World Health Organization, 1994.

13. World Health Organization. *World Health Report 2000 – Health systems: improving performance.* Available at: www.who.int/whr/2000/en/

14. Bobadilla JL, Cowley P, Musgrove P, et al. Design, content and financing of an essential national package of health services. *Bulletin of the World Health Organization.* 1994; **72**(4): 653–62.

15. World Health Organization. *World Health Report 2008 – Primary health care (now more than ever).* Available at: www.who.int/whr/2008/en/

16. World Health Organization. *World Health Report 2006 – Working together for health.* Available at: www.who.int/whr/2006/en/index.html

17. World Health Organization. The reorientation of medical education and medical practice for Health for All. World Health Assembly Resolution WHA48.8. Geneva: World Health Organization, 1995 (WHA48/1995/REC/1: 8-10).

18. World Health Organization. *Doctors for Health: a WHO global strategy for changing medical education and medical practice for health for all.* Geneva: World Health Organization, 1996.

19. World Health Organization. International migration of health personnel: a challenge for health systems in developing countries. World Health Assembly Resolution WHA57.19. Geneva: World Health Organization, 2004. Available at: apps.who.int/gb/ebwha/pdf_files/ WHA57/A57_R19-en.pdf

20. World Health Organization. Reducing health inequities through action on the social determinants of health. World Health Assembly Resolution WHA62.12. In: Sixty-second World Health Assembly, Geneva, 18–22 May 2009, Volume 1: Resolutions and decisions, Annexes. Geneva: WHO, 2009: (WHA62/2009/REC/1) 16–19.

21. *The Global Consensus for Social Accountability of Medical Schools, 2010.* Available at: www. healthsocialaccountability.org

22. Frenk J, Chen L, Bhutta ZA, et al. Health professionals for a new century: transforming education to strengthen health systems in an interdependent world. *Lancet.* 2010; **376**: 1923–58.

23. Royal College of General Practitioners. Physician funding and health care systems – an international perspective. A summary of a conference hosted by the WHO, WONCA and RCGP at St John's College, Cambridge, 1999.

24. Organisation for Economic Co-operation and Development Paris declaration 2005 and Accra agenda for action 2008. Available at: www.oecd.org/dac/aideffectiveness/paris declarationandaccraagendaforaction.htm

25. Preker A, Feachem R, DeFerranti D. *Health, Nutrition and Population Sector Strategy.* Washington DC: World Bank, 1997.

26. United Nations Development Programme. *Human Development Report 1996.* Oxford University Press, 1996.

27. World Health Organization. *The Global Burden of Disease 2004 Update*. Available at: www. who.int/healthinfo/global_burden_disease/2004_report_update/en/index.html

28. Horton R. GBD 2010: understanding disease, injury, and risk. *Lancet*. 2012; **380**: 2053–4.

29. Starfield B. Is US health really the best in the world? *Journal of the American Medical Association*. 2000; **284**: 483–5.

30. UNAIDS/WHO. *AIDS Epidemic Update: December 2000*. Geneva: UNAIDS/WHO, 2000 (document UNAIDS/00.44E-WHOICDS/EDCl2000.9).

31. United Nations Department of Economic and Social Affairs. *World Population Prospects: the 2010 revision*.

32. Yach D, Hawkes C, Gould L, et al. The global burden of chronic diseases: overcoming impediments to prevention and control. *Journal of the American Medical Association*. 2004; **291**(21): 2616–22.

33. United Nations. Political declaration of the High-Level Meeting of the General Assembly on the prevention and control of non-communicable diseases, 2011. Available at: www. un.org/ga/search/view_doc.asp?symbol=A/66/L.1

34. De Maeseneer J, Boeckxstaens P. James Mackenzie Lecture 2011: multimorbidity, goal-oriented care and equity. *British Journal of General Practice*. 2012; **62**: 522–4.

35. Adams O, Kinnon C. A public health perspective, perspective. In: Zarrilii S, Kinnon C, Ricupero R (eds). *International Trade in Health Services: a development perspective*. Geneva: World Health Organization, 1998 (document no. WHO/TFHE/98.1): 37.

36. Karle H. Globalisation of medical education. *Journal of the World Medical Association*. 2001; **47**(1): 3–7.

37. Boelen C. Adapting health care institutions and medical schools to societies' needs. *Academic Medicine*. 1999; **74**(8): S11–20.

38. AMEE: Association of Medical Education in Europe. ASPIRE project, 2012. www.aspire-to-excellence.org

39. Pandurangi VR. Basic health services: why we are not making greater progress. *Towards Unity for Health*. 2000; **2**: 34–5.

40. World Health Organization/UNICEF. *Primary Health Care 21: everybody's business: an international meeting to celebrate 20 years after Alma Ata, Almaty, Kazakhstan, 27–28 November 1998*. Geneva, World Health Organization, 2000. Available at: http://apps.who.int/iris/bitstream/10665/66306/1/WHO_EIP_OSD_00.7.pdf

41. Starfield B, Shi L, Macinko J. Contribution of primary care to health systems and health. *Milbank Quarterly*. 2005; **83**: 457–502.

42. Abramson JH. Community-oriented primary care: strategy, approaches and practice – a review. *Public Health Reviews*. 1988, **16**: 35–98.

43. Nutting PA (ed). *Community-Oriented Primary Care: from principle to practice*. Washington DC, Health Resources and Services Administration, Public Health Services, 1987.

44. Longlett SK, Kruse JE, Wesley RM. Community-oriented primary care: historical perspective. *Journal of the American Board of Family Practice*. 2001; **14**(1): 54–63.

45. Donaldson MS, Yordy KD, Lohr KN, et al. (eds). *Primary Care: America's health in a new era*. Washington DC: Institute of Medicine, National Academy Press, 1996.

46. Gofin J, Gofin R, Abramson JH, et al. Ten-year evaluation of hypertension, overweight, cholesterol and smoking control: the CHAD Programme in Jerusalem. *Preventive Medicine*. 1986; **15**: 304–12.

47. Gofin J. The community-oriented primary care (COPC) approach and Towards Unity for Health: unity of action and purpose. *Towards Unity for Health*. 2001; **1**: 9–10.

48. Cassels A. *A Guide to Sector-Wide Approaches for Health Development: concepts, issues and*

working arrangements. Geneva: World Health Organization, 1997 (document no. WHO/ARA/97.12).

49. World Health Organization. *Commission on Social Determinants of Health Final Report: Closing the Gap in a Generation: health equity through action on the social determinants of health, 2008.* Available at: www.who.int/social_determinants/thecommission/finalreport/en/index.html

50. De Maeseneer J, Roberts RG, Demarzo M, et al. Tackling NCDs: a different approach is needed. *Lancet.* 2012; **379**: 1860–1.

51. World Health Organization. *Action Plan for the Global Strategy for the Prevention and Control of Noncommunicable Diseases, 2008.* Available at: www.who.int/nmh/publications/9789241597418/en/

52. Schieber G, Maeda A. A curmudgeon's guide to financing health care in developing countries. In: Schieber G (ed). *Innovations in Health Care Financing. Proceedings of a World Bank Conference, 10–11 March 1997.* Washington DC: World Bank, 1997 (World Bank Discussion Paper No. 365).

53. Kark SL. *The Practice of Community-oriented Primary Care.* New York: Appleton-Century-Crofts, 1981.

CHAPTER 3

Family doctors in health systems

This chapter describes the nature of family medicine and how family doctors contribute to optimal primary health care systems. It focuses on the functions, roles, and effective clinical care provided by family doctors. Furthermore, it looks at the quality of their work and their contributions within their many roles as health care providers, leaders, managers and supervisors, and overall coordinators of individual and community health care.

3.1 THE NATURE OF FAMILY MEDICINE

The characteristics of family medicine are guided by a few fundamental concepts including a commitment to ongoing personal care (longitudinality), a comprehensive approach, and acceptance of all patients regardless of their gender, age, or type of health concern. Family doctors most frequently care for this rich mosaic of patients in community-based, ambulatory practice settings. Shared experiences establish a common viewpoint among family doctors around the world despite their diverse educational backgrounds and different cultures. Consequently, the characteristics, knowledge, skills, and practice patterns appear to be remarkably comparable throughout the world.[1] This uniform approach to care is summarized in the World Organization of Family Doctors (WONCA) definition of the family doctor in Box 3.1.

The role of family doctors initially evolved from traditional general practice, when most doctors were considered general practitioners immediately after medical school or after a relatively short internship period.[3] Today, an increasing number of countries require formal training in family medicine as for other medical specialties, and curricula have been developed in many countries,

---

BOX 3.1 Definition of general practitioners/family physicians

The general practitioner/family physician is the physician who is primarily responsible for providing first contact and comprehensive health care to every individual
seeking medical care and advice, and arranging for other health personnel to
provide services when necessary. The general practitioner/family physician functions as a generalist who accepts everyone seeking care in contrast to other
physicians who limit access to their services on the basis of age, sex and/or type
of health problem.

The general practitioner/family physician cares for the individual within the context of the family, for the family within the context of the community, and for the
community in the context of public health, irrespective of race, culture or social
class. He or she is clinically competent to provide the greater part of their care,
taking into account the cultural, socioeconomic and psychological background. In
addition, he or she takes personal responsibility for providing comprehensive and
continuing, person-centered care for his or her patients, and in helping coordinate
and integrate care.

The general practitioner/family physician exercises his or her professional role
by providing care either directly to patients or through the services of others
according to the health needs and resources available within the community he
or she serves.

Adapted from: The Role of the General Practitioner/Family Physician in Health Care
Systems: A Statement from WONCA, 1991.[2]

---

certification procedures established, and continuing medical education programs instituted. All of these developments relate to the changing health needs
and expectations of populations around the world.

3.2 FAMILY DOCTORS' CONTRIBUTIONS TO HEALTH CARE

The unique combination of attributes that characterize family doctors also
describe their contributions to health care. These characteristics provide the
foundation for their roles as health care providers and for their functions in primary care teams. Their contributions also relate to the manner in which patients
seek care within their particular communities.

The 2008 World Health Report reminded the world that primary health care
was needed "Now More Than Ever" in order to achieve equitable access to health
for all. In order to achieve this universal coverage, leadership and public policy

reforms are needed, and recognition that the heart of health service delivery that "puts people first" is primary care.[4] Family doctors are at the heart of primary care in many health systems.

The attributes of family doctors

The fundamental characteristics and attributes of family medicine allow family doctors to contribute substantially to health systems, not just in terms of service delivery, but also in terms of influencing public policy and through leadership by being advocates for their patients.

In addition, despite differences between countries, the fundamental characteristics and attributes of good family medicine are similar. This allows all family doctors to contribute should they wish to do so to the betterment of health systems in their own country and beyond.

The Framework for professional and administrative development of general practice/family medicine in Europe[5] reflects the culmination of a European-wide consultative process over almost a decade, initiated by the World Health Organization Regional Office for Europe. This group summarized the attributes of family practice as follows.

➤ **General**: family practice addresses the unselected health problems of the whole population; it does not exclude certain categories of the population because of age, sex, social class, race or religion, or any category of complaint or health-related problem. It must be easily accessible with a minimum of delay; access to it is not limited by geographical, cultural, administrative, or financial barriers.

➤ **Continuous**: family practice is primarily person-centered rather than disease-centered. It is based on a long-standing personal relationship between the patient and the doctor, covering individuals' health care longitudinally over substantial periods of their lives and not being limited to one particular episode of an illness.

➤ **Comprehensive**: family practice provides integrated health promotion, disease prevention, curative care, rehabilitation, and physical, psychological, and social support to individuals. It deals with the interface between illness and disease, and integrates the humanistic and ethical aspects of the doctor-patient relationship with clinical decision making.

➤ **Coordinated**: family practice can deal with many of the health problems presented by individuals at their first contact with their family physician but, whenever necessary, the family physician should ensure appropriate and timely referral of the patient to specialist services or to another health professional. On these occasions, family physicians should inform patients about available services and how best to use them, and should be the coordinators of the advice and support that the patients receive. Family physicians should act as care managers in relation to other health and social care providers, advising their patients on health matters.

➤ **Collaborative**: family physicians should be prepared to work with other medical, health, and social care providers, delegating to them the care of their patients whenever appropriate, with due regard to the competence of other disciplines. They should contribute to and actively participate in a well functioning multidisciplinary care team and must be prepared to exercise leadership of the team.

➤ **Family-oriented**: family practice addresses the health problems of individuals in the context of their family circumstances, their social and cultural networks, and the circumstances in which they live and work.

➤ **Community-oriented**: the patient's problems should be seen in the context of his or her life in the local community. The family doctor should be aware of the health needs of the population living in this community and should collaborate with other professionals, agencies from other sectors, and self-help groups to initiate positive changes in local health problems.

An additional key point is:

➤ **First contact**: when needed, patients and populations know the family doctor is the first point of contact, who can refer, if necessary, to other providers and health care services.

Working from a similar conceptual framework, the College of Family Physicians of Canada has defined four principles that underlie family medicine (*see* Box 3.2).

BOX 3.2 Underlying principles of family medicine[6]

1. The patient-doctor relationship is central to family medicine.
2. The family doctor is an effective clinician.
3. Family medicine is community based.
4. The family doctor is a resource to a defined practice population.

These attributes and principles are imbued with a commitment to the whole person.[3] The scope of the family doctor's practice is defined in large part by human needs.[7] The approach to these needs, however, reflects rigorous medical training that provides the necessary foundation to provide competent care in primary care settings, where patients present with a wide range of health concerns.

Family doctors combine breadth of practice with depth of expertise. In so doing, they add value to primary health care systems, thereby enhancing the contributions of similarly oriented health professionals such as nurses, social workers, and community health workers – all of whom empower one another in a mutually reinforcing manner.

Family doctors are in an ideal position to improve the health of people in their practices, by considering them as a defined group. This may allow them to analyze the needs and health risks of a particular population, to provide effective disease prevention measures, and to advocate health promotion strategies, particularly if they have training in population health promotion or prevention.

The family physician is trained in cultural competency. The value of diversity is reflected in communication, listening skills, and person-centric care.[49]

The population's health needs can also provide the focus for educating family doctors and guiding primary health care research (*see* Box 3.3).

BOX 3.3 The JANUS project: family doctors meeting the needs of tomorrow's society[8]

In Roman mythology, Janus was the god of good beginnings, and the Romans believed that good beginnings ensured good endings. Like its namesake, the JANUS project – an initiative of the College of Family Physicians of Canada – looks to the past and present to help Canadian family physicians meet their patients' future health care needs. It is designed to ensure that education and research are appropriate and relevant to the changing needs of patients in today's society. It includes:

- ensuring family physician participation in an ongoing, comprehensive National Physician Survey
- development of educational and research opportunities for practicing family doctors based on the identified needs of their patients and communities
- making National Physician Survey results available to physician leaders, health care planners, researchers, and health policy decision makers; these lessons from Canada are available to all countries through the development of a functional template that countries can use to assess their health needs, evaluate their current services, and train family doctors accordingly.

Many of the attributes outlined are shared by other physicians and health care providers. Yet, when taken as a whole, they define the type of physician whose expertise is remarkably congruent with the requirements for optimal primary health care envisaged in the Declaration of Alma-Ata (*see* Annex A).

Distinguishing characteristics such as first contact, accessibility, person-focused, longitudinal care, comprehensiveness and coordination of care define an approach that is unique to primary care. Health care systems with these characteristics are associated with better outcomes, increased patient satisfaction, less hospitalization and lower costs.[9-11]

Furthermore, international comparisons of primary health care outcomes[12] suggest that the greatest differences in health between countries are associated with the degree to which the following principles of their health services delivery system have been implemented:

➤ equitable distribution and financing of health care services
➤ similar level of professional earnings of primary care physicians and specialists
➤ comprehensiveness of primary health care services
➤ absent, or very low, requirements for co-payments for primary health care services
➤ primary care physicians providing first-contact care and entry into the health delivery system
➤ person-focused longitudinal care.

Family medicine can play an integral role in helping a country organize its health system to implement these principles. In order to achieve these positive outcomes, however, it is necessary for family doctors to work in unison with community representatives, public health professionals, and allied health workers.[50]

Also it will be necessary to develop a system of reimbursement, appropriate incentives, and positive working conditions in order to carry out activities that, although broader than individual patient care, may nevertheless have an even greater impact on the health of individuals. These activities include involvement in analyzing the needs of the population, working in teams, and providing supervision of other health workers.

The roles of family doctors as health care providers

As providers of care, family doctors work with other members of the primary care team to increase access, continuity, and comprehensiveness of health care services.

Access to care is determined by the way family doctors provide a variety of person-centered care services at the community level, usually in partnership with team members. It is determined by hours of availability, convenience, proximity, affordability, and acceptability.[12] Continuous access to health care services is provided for patients through coverage arrangements at the point of first contact, along with referral for patients who require services that are not available at the community level. Continuous coverage is usually shared among team members or by pooling the efforts of several teams and ensuring effective communication. After-hours coverage may be provided through on-call systems, or through emergency care services or hospital emergency rooms. When patients can readily access primary care services in the community, they are less likely to seek hospital services which are often less convenient and more expensive.

Continuous care involves an ongoing personal relationship with an individual doctor, or it may be shared among team members. It is enhanced when patients can identify and readily access their own primary care providers. Similarly, continuity is expedited when providers identify a specific group of patients for whom they are responsible. Ideally, people should be able to select the family doctor whom they prefer. In some areas, these choices may be limited by financial or geographical factors. In some practice arrangements, family doctors may supervise the care provided by nurse practitioners, medical assistants, and other health team members, to ensure continuity of care for a greater number of patients. In these situations, family doctors will focus more of their efforts on the care of patients with more severe conditions and on the most complex patients.

Family doctors are well prepared to provide comprehensive care to the whole person taking into account biological, psychosocial, and cultural influences on health and disease. They can treat the majority of their patients' problems in the consultation room or in the patient's home while arranging for appropriate assistance or referral for those with clinical problems outside their expertise.

In addition to individual patient care, family doctors can provide community health services through partnership with community health workers, health educators, and other community-oriented team members. In many communities, family doctors serve as public health or district medical officers (particularly if they have formal public health training), as coroners, or as public health educators. Box 3.4 outlines ways in which family doctors can contribute to providing effective and efficient health services. For example, some family doctors in New Zealand work with high school nurses to provide health care using standing orders for emergency contraception, regular contraception, treatment of sexually transmitted disease, treatment of skin, throat, and urinary tract infections.

Effective family medicine can deliver what may be considered as generalist care. However the ability of family doctors to do so effectively can be limited because of a number of external factors such as access to training and resources. A recent study by the Royal College of General Practitioners in the United Kingdom on medical generalism looked at why expertise in whole person medicine matters, and identified that, despite already having a relatively well developed primary care system in that country, certain preconditions were needed in order to consistently deliver excellent generalist care. These included longer training, working as a team of generalists, more time with patients, better access to additional near-patient or ambulatory diagnostics, and better communication with specialists.[13]

BOX 3.4 How to provide effective and efficient health care services with family doctors

- Assess local health needs to determine which health services should be provided at the community level; this may apply more to public health doctors, but family doctors should certainly be among stakeholders consulted. The government in the United Kingdom has made general practitioners responsible for commissioning services for their patients.
- Prepare family doctors with specific competencies to meet the needs of their practice environment.
- Integrate family doctors into primary care teams to share 24-hour coverage in order to provide continuous access to care at the community level.
- Develop and maintain lists of patients and their primary care team to promote continuity of care.
- Educate patients and other health professionals about the benefits of continuity of care.
- Provide funding mechanisms to attract family doctors and to support comprehensive primary care.
- Provide incentives for the primary care team to be the first point of call for patients with conditions that do not require urgent attendance at a hospital emergency room.

The functions of family doctors in primary care teams

A primary care team is composed of people who contribute to delivering health services.[14] Each team is unique; local conditions determine the members, relationships, and responsibilities of the team; regional and national conditions influence the resources and contexts in which the teams operate. There are many types of primary care teams ranging from small teams with a few members who fulfill multiple functions, to large teams with many members serving larger communities of patients. The basic team may consist of physicians, nurses, medical assistants, midwives, social workers, community health workers, and others who provide direct patient care. Support members of the team may include

> **BOX 3.5** Profile of the "five-star" doctor
>
> The "five-star" doctor has the desirable profile for a health care professional in a system that is based on responding to people's needs. The roles of the "five-star" doctor include the following.
>
> - **Care provider**, who considers the patient holistically as an individual and as an integral part of a family and the community, and provides high-quality, comprehensive, continuous, and personalized care within a long-term, trusting relationship.
> - **Decision maker**, who makes scientifically sound judgments about investigations, treatments, and use of technologies that take into account the person's wishes, ethical values, cost-effective considerations, and the best possible care for the patient.
> - **Communicator**, who is able to promote healthy lifestyles by effective explanation and advocacy, thereby empowering individuals and groups to enhance and protect their health.
> - **Community leader**, who, having won the trust of the people among whom he or she works, can reconcile individual and community health requirements, advise citizen groups, and initiate action on behalf of the community.
> - **Manager**, who can work harmoniously with individuals and organizations both within and outside the health system to meet the needs of individual patients and communities, making appropriate use of available health data.

receptionists, secretaries and administrators, health educators and laboratory, pharmacy, and radiology personnel. Consultant members of the team may include those who provide specialized health services, or those with expertise in community health.[14,15] When each member of a primary care team is well prepared and has adequate resources, the team can effectively respond to the majority of a community's health needs.[16]

Primary care teams must remain flexible in order to respond to the unique circumstances and resources available in a particular community. For instance, not all of the aforementioned personnel may be available, in which case others may assume essential roles. Nurses or health center staff may arrange for placement of patients with social service agencies, or assume a greater role in health education or in surveillance regarding domestic violence and many other problems. Likewise, solo practitioners who are not part of geographically located teams may make alliances with other professionals in a manner that provides their patients with many of the advantages of a primary care team.

When integrated into primary care teams, family doctors can function more effectively and enhance the capacity of the team to deliver more comprehensive services to patients. The theoretical advantages of effective teamwork[17] include:

➤ care given by a group is greater than the sum of individual care
➤ rare skills are used more appropriately
➤ peer influence and informal learning within the group raise the standards of care and status of the team in the community
➤ team members have increased job satisfaction and are less likely to become overwhelmed
➤ team working encourages coordinated health education and treatment.

Family doctors provide a variety of services for individuals, families, and communities, including preventive and curative health care. As coordinators, they can connect primary, secondary, and tertiary health care services. As leaders, managers, and supervisors, they can enhance the quality and effectiveness of team efforts. As described in the profile of the "five-star" doctor (*see* Box 3.5), these interrelated functions allow family doctors to work with primary care teams to integrate commonly fragmented elements of the health system.[18]

The ecology of primary care

Primary care can address the vast majority of the population's presenting health concerns. Nevertheless, the potential of effective primary care to prevent premature morbidity and mortality has not been always been recognized and supported by those responsible for teaching and research in medical centers or by those responsible for allocating and financing health care services. The majority of academic efforts have concentrated on the relatively small number of patients who are referred to teaching centers or hospitalized in academic medical centers.

Kerr White and colleagues graphically illustrated this phenomenon in their analysis of community health data from the United Kingdom and the United States.[19] They found that in an adult population of 1000 people, 750 experienced some form of illness each month. Of these ill patients, 250 consulted a physician, only five were referred to a consultant and just one was hospitalized at a university medical center. Yet most of teaching and research is based on this limited referral population that does not accurately represent the community at large.

Green and colleagues found remarkably similar results when they recently repeated this study in the United States and found that more women, men, and children receive medical care each month in the offices of primary care physicians than in any other professional setting.[20] More than 12 times as many people are seen in primary care physicians' offices as in hospitals. The bulk of health care remains in primary care, self-care, and ambulatory care. The health problems most commonly faced by the majority of the population would escape detection, analysis, and response by health care efforts restricted to hospitals and academic health centers. This study shows that despite substantial changes in the organization and financing of health care, utilization has remained remarkably consistent over the last 40 years (*see* Box 3.6).

The experience and expertise of the family doctor is very different from that of the specialist consultant who cares for a small proportion of diseases occurring within the community. In the words of Dr Iona Heath, "in hospitals diseases stay and patients come and go. In general practice, patients stay and diseases come and go."[21]

Family doctors' practices reflect the wide range of problems encountered in primary care, and family doctors often work at the interface of public health, preventive medicine, and self-care. This has implications for the education of physicians and highlights the importance of training generalists in community practice settings where they will encounter patients with the types of problems that they will be called upon to manage in their future practices.[22,23]

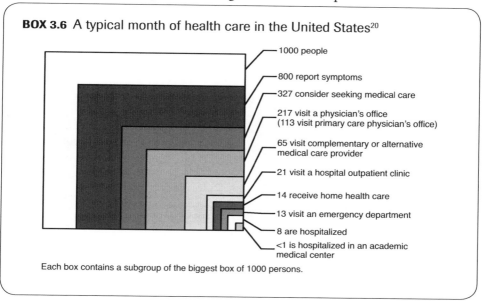

BOX 3.6 A typical month of health care in the United States[20]

- 1000 people
- 800 report symptoms
- 327 consider seeking medical care
- 217 visit a physician's office (113 visit primary care physician's office)
- 65 visit complementary or alternative medical care provider
- 21 visit a hospital outpatient clinic
- 14 receive home health care
- 13 visit an emergency department
- 8 are hospitalized
- <1 is hospitalized in an academic medical center

Each box contains a subgroup of the biggest box of 1000 persons.

3.3 FAMILY DOCTORS AS EFFECTIVE CLINICIANS

The effectiveness of primary care and family doctors is reflected in their ability to adapt to the health care needs of diverse countries around the world, in the scope of their activities, and in the quality and cost-effectiveness of their efforts.

Family practice activities around the world

While family doctors may also need to deliver specialized services and provide care for hospitalized patients, due to working in resource-limited settings and/or rural communities, they are most frequently engaged in delivering primary care services at the community level in the office and in the patient's home. To provide a benchmark and better understand the common activities of family doctors in different countries, WONCA administered a global survey on family practice through its member organizations.[1] This cross-sectional study included a self-administered questionnaire that was mailed to 130 WONCA members in 66 member countries; 66 individuals representing 51 countries (4 Africa, 7 Americas, 21 Asia-Pacific, 19 Europe) responded. It is important to note that those surveyed represent countries where family medicine generally is well developed. The survey indicated that, in these countries, family doctors practice

TABLE 3.1 Percentage of countries in which the majority of family doctors include this knowledge in their practices

Knowledge	Percentage
Internal medicine	100
Preventive medicine	96
Pediatrics	94
Psychiatry	92
Gynecology	90
Obstetrics	80
Orthopedics	80
Surgery	78
Community medicine	77
Public health	67

TABLE 3.2 Percentage of countries in which the majority of family doctors provide these services

Service	Percentage
Office practice	98
Emergency care	90
Home visits	90
After-hours coverage	59
Nursing home care	43
Hospital care	29

primarily in the community, providing care to children and adults of both sexes. Their scope of practice is quite broad, as indicated in Tables 3.1, 3.2, and 3.3 that deal, respectively, with the knowledge, services, and procedures offered by most family doctors in these nations.

TABLE 3.3 Percentage of countries in which the majority of family doctors perform these procedures

Procedure	Percentage
Individual preventive services	98
Office diagnostic procedures	94
Office surgical procedures	90
Control of laboratory testing	73
Supervision of other health workers	63
Preventive services to communities	51
In-patient surgery	12

Scope of family practice

Although family doctors around the world have much in common, the actual scope of family practice services can vary significantly within countries and communities, depending on many factors. The services provided by family doctors depend on the local prevalence of diseases and health problems, the availability of resources (such as office equipment, supplies and the ability to pay staff), the extent of their training, the organization and funding of health services, and the roles, responsibilities, and availability of other health professionals (*see* Box 3.7).

Family doctors often also perform a variety of procedures including skin biopsies of potential malignant lesions, repair of lacerations, application of casts, obstetric deliveries, giving cortisone injections, applying liquid nitrogen, carrying out dermoscopy, vasectomy, retinography, and so forth. Depending on the community's needs they may be trained in more specialized procedures such as endoscopy or caesarean sections.

They also manage and coordinate care for many complicated and severe disorders including acute emergencies, serious infections, cardiovascular diseases, or stabilization of trauma victims (*see* Tables 3.4 and 3.5 and Boxes 3.7 and 3.8).

In addition, family doctors may focus their practices in different ways. For example, they may develop a special interest and expertise in the care of adolescents, elderly people, or patients with behavioral and psychiatric disorders. They may choose to work full- or part-time in public health departments, in institutional settings (such as nursing homes or workplaces), or as faculty in medical schools. With their broad training and experience as generalists, some family

BOX 3.7 The work of a family doctor in South Africa

The work of Dr Ian Couper, a family doctor in KwaZulu-Natal in South Africa, demonstrates the range and flexibility of family practice. Dr Couper is a family doctor who works as a member of a team of generalist doctors, nurses, and allied health professionals caring for a population of 100 000 people in a provincial health department. His sub-district health department includes a 280-bed hospital, nine fixed location clinics, and three mobile clinics. It is 300 km from the nearest specialists.

The following patients were among those seen by Dr Couper in a typical week.

- An 8-year-old boy who had collapsed at school was found to be suffering from cerebral malaria. Dr Couper treated the child and also discussed strategies for prevention with the school principal.
- A family of five suffered from burn wounds after their hut burned down. Dr Couper treated the wounds and arranged for a social worker to assist with temporary housing.
- A young man was referred by a traditional healer because of concerns about possible tuberculosis. He was found to have both tuberculosis and HIV/AIDS, and arrangements were made to provide treatment and counseling to the patient and his family.
- A middle-aged woman dying of cancer of the cervix needed help with pain control and home assistance. She was admitted to the hospital for respite care.
- A dehydrated infant was brought in with diarrhea and acidosis, exacerbated by herbal enemas. The infant required emergency intraosseous rehydration and Dr Couper also discussed appropriate management of future episodes with the mother.
- An agitated man was brought in with his hands tied up because he was confused and destroying things in the home. He was sedated and admitted for further psychiatric assessment and management.

Sources: Mfenyana K (personal communication), Mash B[24]

doctors assume administrative positions as leaders in health care systems, public health departments, and government. In some countries, there are formalised training programs that encourage subspecialization within family medicine. For instance, in Canada, there is a growing number of family medicine trainees who do an additional year of training in order to develop additional skills in areas such as emergency medicine, geriatrics, palliative care, obstetrics, or anesthesia.

Practice arrangements also vary. For example, a family doctor may work alone in solo practice or with other family doctors in a group practice. Alternatively, a family doctor may work with doctors from other specialties in a multispecialty group practice or in a hospital, nursing home, or other facility. Regardless of practice arrangements, the need to address lifelong learning needs must always be present.

Despite these differences, the core elements of family medicine around the world are similar. These elements provide the foundation that is necessary to care for the majority of people's health needs and to integrate individual and community health systems in concert with the roles of other health professionals.

Family doctors must possess the skills, knowledge, and clinical judgment to deal with a wide range of problems in the family practice setting.[25] They often care for patients who present with undifferentiated problems, at which time it is necessary to distinguish between variations in normal physiology and diseases in their earliest stages. This requires training specially designed to provide expertise in managing problems that are frequently encountered in the community, acknowledgment of skill limitations, and an ability to refer patients when indicated.

Generalist doctors acquire expertise in managing problems that occur frequently in their patient populations. A variety of studies indicate that about 30–40 conditions account for over half of the medical encounters in family practice, as exemplified by analysis of electronic patient records in the Netherlands, Japan, Poland, Malta, and Serbia. The most frequent 20 conditions are listed by order of frequency in Tables 3.4 and 3.5. By dealing with familiar problems, family doctors become experts in the diseases they treat. Additionally, studies from many countries confirm that most people's problems can be managed by family doctors in the community, without requiring referral (*see* Box 3.8).

Developing long-term therapeutic relationships requires an ability to relate to patients from a position of unconditional respect.[3] In order to do so, family doctors need self-awareness and insight into how their own attitudes and life experiences affect the patient-doctor relationship. As with all physicians, the family doctor must also be a self-directed learner who stays up to date with medical knowledge, maintains diagnostic and therapeutic skills, and recognizes his or her own limitations.

What family practice means to the patient

The challenges to health service delivery systems, described in Chapter 2, are experienced in a personal manner by patients seeking care within these systems. Problems include:

TABLE 3.4 Top 20 episodes of care

	Code	Label	Total
1	A97	Prevention activity	33 292
2	R74	Upper respiratory tract infection	14 168
3	K86	Uncomplicated hypertension	11 572
4	R78	Acute bronchitis/bronchiolitis	9420
5	L03	Low back symptoms, excluding radiation	8518
6	S88	Contact dermatitis and eczema	8182
7	H81	Excessive ear wax	8174
8	W11	Family planning and oral contraceptive advice	7352
9	U71	Cystitis and other urinary tract infections	6718
10	A04	General weakness/tiredness	6621
11	S74	Dermatophytosis	6557
12	R75	Acute/chronic sinusitis	6383
13	L81	Musculoskeletal injury	6027
14	R05	Cough	5793
15	A85	Adverse effects of medications	5515
16	P06	Disturbances of sleep/insomnia	5130
17	S03	Warts	4930
18	L01	Neck symptom excluding headache	4808
19	L89	Osteoarthritis	4567
20	T90	Diabetes mellitus	4332
		Total	535 876

Source: Transition Project (www.transitieproject.nl)[26]

➤ fragmentation of services
➤ lack of a personal relationship with a physician
➤ escalating costs
➤ insufficient coordination of care
➤ difficulty knowing which health provider to contact
➤ having to consult several health providers for common problems
➤ inadequate access to care, especially in inner city and rural areas.

All members of a family should be able to rely on the well-trained family doctor to provide competent help with the majority of their problems, as well as caring for their psychological and physical well-being, while taking into account their cultural, spiritual, and personal values. Care extends from providing prenatal

TABLE 3.5 Top 20 reasons for encounter (N = 829 572)

	Code	Label	Total
1	*31	Medical examination and/or health evaluation	113 261
2	*50	Medication/prescription/injection	76 408
3	*64	Provider initiated episode of care, either new or ongoing	34 839
4	R05	Cough	31 375
5	*45	Advice/health education	26 086
6	*62	Administrative procedure	20 166
7	*34	Blood test	18 389
8	A04	General weakness/tiredness	16 888
9	*60	Results test/procedures	13 833
10	03	Fever	13 141
11	L03	Low back symptoms, excluding radiation	13 133
12	R02	Shortness of breath/dyspnoea	12 702
13	S06	Local redness/erythema/rash	12 595
14	R21	Throat symptoms or complaints	11 222
15	S04	Local swelling/lump/mass	11 149
16	N01	Headache	11 075
17	D06	Localized abdominal pain	11 016
18	L15	Knee symptoms/complaints	9553
19	L14	Leg/thigh symptoms/complaints	8777
20	L08	Shoulder symptoms/complaints	8763
		Total	946 142

Source: Transition Project (www.transitieproject.nl)[26]

care to helping patients die with dignity. People should be confident that their family doctor will refer them when necessary, coordinate multidisciplinary care, and guide them through the maze of specialties and medical technology when indicated. In order to do so, the family doctor often will need to involve other team members such as nurses and social workers in the care of their patients.

In all countries, family doctors should mobilize available resources to provide, in addition to essential medical care, relevant health education and preventive services. Effective clinicians enable screening where appropriate yet avoid unnecessary investigations ensuring their patients are reassured appropriately and protected from life-threatening harms.

In some countries, patients may receive their primary care from community workers, often with surveillance, consultation, and assistance from the family

BOX 3.8 Scope of family practice: an analysis in Australia, Germany, and South Africa

Australia

Reliable data about morbidity and its management in general practice are essential for assessment of the community's health, for planning future health services, and for measurement of change and quality of care. Since 1998, an annual random sample of about 1000 general practitioners' complete structured encounter forms on 100 consecutive patients, producing an annual database of 100 000 encounters. In 1999–2000, 60% of the patients were female and 155 690 patient reasons were given for the encounter. Medications were prescribed (95%), advised for purchase over the counter (8.5%) or provided (6.3%) for a rate of 110 per 100 encounters. Other treatments were provided at a rate of 42.1 per 1000. Referrals to specialists were made at a rate of 7.3 per 100 encounters and to other health professionals at a rate of 3.1 per 100. Laboratory (i.e., pathology) testing was ordered in 13.8% and imaging (e.g., radiology) studies in 6.7% of encounters. The study indicates that 90% of visits are managed by the family doctor.

Source: Britt H, Miller GC, Charles J, et al. The BEACH (Bettering the Evaluation and Care of Health) Study, Family Medicine Research Centre, Australia.[27]

Germany

To evaluate patient characteristics and care in 20 general practitioner offices, all patients in 20 offices and their general practitioners were administered questionnaires. A total of 1593 patients were seen, of whom 58% were female, the mean age was 47 years, and 2% were children. In 59% of the office visits, the general practitioner (GP) already knew both the patient and his or her health problem from previous visits; in 37% the GP knew the patient but not the problem; and in 4% the GP knew neither the patient nor the problem. About 40% of the problems were acute, 35% were short-term chronic (less than 6 months), and 25% long-term chronic. General advice (65%), drug prescriptions (59%), and condition-specific counseling (28%) were the most frequent interventions.

Family doctors scheduled follow-up appointments in 25% of the visits, an inpatient hospital evaluation in 0.5% of cases, and specialist referrals in 9% of cases. The study suggests that most patients' presenting problems were already known by the general practitioners, making "known history" an important diagnostic tool. Furthermore, the unselected patient population brings a wide spectrum of complaints requiring the special skills of a generalist. Over 90% of visits were managed by the family doctor with few patients referred for secondary or tertiary care.

Source: Karg T, Sandholzer H (personal communication with authors).

South Africa

To analyze the scope of care provided in an outpatient clinic operated by the Department of Family Medicine, comprehensive statistics were taken of all patients seen over a 21-working-day period. A total of 6864 patients were seen, an average of 327 patients per day. A total of 627 (9%) of the patients were referred to other physicians for consultation, the most common being internal medicine (22% of total referrals). If facilities such as a procedure room and observation beds had been available, an estimated 40% of the referrals could probably have been cared for in the family practice clinic. This study indicates that, in this urban, academic outpatient clinic, over 90% of people's health problems could be managed by a family doctor.

Source: Loots SJ, Steenkamp B (personal communication with authors).

doctor. In some countries, the family doctor is trained to provide coordination and hospital care when necessary, to deliver babies, and to perform surgical procedures when indicated. In all circumstances, the family doctor is expected to serve as an adviser and advocate for individual patients as well as for the health of the community (*see* Box 3.9).

BOX 3.9 The family doctor's role in smoking cessation counseling in Denmark

To evaluate the family doctor's impact in reducing smoking prevalence, researchers conducted a randomized controlled trial in all general practitioner offices in Ebeltoft, Denmark. A total of 3464 inhabitants aged 30–50 were randomly allocated to either a control group, a group receiving an office health check but no smoking cessation counseling, or a group receiving a health check plus a smoking cessation talk with their family doctor. At baseline, 50.8% of the participants were smokers and the groups were comparable. After 1 year, there was a 3.5% reduction ($p < 0.02$) in smoking in the group which spoke with their family doctor compared with a 1.7% reduction in the control group, a 0.9% reduction in the health check group and a 1% reduction in the general population in Denmark. The study results indicate that brief smoking cessation talks during the regular GP office health check can significantly reduce the prevalence of smoking.

Source: Refsgaard LJ, Karlsmose B, Engberg M, Lassen JF, Lauritzen T (personal communication with authors).

The quality of family practice

The difference in prevalence of diseases encountered by the generalist physician and the more narrowly focused specialist physician explains much of the misunderstanding between these different approaches to clinical medicine. The consultant specialist sees patients who have usually been screened and who are thus in a different prognostic category from that of patients seen by a generalist family doctor. Among the patients of a family doctor presenting with headache, the probability of the pain being due to a brain tumor is extremely low: probably less than 1 in 1000.[28,29] The patients of neurosurgeons, who have usually been filtered through a referral process, have a higher probability of having a brain tumor. Thus family doctors and neurosurgeons are likely to respond in different ways to patients with headache. If the family doctor approached each of these patients with the mindset of a neurosurgeon, the cost of testing would be prohibitive. Furthermore, the greater number of invasive and expensive diagnostic tests would increase the likelihood of iatrogenic complications and false positive results, requiring even further testing.

The type of appropriate evaluation by generalists and specialists is in large part determined by the prevalence of diseases in their practices. Caution is therefore needed in generalizing standards of quality from a limited, highly specialized practice to the undifferentiated population covered by primary care. In practice, both approaches are necessary to provide high-quality care to patient populations, and family doctors work in synergy with specialists in a variety of consultative arrangements and group practices. For example, family physicians may end up managing many cases of plaque psoriasis, but may be expected to refer cases of plaque psoriasis

> when disease is extensive, distressing, or unresponsive, or when the patient requires in-depth counseling or education outside the scope of primary care practice, or to confirm a diagnosis, to assess or help establish an appropriate therapeutic regimen, or to help manage more complex cases, or in patients who become unresponsive to previously successful treatments or who experience other adverse reactions to topical medications, or in response to a patient's request for a referral to a dermatologist.[30]

Family doctors get to know their patients well through long-term continuous relationships. A wealth of unique knowledge is accumulated from these interactions that attunes the family doctor to the context and significance of the patient's complaints and to deviations from normally expected behavior.[31] This knowledge is an invaluable aid in making accurate diagnoses and in determining how rapidly to respond with interventions.

Furthermore, when caring for patients, continuity serves as an additional diagnostic aid, allowing time for ongoing observation to clarify the nature of the patient's problem (described by some authors as the "permitted delay" or "tincture of time"). If there is no immediate threat to life, close follow-up provides the opportunity for the astute physician to sort out probabilities while watching the patient closely for developments suggesting need for more active intervention. In this way, high-quality care is provided without excessive diagnostic testing, many problems are clarified or resolve spontaneously, trust is established, costs are reduced, and iatrogenic risks are diminished. Continuity is associated with a variety of positive outcomes, including reduced number and duration of hospital admissions,[32] less testing[33,34] and improved trust in the patient's physician.[35,36]

Access, longitudinality, and comprehensiveness are the hallmarks of family medicine and primary care. Studies correlate these characteristics with improved outcomes in patients of all ages, including higher birth weight, reduced morbidity in children, and reduced hospitalization in the elderly.[37] Continuity and coordination of care have been found to be associated with higher compliance with therapeutic plans, fewer hospitalizations, decreased costs,[37] and up to a 53% reduction in expenditures when health care is initiated with the patient's primary care physician.[10]

Community-wide studies of whole populations also reflect the impact of primary care physicians on the quality of care. An analysis of mortality rates from cancer, heart disease, and stroke, the three primary causes of death in the United States, showed a consistent relationship between availability of primary care physicians and positive health levels, including a decrease in the number of residents stricken with or dying from these diseases.[38] This study also showed that higher numbers of primary care physicians correlated with lower infant mortality rates, lower overall mortality, and higher life expectancy. Sub-analyses of the data indicated that these results were primarily due to the influence of the family doctor, an association that held after correcting for the effect of urban-rural differences, poverty rates, education, and lifestyle factors. It is of interest that a higher number of hospital beds or of specialists was not associated with a lower death rate or longer life span.

Other investigators have shown that expenditure on care for the elderly in the United States was lower in areas of the country with high ratios of primary care physicians to population,[39] and this ratio was found to be the only consistent predictor of improved age-specific mortality rates, even when considering such variables as educational levels, poverty, and living in rural areas.[40]

A study on the impact of primary care in 12 European and North American countries showed that those with more highly developed systems of primary care (mainly composed of general practitioners) tend to have lower health care costs, and that the lower cost is achieved without an increase in mortality rates and with significantly improved health outcomes as measured by 14 health indicators, including birth weight, neonatal mortality, infant mortality, and age-adjusted life expectancy.[41] This makes a compelling case for a health service delivery system that is based on a strong infrastructure of generalist physicians.

3.4 FAMILY DOCTORS AS HEALTH CARE COORDINATORS

In every part of the world, when people fall ill, they look for someone to listen, to understand, and to help. If these needs cannot be met in the family, people turn to community health services and the nearest available health professional, and if necessary, they seek assistance from specialists or in hospitals. An optimal health system should provide equitable access to this comprehensive continuum of health services for everyone.

Comprehensive primary care seeks to provide essential services when the patient makes first contact with the health system, usually at the local level, and to integrate primary with secondary and tertiary levels of care through appropriate referrals. Integrated primary care services provide many advantages over separate, vertically organized programs; people come to one location for most of their health care needs and limited health care resources are used more efficiently and cost-effectively. A number of studies have demonstrated that systems with primary care at their heart improve health outcomes and lower the costs of care.[12] Coordinating primary care services nevertheless remains a challenge in many systems.

Family doctors are ideally suited to serve as coordinators in primary care teams because of their familiarity with all levels of the health system and their involvement in a wide range of clinical services. They frequently coordinate clinical services for the care of individuals, involving family members, health team members, and specialty or hospital services. Because of their familiarity with both the patient and the health system, family doctors are in an excellent position to decide when and how to engage specialized services as necessary. The family physician serves as a critical link, communicating, educating, and establishing a shared understanding among these entities for the benefit of the patient (*see* Box 3.10).

Patient lists or registries enable family doctors to identify all the people in their practice with a given health condition, such as diabetes. When resources permit, electronic medical records or information systems can be used as tools to collect and summarize information about patients with specific conditions. Nurses or medical assistants within the primary care team can regularly review these lists to ensure that all patients with, for example, diabetes have been seen and are receiving appropriate management and follow-up. They can contact all the patients that have not been seen to provide recommended screening, immunizations, and chronic care management. This kind of population-based health care can be applied to many common conditions for which medical evidence is available as to the best way to monitor and treat patients.[42]

BOX 3.10 Coordinated care for a patient with tuberculosis

Mr Y, a 40-year-old married father of six, presented to his family doctor with a backache, which had been worsening over several weeks. On examination, his family doctor, Dr M, noted a draining abscess in the lumbar region. Cultures revealed active tuberculosis, and X-rays demonstrated partial destruction of the fourth lumbar vertebral body. Dr M admitted Mr Y to the hospital for consultation with radiologists, orthopedic surgeons, neurologists, and infectious disease specialists to determine the best treatment plan. At one point, Mr Y was so frightened and worried about his family that he wanted to leave the hospital. After a meeting with Dr M, a social worker, and family members, family assistance was arranged, and he completed his hospital course.

Prior to Mr Y's discharge from the hospital, Dr M contacted the public health department. He arranged for community nurses to test Mr Y's family for tuberculosis, arranged for outpatient treatment and supervision of drug therapy, and followed the patient and family until the infection was resolved. At several points, as Mr Y was improving, he wanted to stop taking his drugs, but after discussion with Dr M and community health nurses he agreed to complete the course. Mr Y's tuberculosis was cured and he was able to return to work and family life without disability.

Source: Matthews R (personal communication).

Some health care systems designate the family doctor as the entry point into the health system. In these systems, all individuals select or are assigned to a specific family doctor or group practice. The family doctor maintains a list or registry of their assigned population. Except for emergencies, individuals must initially contact their family doctor for all health-related concerns. The family doctor evaluates and treats the patient and then decides when and if specialty consultation or other diagnostic tests are necessary. When family doctors or other generalist physicians serve as the initial source of care, patients have lower rates of unnecessary consultation and lower costs of health care.[43]

A survey conducted among family doctors in 51 countries indicated that 8% of countries responding designated family doctors as the entry point for all patients, 24% designated family doctors as the entry point for all patients except those seeking care privately, and 39% designated family doctors as the entry point for some patients, while 29% did not designate an entry point role for family doctors.[1]

In countries where the function of the family doctor as the entry point to care is not established, other strategies strengthen the coordinating role of family doctors. These may include negotiation of the roles and responsibilities of family doctors and their relationships to other health professionals. Specialty consultants can provide assessments and recommendations for continuing patient care to family doctors, thereby focusing the efforts of consultants in their areas of expertise while enhancing the role of family doctors as coordinators of care. The approaches that enable family doctors to fulfill their function as coordinators of patient care are listed in Box 3.11.

BOX 3.11 How to enhance family doctors' coordination of care

Provide continuity of care for a specific group of patients to:
- develop an understanding of patients, their family, and community contexts
- establish trust and rapport
- follow patients over the progression of an illness
- collaborate with specialty consultants and community health resources.

Care for entire families to:
- become familiar with many family members
- understand family dynamics
- provide education and other services effectively for families.

Develop communication and organizational skills to:
- conduct family meetings
- organize teams and conduct team meetings
- enhance relationships with specialty consultants.

Establish and maintain comprehensive medical records to:
- organize information about the patient, family, and history
- assemble information from multiple health care sources in one location
- maintain problem and medication lists
- optimize therapy
- avoid adverse drug interactions
- record patient preferences for therapies.

Develop lists of patients in the practice with common chronic conditions to:

- ensure that all patients with these conditions receive high-quality care based on the best medical evidence
- establish mechanisms to regularly measure the health status of these patients and the quality of care according to established guidelines.

Delineate the roles and responsibilities of family doctors in relation to other health providers to:

- enhance consultation skills, prepare patients for consultation, summarize the patient's history and identify questions for the consultant, and resume care after hospitalization or consultation
- coordinate efforts between specialty consultants, family doctors, and other health team members.

Educate family doctors about community resources to:

- know how and when to access community health resources to benefit patients
- mobilize available resources
- identify unmet health care needs
- develop new health care resources when needed.

The best national health strategies are ineffective unless health care services are implemented when and where they are needed at the community level. While family doctors and primary care teams focus their energies on individuals, families, and communities, they rely on coordination with health programs at the district and regional level to provide the entire spectrum of necessary health services. Effective implementation of primary care requires integrating services within these networks of community and regional providers.[22,44]

Family doctors and primary health care teams are ideally situated to integrate individual and community health services. However, while family doctors and other primary care team members provide preventive and curative services, the majority of their time is usually devoted to providing care for individuals. Various skills and activities are involved in community health, including epidemiology, community diagnosis, community health education, community organization, and promotion of family and community involvement in health.[15] It is not necessary for each member of a primary care team to have all of these skills, yet the family doctor can contribute substantially to the community orientation of a primary health care team if he or she possesses some of these skills and encourages community health activities among team members (*see* Table 3.6).[16]

TABLE 3.6 Complementary clinical and community health skills

Clinical skills	Community skills
Examination of a patient	Assessment through analysis of indicators, surveys and community-wide sampling
Diagnosis of a patient's problem	
Health assessment and maintenance for an individual	Identification of types of health problems and their distribution in the community
Treatment according to diagnosis, preferences and resources of patient	Health assessment of entire community or sub-groups
Interventions, usually following patient-initiated concerns	Treatment based on community health problems, priorities, and resources
Follow-up observation, determining need for continued investigation or treatment	Interventions, following data analysis and identification of trends within the community
	Continued surveillance, determining follow-up actions and programs

Source: adapted from Kark SL, 1981.[15]

Family doctors can serve as bridges, linking individual and community health services at the community and regional levels. They are in an ideal position to observe the interactions between individual and community health efforts and to identify strategies to link related programs for the benefit of the entire community. Coordinating the delivery of individual primary care services with community-oriented programs takes time and consideration of the costs and benefits. Nevertheless, community-oriented programs cannot replace individual care.

Initially, family doctors, team members, and community and public health staff may meet to share common interests and concerns. Over time, as benefits are realized, these partners may plan more comprehensive collaborative projects. Box 3.12 describes strategies that facilitate interactions among family doctors, other primary care providers, and the community.

BOX 3.12 How to increase the community orientation of family doctors and primary care teams

- Educate family doctors in community health, epidemiology, community organization, and health development strategies.
- Provide time for family doctors to meet regularly with community leaders and key informants to discuss community health concerns and explore potential collaboration.
- Invite community participation in health assessments and program planning.

- Encourage the primary care team members to participate in community meetings, organizations and health-related programs, to present community health assessments, discuss risks and determine appropriate responses.
- Recruit community health workers to participate in implementing primary care programs.
- Use existing community organizations to mobilize support and resources for health education and prevention programs.
- Establish coalitions among independently functioning health programs to share information and develop shared goals.
- Delineate responsibilities of family doctors and primary care team members as community health coordinators.
- Designate resources, measure outcomes, and provide incentives for collaborative community health projects.

3.5 FAMILY DOCTORS AS LEADERS, MANAGERS, AND SUPERVISORS

Because of their holistic orientation and training to serve people of all ages, family doctors are well suited to lead clinical and community health services for the benefit of an entire community.

From patient interactions, family doctors may note anomalies, and have a role in reporting clusters or unusual rises. They may, less often, sometimes note trends in diseases, injuries, or risks before others are aware of such problems. These in turn can spur public health action or research projects. From interactions with other health professionals, family doctors may note problems in service delivery or quality. Their combination of knowledge, skills, experience, and authority positions family doctors to assume leadership roles in order to improve the quality, organization, management, integration, and evaluation of health services provided to their community. Their management skills can be improved through courses, consultations, and reading relevant literature such as journals that focus on practice management (*see* Box 3.13).

Family doctors can provide, share, or delegate some of the following leadership functions[46] necessary for effective primary care delivery.

➤ Planning and setting objectives
➤ Organizing and implementing services and plans
➤ Recruiting personnel
➤ Training and providing continuing education for health workers
➤ Monitoring working conditions
➤ Supervising and assuring competent performance of all tasks
➤ Promoting community involvement

BOX 3.13 Practice management for family doctors

The American Academy of Family Physicians launched its Family Practice Management program to help family doctors practice effectively in the continually evolving health system. The program is available online through the website of the American Academy of Family Physicians.[45] Family doctors can take an online "practice self-test" to assess the effectiveness of their office practice and identify areas for improvement. The program follows the following areas.

- **Measuring and improving clinical care** – guidelines on best practice and quality improvement.
- **Improving patient satisfaction** – communication skills, patient education, patient satisfaction surveys.
- **Running an effective practice** – effective appointment scheduling, personnel issues, telephone management, texting to remind patients of appointments both with specialists and the family physician.
- **Financial management** – proper coding and documentation, contract negotiation, understanding financial statements.
- **Medical ethics and regulations** – maintaining patient confidentiality, medical record security, and compliance with office and laboratory regulations.
- **Using computers and information systems** – comparison of office computers, electronic medical records, using the Internet, useful websites for the family doctor, facilitating links with radiology, laboratory, and secondary care.
- **Monitoring health care trends** – news and analysis of health system legislation.
- **Leadership:** strategic planning, running meetings effectively, forming and operating group practices.
- **Career and practice development** – evaluating practice opportunities, effective teaching skills.
- **Life balance** – how to balance the demands of professional and personal life, stress management, time management.

➤ Developing collaborative programs among different health groups
➤ Maintaining relationships
➤ Evaluating programs
➤ Inspiring and motivating workers.

Family doctors are often ultimately responsible for the quality of clinical services delivered by their teams and the satisfaction of their patients with the services provided. They often work and lead a collaborative effort. Some of those functions of family doctors may include direct observation of clinical care, providing feedback, reviewing processes, developing protocols, and conducting regular in-service training programs.

Family doctors may become involved in a variety of leadership roles in the community, from providing informal advice to acting as designated public health managers. Some health systems are now supporting and promoting family doctors as health system including as deans of medical schools (*see* Box 3.14). If family doctors are not prepared, or if they spend all their time providing individual patient services, their leadership potential may not be realized.

BOX 3.14 Family health program in Brazil[47,48]

Brazil's epidemiological profile reveals marked disparities in health status and outcomes among its people; mortality rates are greater for working men, childbearing women and children in poor urban and rural areas. To address these disparities, a National Health System (SUS) was established in Brazil in 1988. The SUS, which provides primary, secondary, and tertiary health care for a population of more than 190 million inhabitants, is based on the concepts of universally accessible essential care, decentralization, and community participation. The SUS is organized at federal, state, and municipal levels, with autonomy among managers at each level.

In 1994, Brazil launched an intensive effort to provide primary care through its family health program, "Programa Saúde da Família" (PSF). The PSF aims to provide family health teams for the entire population. Each team consists of a physician, a nurse, nursing assistants, and community health agents, and cares for a defined population of up to 4000 people. Team members collaborate to provide essential health services, health education and promotion, integrate services between the primary, secondary, and tertiary levels and reduce health risks with community participation. Family doctors were added to complement the skills of other health workers, enhance program effectiveness, improve technical skills of team members, and to link PSF services with the health system. To date, more than 32 000 teams have been established and have achieved significant improvements in health outcomes. Challenges include establishing optimal systems for coordinated health service delivery, strengthening local management capacities, and development of human resources. Intensive training, development, and research efforts are in progress to expand and improve the outcomes of the PSF. Many publications show the effectiveness of the strategy through a decrease in the infant mortality rate. For instance, a 10% increase in the Family Health Program coverage was associated with a 4.5% decrease in the infant mortality rate.

Source: Departamento de Atenção Básica, 2012.

While family doctors are uniquely positioned to lead and improve primary care programs, they require support and skills to fulfill these functions. Some steps that will enable family doctors to become leaders are delineated in Box 3.15.

BOX 3.15 How to enable family doctors to become leaders

- Provide education to prepare family doctors with specific leadership skills in health program development, resource allocation, management, and intersectoral collaboration.
- Promote continuing education to inform family doctors about health system changes, evolving needs, and how to improve the quality of health care services.
- Delegate patient care responsibilities so family doctors share the tasks of health service provision with other team members, to allow time for family doctors to assume leadership roles.
- Provide incentives to motivate family doctors to undertake leadership activities and to reward them for doing so.
- Develop community partnerships to integrate clinical and community health services.
- Designate authority to recognize and delineate the specific leadership responsibilities of family doctors.
- Provide focused training to family doctors about working in teams, consensus management, and conflict resolution.

The education and professional development of family doctors that will prepare them for these multiple roles in health systems are reviewed in the following chapter.

REFERENCES

1. Gilbert T, Culpepper L. World survey of family practice and general practice. In: *Proceedings of the International Conference on the Education of Family Physicians, 26–28 October 1993, Bethesda, MO, USA*. Bethesda: National Institutes of Health, 1993: 16.
2. Bentzen BG, Bridges-Webb C, Carmichael L, et al. *The Role of the General Practitioner/ Family Physician in Health Care Systems: A Statement from WONCA, 1991*. Available at: medfamcom.files.wordpress.com/2009/10/wonca-statement-1991.pdf
3. McWhinney IR. *A Textbook of Family Medicine*. Oxford University Press, 1997.
4. World Health Organization. *World Health Report 2008 – Primary health care (now more than ever)*. Available at: www.who.int/whr/2008/en/
5. WHO Regional Office for Europe. Framework for professional and administrative development of general practice/family medicine in Europe. In: *Draft Charter for General Practice/ Family Medicine in Europe*. Copenhagen: World Health Organization Regional Office for Europe, 1998 (document EUR/ICP/DLVR/01 0301: Annex 3).

6. College of Family Physicians of Canada. Four principles of family medicine. In: *Section of Teachers of Family Medicine Committee on Curriculum. The postgraduate family medicine curriculum: an integrated approach.* College of Family Physicians of Canada, 2003: 8–10.

7. Phillips WR, Haynes DG. The domain of family practice: scope, role and function. The Keystone papers: formal discussion papers from Keystone iii, 2001; **33**(4): 273–7.

8. JANUS Project. College of Family Physicians of Canada, 2012. Available at: www.cfpc.ca/Janus/

9. Bindman AB, Grumbach K, Osmond D, et al. Preventable hospitalizations and access to health care. *Journal of the American Medical Association.* 1995; **274**(4): 305–11.

10. Forrest CB, Starfield B. The effect of first-contact care with primary care clinicians on ambulatory health care expenditures. *Journal of Family Practice.* 1996; **43**(1): 40–8.

11. Starfield B. Primary care: an increasingly important contributor to effectiveness, equity, and efficiency of health services. SESPAS report 2012. *Gaceta Sanitaria.* 2012; **26**(Suppl. 1): 20–6.

12. Starfield B. *Primary Care: balancing health needs, services and technology.* Oxford University Press, 1998.

13. Howe A. Medical generalism: why expertise in whole person medicine matters. Royal College of General Practitioners, 2012. Available at: www.rcgp.org.uk/policy/rcgp-policy areas/~/media/Files/Policy/A-Z%20policy/Medical-Generalism-Why_expertise_in_whole_person_medicine_matters.ashx

14. Pritchard P. *Manual of PHC: its nature and organization.* 2nd ed. Oxford Medical Publications, 1981.

15. Kark SL. *The Practice of Community-oriented Primary Care.* Appleton-Century-Crofts, 1981.

16. Wagner EH. The role of patient care teams in chronic disease management. *British Medical Journal.* 2000; **320**(7234): 569–72.

17. World Health Organization. Patient safety curriculum guide: multi-professional edition (Part B: Curriculum Guide Topics, Topic 4: Being an effective team player), 2011. Available at: www.who.int/patientsafety/education/curriculum/who_mc_topic-4.pdf

18. Boelen C. *Towards Unity for Health: challenges and opportunities for partnership in health development. A working paper.* Geneva: World Health Organization, 2000.

19. White KL, Williams F, Greenberg BG. The ecology of medical care. *New England Journal of Medicine.* 1961; **265**(18): 885–92.

20. Green LA, Fryer GE Jr, Yawn BP, et al. The ecology of medical care revisited. *New England Journal of Medicine.* 2001; **344**(26): 2018–20.

21. Heath I. *The Mystery of General Practice.* London: Nuffield Provincial Hospitals Trust, 1995.

22. Kahssay HM, Taylor ME, Berman PA. *Community Health Workers: the way forward.* Geneva: World Health Organization, 1998 (Public Health in Action, No.4).

23. Schmidt HG et al. Network of community-oriented educational institutions for the health sciences. *Academic Medicine.* 1991; **66**(5): 259–63.

24. Mash B (ed). *Handbook of Family Medicine.* Cape Town: Oxford University Press, 2000.

25. Flocke SA. Frank SH, Wenger DA. Addressing multiple problems in the family practice office visit. *Journal of Family Practice.* 2001; **50**(3): 211–15.

26. Transitieproject. *TranHis for Windows.* Available at: www.transitieproject.nl

27. Britt H, Miller GC, Charles J, et al. *The BEACH (Bettering the Evaluation and Care of Health) Study.* Available at: sydney.edu.au/medicine/fmrc/beach/

28. Becker LA, Green LA, Beaufait D, et al. Use of CT scans for the investigation of headache: a report from ASPN, Part 1. *Journal of Family Practice.* 1993; **37**(2): 129–34.

29. Becker LA, Green LA, Beaufait D, et al. Detection of intracranial tumors, subarachnoid hemorrhages, and subdural hematomas in primary care patients: a report from ASPN, Part 2. *Journal of Family Practice.* 1993; **37**(2): 135–41.

30. Poulin Y, Wasel N, Chan D, et al. Evaluating practice patterns for managing moderate to severe plaque psoriasis: role of the family physician. *Canadian Family Physician.* 2012; **58**(7): 390–400.

31. Stange KC, Jaén CR, Flocke SA, et al. The value of a family physician. *Journal of Family Practice.* 1998; **46**(5): 363–8.

32. Wasson JH, Sauvigne AE, Mogielnicki RP, et al. Continuity of outpatient medical care in elderly men: a randomized trial. *Journal of the American Medical Association.* 1984; **252**: 2413–17.

33. Freeman G, Hjortdahl P. What future for continuity of care in general practice? *British Medical Journal.* 1997; **314**(7098): 1870–3.

34. Hjortdahl P, Borchgrevink CF. Continuity of care: influence of general practitioners' knowledge about their patients on use of resources in consultations. *British Medical Journal.* 1991; **303**: 1181–4.

35. Mainous AG, Baker R, Love MM, et al. Continuity of care and trust in one's physician: evidence from primary care in the United States and the United Kingdom. *Family Medicine.* 2001; **33**(1): 22–7.

36. Thomas P, Griffiths F, Kai J, et al. Networks for research in primary health care. *British Medical Journal.* 2001; **322**: 588–90.

37. Starfield B, Shi L, Macinko J. Contribution of primary care to health systems and health. *Milbank Quarterly.* 2005; **83**: 457–502.

38. Shi L. Primary care, specialty care, and life chances. *International Journal of Health Services.* 1994; **24**(3): 431–58.

39. Welch WP, Miller ME, Welch HG, et al. Geographic variation in expenditures for physicians' services in the United States. *New England Journal of Medicine.* 1993; **328**: 621–7.

40. Farmer FL, Stokes CS, Fisher RH. Poverty, primary care and age-specific mortality. *Journal of Rural Health.* 1991; **7**: 153–69.

41. Starfield B, Shi L. Policy relevant determinants of health: an international perspective. *Health Policy.* 2002; **60**(3): 201–18.

42. Rivo ML. It's time to start practicing population-based health care. *Family Practice Management.* 1998; **5**(6): 37–46.

43. Starfield B. International comparisons of primary care systems. In: *Proceedings of the International Conference on the Education of Family Physicians, 26–28 October 1993, Bethesda, MD, USA.* Bethesda: National Institutes of Health 1993: 17–18.

44. Janovsky K. The challenge of implementation: district health systems for primary health care. Geneva: World Health Organization, 1988 (document WHO/SHS/DHS/88.1, Rev. 1).

45. American Academy of Family Physicians. *Family Practice Management.* Available at: www.aafp.org/online/en/home/publications/journals/fpm.html

46. Flahault D, Roemer MI. *Leadership for Primary Health Care. Levels, functions and requirements based on 12 case studies.* Geneva: World Health Organization 1986 (Public Health Papers, No. 82).

47. Viana AL, Dal Poz MR. *Family health program as a strategy to reform the health system in Brazil. Brazil towards a new health care model.* Ministerio da Saude, Governo Federal Brasil, 2000.

48. Macinko J, Guanais F, Souza M. Evaluation of the impact of the Family Health Program on infant mortality in Brazil, 1990–2002. *Journal of Epidemiology and Community Health*. 2006; **60**: 13–19.

49. Sutton M. Improving patient care. Cultural competence, it's not just political correctness, it's good medicine. *Family Practice Management*. 2000; **7**: 58–60.

50. Folsom Group. Communities of solution: The Folsom Report revisited. *Annals of Family Medicine*. 2012; **10**: 250–60.

CHAPTER 4

Education and professional development

This chapter focuses on education and professional development in family medicine, and will seek to answer three primary questions:

1. What is family medicine education and training?
2. Why is family medicine education and training different from other types of medical education?
3. How should family medicine education and training be implemented?

While answering these questions, this chapter will cover a variety of issues in the education of family doctors, including basic undergraduate medical education; postgraduate medical education and vocational training; and continuing professional development. It aims to place family medicine and primary care education in the context of both complete medical education and health delivery systems, describe the content and structure for high-quality training in family medicine, and outline critical issues in developing a system-wide approach to primary care medical education.

It should be noted that while this chapter focuses specifically on the education and professional development of the family doctor as the core medical specialist in many primary care systems, the field of family medicine should not be seen as exclusive to the physician. The family doctor can only be as successful as the team that surrounds them, and there can be little doubt that the primary care team should be well versed in the principles and practice of family medicine. While a comprehensive review of interdisciplinary education is beyond the scope of this chapter, it is important to recognize that primary care staff members of all types can benefit from education and professional development in family medicine, including nurses, midwives, mid-level providers such as physician assistants, medical assistants, community health workers, and others working with the primary care team.

4.1 WHAT IS FAMILY MEDICINE EDUCATION AND TRAINING?
The common foundation of medical education

To begin to understand the specifics of family medicine education and training, one must first understand the core concepts of education and training, particularly as they relate to medicine. Traditionally, education refers to the formal academic education of individuals. Initially, education teaches the basics of how to live a good and productive life.[1–3] As we grow, we begin to focus beyond the basics to specifics such as in what areas we might focus our productive efforts and how to be successful. As we become more specific in our focus, educational goals narrow from the very broad to more defined goals.

In the field of medicine, the overall goals of medical education are to:
➤ prepare physicians with appropriate knowledge, attitudes, and skills to meet the health needs of the individuals and communities in which they will serve;
➤ establish, maintain, and improve standards for high-quality medical practice and health care;
➤ attract and prepare new learners who will then go on and renew the profession into the future.

In pre-service undergraduate medical education, schools of medicine focus on providing a minimum breadth of learning and experience in medicine sufficient to confer a medical degree. Such a degree is commonly intended to indicate that a learner has achieved an academic understanding of the profession that represents the minimum qualifications necessary to pursue future endeavors in medicine, such as clinical practice or medical research.

It is worth noting that the goals of pre-service medical education as an endeavor may not be precisely the same as the goals of the medical student, although they should be closely aligned. The typical primary goal of the medical student is to become competent in the very basics of providing high-quality health care, ranging from acquiring adequate medical knowledge to the basic provision of patient care and to familiarity with navigating the practice of medicine within a dynamic health care system.

Once learners have completed a basic pre-service medical education, they then begin to transition from academic student to active practitioner of medicine. Similarly, the overall endeavor of medical education begins a transition as well from more traditional academic education toward continuing professional development through specific vocational skills training. The goals of the training system in medicine shift from primarily broad-based theoretical learning coupled with the most basic medical competencies toward the subsequent achievement of advanced skills and a level of competency consistent with a minimum acceptable standard of quality in a specific area of medical practice. Toward this end, the training site often shifts from the learning-based environment of medical schools to the practice-based setting of clinics and hospitals. In many places around the world, although not all, this training is provided through structured postgraduate in-service training programs in a focused specialty area of medicine, sometimes referred to as a residency.

Coincident with this shift in the educational system, learners also begin to look forward to the setting in which they plan to work and the type of practice they hope to pursue. Their own learning style and interest transitions more aggressively from pedagogy, traditional methods of teaching often founded on original principles of teaching children, to andragogy, or adult learning. In making this shift to andragogy from pedagogy, learners become more focused on participating in decisions about their own learning. They are more goal-oriented, and begin to demand more relevancy and respect while seeking education that focuses more on the practical aspects than the academic. Learners will begin to develop a more individual concept of their future type of medical practice and thus seek additional training that is specifically targeted at achieving complete competency in providing this type of practice. In practical terms, it often means entering a postgraduate in-service vocational training program focused on learning more in a specialty field of medicine.

Once in practice, the learner's goal typically then becomes the lifelong maintenance of competency in their chosen field of medical practice, although the further acquisition of new skills may also be desirable at times to enhance their current practice. Educational systems have grown to meet these additional in-service training needs through the advent of continuing professional development, also sometimes referred to as continuing medical education or CME. These programs are usually highly practical, time-limited, and offer a wider variety of settings and formats.

One must also consider, however, the goals of a nation's health system and population when considering overall medical education goals. For any health system, the combination of pre- and in-service training should provide an adequate number of health professionals with a range of skills matched to the specific health needs of the population. Last but not least, the patient's goal should be considered. For the individual patient, they would like medical education to result in a well-trained provider competent in helping them achieve the maximal level of health they desire.

The evolution of medical education and family medicine

Initial reform

Medical education has undergone several transitions in the twentieth century, resulting in a number of worldwide movements. The first involved establishing a solid scientific foundation for clinical medicine, organizing the preclinical curriculum around basic sciences, and incorporating medical education in the university system in order to assure quality and accountability. In Western countries, this movement was influenced by the accomplishments of the leading German medical schools in the latter part of the nineteenth century, the Medical Act of 1880 in the United Kingdom, and Abraham Flexner's influential publication in 1910. Flexner described deficiencies in medical schools throughout the United States, delineated the inherent weakness of proprietary schools, and provided recommendations for reform. Flexner's model was adopted rapidly in the United States and eventually throughout the world.[4]

These reforms in medical education imbued physicians with the importance of basing clinical decisions on a sound scientific foundation and encouraged specialization. Health systems were impressed with the remarkable progress in research and clinical outcomes. However, these reforms also led to an artificial separation between the basic sciences and the clinical disciplines. Financial and academic incentives reinforced the emphasis on in-depth investigation and research, further increasing subspecialization within medical professions and schools. Remarkable technical achievements and impressive scientific advances overshadowed the fact that care was becoming fragmented, depersonalized, and costly. It is therefore worthwhile revisiting Flexner's report for a better match of medical schools' missions to new challenges for health systems.[112] The subsequent explosion of medical knowledge resulted in further expansion and subdivisions of the medical school curriculum. Students naturally emulated their academic mentors, while the generalist clinician gradually became less valued as a teacher or role model.

Medical schools and social accountability

Medical schools both shape the health system and are shaped by it. Physicians are granted substantial privileges and resources by society. These privileges imply a corresponding responsibility to participate in improving health systems and training physicians to meet the needs of society. While academic medical institutions have the capacity to influence health care systems, they do not always choose to do so. Many centers tend to pursue research and technological developments that have limited relevance to urgent, unmet community health care needs.[5]

Social accountability involves commitment by medical schools to direct their education, research, and service activities toward the priority health concerns of the community, region, or nation that they serve. Such responsibility to society guides every socially accountable academic medical institution and permeates its entire scope of activities. The four values used to assess progress in health systems – relevance, quality, equity, and cost-effectiveness – are equally important for medical schools. These values can be delineated according to each of the three domains of academic medicine: (1) education, (2) research, and (3) service.[6]

The second worldwide movement addressed the social relevance of medical education. By the 1950s some medical educators and practitioners recognized problems with a disease-oriented education model that focused on the unusual conditions of hospitalized patients and treatment of disease with concomitant lack of emphasis on the health of individuals and populations.[7] They sought ways, during the latter half of the twentieth century, to adapt medical curricula to become more responsive to the health needs of people and communities, and to prepare physicians to provide high-quality, comprehensive medical care.[8]

Teaching methods were developed to integrate basic sciences with clinical problem solving and engage learners with patients in the context of the patients' families and environment. Community-oriented education was designed to help students understand the complexities of interactions between the health of the individual, the population and the environment, how illness presents differently in various settings, and how to intervene in ways that are acceptable and efficient. Population-based approaches were developed to assess the needs of the population, consider options to address priority problems, and allocate personnel and resources accordingly.[7]

In addition, over the years, the World Health Organization (WHO) fostered a variety of related educational activities. In the late 1960s, it initiated a network of teacher training centers and programs throughout the world. Innovative teaching methods were described and tested to provide educators with a wide range of options for preparing learners to deal effectively with the priority health problems of individuals and communities. In 1979, the WHO supported the establishment of the Network of Community-oriented Educational Institutions for Health Sciences, now known as The Network: Towards Unity for Health, a global association of institutions and educators committed to the improvement of health in communities they serve through education, research, and service. Over the past 2 decades, members from more than 80 countries have advanced community health through linkages with other stakeholders in the community (www.the-networktufh.org). All of these efforts have had a cumulative effect on the substance, efficacy, and vitality of this worldwide movement toward social relevance in medical education.

More recently, there has been a growing appreciation of the overall social impacts on health. The Global Consensus for Social Accountability of Medical Schools is an important initiative illustrating this trend.[113] Beyond just medical education, there is an increasing focus on the political, economic, and social influences on individual's health, often referred to as social determinants of health. It is recognized that not only do health care providers need to consider these social determinants of health in their health management plans but also the health system itself acts as one of these important determinants of health. Medical education must be provided in a context that helps address the inadequacies of health systems as a social determinant of health, and many institutions have begun to include this as a formal component of medical education programs.[9]

BOX 4.1 Aligning family medicine efforts in Brazil

In 1988, access to comprehensive care, preventive and health promotion services became a constitutional right in Brazil. To try to operationalize this, the Brazilian government began the Family Health Program, involving primary care teams of health professionals that would be responsible for a panel of people and families within a community. The family health team is intended to typically consist of one family doctor, one nurse, two auxiliary nurses, and several health agents. As a result of this national support, postgraduate training programs in family medicine have grown around the country, and the Brazilian Society of Family and Community Medicine (SBMFC) now has over 3500 members. The model has been lauded as an admirable construct, but has faced a number of limitations.

While the public health sector has promoted this model for the combination of health promotion, preventive care, and treatment of illness, the academic establishment has generally been slow to follow. Medical schools generally lack academic departments of family medicine and there has been slow penetration of family medicine and community medicine into educational institutions, leading to a discrepancy between the national health strategy and the types of physicians being produced by the academic medical system. On the other hand, there are new national guidelines for undergraduate medical education in Brazil, supported by the government, promoting a health system-oriented curriculum for each medical school based on primary care and general practice. As a result, most medical schools have begun curriculum reforms, and developed formal partnerships with the regional and local health stakeholders with community people active participation.

Until there are standards supported by strong departments of family medicine and faculty, however, there will be wide variation in academic programs. The SBMFC and the Brazilian Association of Medical Education (ABEM) have been actively participating in guideline implementation and have developed several workshops and documents in partnership to support primary care development, including a recent guideline on undergraduate medical education in primary care. With the support of the government, SBFMC, and ABEM, there is tremendous potential for the future development of true synergy between academic family medicine in Brazil, primary care, and the Family Health Program.

Source: Demarzo MMP, Gusso GDF, Anderson MIP, et al. Academic family medicine: new perspectives in Brazil (letter). *Family Medicine.* 2010; **42**: 464–5.

Source: Demarzo MMP, Chalegre RC, Marins JJN, et al. Diretrizes para o ensino na atenção primária à saúde na graduação em medicina. *Revista Brasileira de Educação Médica (Impresso).* 2012; **36**: 143–8.

The role of competency

A growing movement in medical education, accelerated in the last decade, has involved an evolution from traditional knowledge-based academic instruction to competency-based training. Traditional medical education focused on gaining a body of medical knowledge through pedagogical didactic instruction combined with an apprenticeship-type model for practical skills acquisition. Evaluation of the former involved knowledge-based summative assessments often using multiple choice questions, and performance in the latter was often judged with vague and subjective criteria by a supervising physician of variable experience. One can imagine that instruction aimed to achieve high scores on multiple choice exams and the generalized approval of one's instructor is unlikely to demonstrate a close correlation with actual daily performance in the work context, and even less so with patient satisfaction or general health outcomes.

As a result, there has now been a greater emphasis on the development of competency, through specific goals and objectives for instruction as well as meaningful evaluation of performance on those objectives. In sum, medical education is now expected to result in the reliable demonstration of competent performance in all the necessary tasks anticipated of a specific type of medical practitioner. In order to accomplish this, competency-based goals and objectives need to be clear and specific in order to be well understood by both learner and teacher, focused on performance of specific observable behaviors, and measurable in a quantifiable and reliable way.

Competency-based training also includes applying methods of teaching that align the learning context or setting where instruction and learning takes place, with the performance context where actual in-service work and clinical practice occurs. This requires looking at all elements of instruction to better match the methods of teaching to the specific types of competencies expected of learners, and incorporating a variety of skills together to teach more complex tasks. Development of new methods of competency-based instruction often requires going well beyond didactic style lectures and incorporating practical skills taught at the site of actual use or alternatively in a safe setting that reasonably simulates real-life practice.

Beyond goals and objectives and a greater focus on complex and practical skills, competency-based training has perhaps had its biggest impact on the methods of evaluation used in medical education. Traditionally, multiple-choice questions have been used to assess medical knowledge, and global rating scales completed by instructors have been a popular method for clinical skills evaluation. These methods are limited in their ability to accurately assess competency in a variety of other skill areas. Other techniques are increasingly being used to evaluate competency in the workplace, providing a more comprehensive assessment of overall competency. These methods include checklists, objective structured clinical exams, simulations and models, 360-degree assessments, and portfolios. Such improved and more comprehensive evaluations now also allow for more robust evaluation of training programs themselves, resulting in continuously improving medical education.

While there have been some efforts within different national health education systems to identify core categories of competencies, at the very least, a physician must be able to take an effective history, perform a relevant physical exam, assess and reason an accurate diagnosis, and based on these develop appropriate short- and long-term management plans for a patient's health within the context of a health system. Certainly, there are many more important competencies based on the specific specialty or anticipated work setting, but these core activities represent a minimum expectation at the conclusion of training.

The advent and continued growth of competency-based training brings multiple advantages to all stakeholders in the medical education system. For learners, it brings medical training closer to the practical and relevant ideal of the adult learner, focusing instruction specifically and efficiently on those tasks that are expected to be performed in future work settings. Learners are also required to be actively engaged in seeking out and obtaining the required competencies. For educators, competency-based training can streamline curricula by focusing on the performance context, and often leads to more valid and reliable methods of evaluation across a wider-range of necessary skills. Health systems see value in the education of medical professionals with greater competency in more practical skills. Most important, the patient experiences a higher-quality medical provider who is more prepared and confident in providing what the patient needs to maximize their health.

Current and future movements

While growing advances in technology and the use of distance education have always been present, they appear to be gaining as another shift in medicine and medical education now appears to be occurring. With the advent of the Internet, a whole range of therapeutic and educational options are now possible that were almost entirely inconceivable only a decade or two ago.

Distance education has been known as an effective method of teaching ever since the development of basic methods of remote communication such as mail delivery, albeit with each method potentially limited in different ways by the modality involved in providing it.[10] Increasing Internet access throughout the world is now beginning to bring the possibility of instant and real-time e-learning directly to learners in remarkably remote settings. These distance education programs delivered through the Internet can increase access to continuously updated evidence-based medical information, especially for those in rural or traditionally inaccessible settings.

A great hope of the provision of Internet-based education is increased access and equality of education across a large variety of health settings, and movements are afoot to offer low-cost or free educational offerings to all.[11] There are challenges, however, yet to be fully addressed in making this transition in medical education complete. Although access to Internet connections is growing and more new graduates are being exposed to online learning, competency in using a computer or the Internet remains low for many in low resource or remote settings. Online training programs have also proven similar to other distance education efforts in that it is difficult for learners to advance completely through a program to completion. With low barriers to enrollment in online training programs, stunningly high incompletion rates have been seen in online education.[12] Furthermore, methods are still limited for effective and comprehensive clinical training through online-only educational programs, with few, if any, capable of assuring complete competency in complex clinical skills at the point of service delivery.

Telemedicine is one developing method of clinical care that may offer some possibility for developing more practical-based training programs. Already, teleconferencing systems are used by subspecialists to provide consultation to referring physicians and examine patients remotely. In some settings, critical care medicine is now monitored and delivered from a remote control center in conjunction with nurses and other medical staff on-site, and in some cases utilizing a robotic proxy operated by a distant critical care physician. Such technological advances not only offer techniques that may be applicable to delivering more practical distance-based medical education programs, they have the potential to transform the basic practice of medicine in many ways.

The general quality and relevance of online educational offerings, however, can also be of concern. Increasingly, a variety of institutions are capitalizing on the promise of the online distance education model, but may not have the necessary interest or investment in determining local needs. In addition, one-size-fits-all programs in medical education are likely to fail to take into account the wide range of resources and capacity in local health systems, nor focus on the clinical topics most relevant to a specific local community. A comprehensive medical education program designed for a high-resourced medical setting in a temperate climate may in fact result in low-quality, dangerous, or even harmful care in a low-resourced tropical setting. Worse, such a program delivered by a prestigious institution may be perceived as a high-quality program and standard of care even though it is entirely inappropriate for the local setting of care distant from the educational institution. Creating online programs that are locally relevant and developed by experts practicing in the same setting can help to address this concern, and such programs are in place in certain countries.[13]

Nonetheless, the types and number of online medical education programs is exploding, and a great number of high-quality programs exist targeted at specific topics and settings, and including access for clinicians in resource constrained low- and middle-income countries.[114] A wide variety of clinicians around the globe have begun to avail themselves of these offerings, and enthusiasm for these types of programs continues to grow, especially for continuing professional development. The incredible promise of this new technology and increasing access is sure to continue the rapid expansion of online distance-based medical education offerings. Current offerings and technological applications may provide some insight into the next instructive movement in medical education.

The emergence of family medicine

Among these other worldwide movements in medical education, family medicine education and training was developed in order to meet the needs of individuals and populations. Programs in primary care and family medicine are a manifestation of the response of academic medical centers to the needs of society.

Basic health needs of populations are best served by highly competent generalists well-trained in primary care.[14-20] Research has shown that increasing access to competent, community-based, affordable primary care is associated with improvement in health indicators, a decrease in cost, and improvement in patient satisfaction.[17,18,20–25] The higher the "primary care score," the better the outcomes. The data shows that success correlates best with the density of trained primary care doctors, especially family doctors.

As early as 1963, a WHO Expert Committee on Professional and Technical Education of Medical and Auxiliary Personnel defined family physicians as

> practicing physicians that have the essential characteristic of offering to all members of the families they serve direct and continuing access to their services. These doctors accept responsibility for total care either personally or by arranging for the use of specialized clinical or social resources.

The committee noted that "in every country of the world there appears to be a dearth of family physicians, this applies to all countries irrespective of their stage of development." It recommended that every medical school provide opportunities for students to train in family practice settings, and that in order to raise the standards of family medicine, all graduates choosing family practice should undergo a period of postgraduate training specifically designed to meet their needs in this field of medicine.[26] This concern was again reflected in the 1995 World Health Assembly Resolution WHA 48.8 that urged all member countries to support reform of basic medical education "to take account of the contribution made by general practitioners to primary health care-oriented services" (*see* Annex B).

Family medicine evolved at different rates in different areas of the world. In 1966, the United Kingdom started a general practice vocational training program. During the same decade Canada, the United States, and several other countries initiated programs specifically designed to train family doctors. By 1995, at least 56 countries had developed specialty training programs in primary care and many more have followed suit.[27] Many family practice training programs were established through partnerships with medical schools, community hospitals, and practicing physicians.[8,28] Yet in many countries of the world, family medicine is still not recognized or established as a distinct medical specialty.

Given the importance of this specialty to creating high-quality health systems, the WHO and the World Organization of Family Doctors (WONCA) have declared: "The family doctor should have a central role in the achievement of quality, cost-effectiveness, and equity in health care systems."[29]

The WONCA Singapore Statement of 2007 states that:

> Every medical school in the world should have an academic department of family medicine/general practice/primary care. And every medical

student in the world should experience family medicine/general practice/ primary care as early as possible and as often as possible in their training.

In 2008, as a response to persistent demand from Member States, the WHO reaffirmed a commitment to, and called upon Member States to support development of, primary care as the foundation of an effective and integrated overall health system, with the specialty of family medicine at its core.[30]

BOX 4.2 Using family medicine to enhance local health human resources in Africa

The Kingdom of Lesotho is completely surrounded by South Africa as a land-locked country in sub-Saharan Africa. Lesotho has been devastated by the HIV crisis, with the third-highest HIV prevalence rate in the world of about 24%. This is despite a very high health expenditure of over 13% of gross domestic product.

Lesotho faces an extreme shortage of health care personnel, not only due to the loss of life among the workforce resulting from the HIV crisis, but also as a result of the health education system. The government of Lesotho has historically sponsored local citizens to pursue medical school training in South Africa, as there is no medical school in Lesotho. There have also been no postgraduate training programs in Lesotho, and so students must remain in South Africa or head to other countries to pursue further postgraduate training. As a result, very few ever return to Lesotho to practice medicine in their home country.

To counter this "brain drain," Lesotho has developed its own postgraduate training program in family medicine in hopes of attracting more locally sponsored medical students to return home for specialty training. Family medicine was chosen as the first postgraduate specialty program in the country in part due to the unique appeal of its clinical breadth, preparing physician providers to manage illness at the highest level possible when no other specialist may be readily available. Recently, the family medicine postgraduate training program became the first formally accredited specialty training program in Lesotho. Coupled with the development of this program, special training programs in family medicine have also been developed for both inpatient and outpatient-based nurses, recognizing the system's dependence on nursing for grassroots-level clinical service delivery and to promote interprofessional teamwork.

The World Medical Association in 2011 stated that "one of the most important components of health care infrastructure is human resources; well-trained and motivated health care professionals led by primary care physicians are crucial to success," and called on medical schools to "focus on providing primary care training opportunities that highlight the integrative and continuity elements of the primary care specialties including family medicine" and "create departments of family medicine that are of equal academic standing in the university."[31] Developing systems and policies to support such complex infrastructure is essential, and requires ongoing work.

The essence of family medicine

At its core, family medicine is the specialty field of medicine focused on primary care. In order to understand what is needed for competency-based education and training in family medicine, one must then first determine what primary care is.

Primary care is essential health care focused on and accessible to individuals and families in the community through a regular point of entry, ideally provided at an affordable cost and with community participation. This includes health promotion, disease prevention, health maintenance, education, and rehabilitation preferably provided in an established medical home. It should be well integrated as the core clinical service delivery model of a comprehensive primary health care approach used for managing a strong health system. Primary care is often delivered by a team of providers, potentially including doctors, nurses, physician assistants, midwives, social workers, pharmacists, licensed counselors, and community health workers.

When WHO renewed the call for development of high-quality primary care throughout the world in 2008, it outlined key components of high-quality primary care, and cited family medicine as a discipline most closely associated with this type of care (*see* Annex C).[30]

In this report, the WHO stated that quality primary care:

➤ provides a place where people can bring a wide range of health problems
➤ is a hub through which patients are guided through the health system
➤ facilitates ongoing relationships between patients and clinicians
➤ builds bridges between personal health care and patients' families and communities
➤ opens opportunities for disease prevention, health promotion, and early detection of disease
➤ utilizes teams of health professionals, including physicians, nurse practitioners, and assistants with specific and sophisticated biomedical and social skills
➤ requires adequate resources and investment but provides better value for money than its alternatives.

This description most closely reflects the practice of family medicine, focused on principles of person-centeredness, comprehensiveness, continuity of care, and integration and coordination of care with other aspects of the health care system, thus aligning family medicine as the one single specialty best prepared to provide optimal primary care.

4.2 WHY IS FAMILY MEDICINE EDUCATION AND TRAINING DIFFERENT?
Principles of primary care

In order to develop competency in providing high-quality primary care as described by the WHO,[104] one needs to be educated in the core principles associated with such care. Family medicine follows eight core principles that guide family medicine education and training:

1. Access or first-contact care
2. Comprehensiveness
3. Continuity of care
4. Coordination
5. Prevention
6. Family-orientation
7. Community-orientation
8. Patient-centeredness.

The establishment of some of these principles in the medical literature as important core principles of primary care began over 40 years ago. The integration of these principles into clinical care has since been shown to result in improved outcomes, and provide a basis for developing curricula and training methods to achieve competency in primary care. It is the focus on the provision of clinical care utilizing all of these eight principles that distinguishes family medicine training from other medical specialties.

Regarding the issue of nomenclature, we recognize that the term family medicine is often interchangeable with general practice in many countries around the world. To the degree that training programs with these varying names are focused on these same principles and represent a single distinct medical specialty focused on the delivery of primary care, there is no meaningful difference between the two terms. Similarly, for providers with dedicated training in and orientation toward the principles of primary care, the use of the terms family doctor, family physician, and general practitioner may be considered fully interchangeable. One needs to be cautious, however, to avoid confusing these with competing terms such as general doctor which may simply refer to a physician who has completed a basic undergraduate medical degree and is perhaps even expected to provide generalized medical care at a grassroots level, but has not received specialized training focused on the core principles of primary care. For the sake of simplicity and to avoid such confusion, we will refer to the specialty of family medicine throughout this chapter as the medical specialty focused on principles of primary care, and we will refer to the group of all other medical specialties as subspecialties in order to distinguish their narrower focus of medical care.

Training in family medicine has traditionally followed the performance context, seeking a direct connection between the type and methods of training provided and the anticipated work setting of the family doctor. Here we will explore the principles by reviewing how they are applied in practice by the family doctor, and identifying training issues relevant to the successful education and achievement of competency in each principle by learners in family medicine.

Access or first-contact care

The principle of access is a core principle not only for family medicine, but also for health systems as a whole. Without access, people are unable to obtain the health care they need. Access itself may refer to reducing a variety of types of barriers to obtaining care, including temporal, geographic, cultural and financial. Such barriers result in suboptimal outcomes for both patients and health systems. Access is especially important for family medicine as a specialty focused on providing health care from the first point of contact. Access to this point of first contact is necessary in order for the patient to obtain effective and high-quality care, making the two concepts completely intertwined.

Special considerations need to be made when training a provider to provide first-contact care. As the entryway to the health care system, a family doctor working at the primary care level of a health care system requires a special set of skills that are somewhat distinct from those of other providers. In this setting, patients present with a wide variety of medical problems and degrees of severity. Patients are typically not experienced at determining which problems require medical care, if a problem might require higher-level specialty care, and how long to wait before presenting for care. As a result, no other medical specialty faces such an extensive range of undifferentiated health problems.

At this point of first-contact care, the first job of a family doctor is to determine who is sick and who is not. For those who are sick, the family doctor may then set about trying to determine a diagnosis and assessing the severity of the condition. Because patients are not sorted prior to presentation, the role of the family doctor is fundamentally different from that of subspecialists. The family doctor must become expert at determining who is well and who is sick, managing a wide range of problems and severity, and identifying those in need of more advanced subspecialist care. To develop competency in these skills, family medicine training must then occur in accessible first-contact environments where these skills can be practiced.

In addition, the family doctor should be trained in how to improve access itself, since they often share some responsibility for enhancing access for patients. Family doctors should be taught ways to improve access such as how to make people from a variety of cultures feel comfortable coming to them to seek first-contact care, the importance of expanded office hours, and mechanisms to facilitate care after-hours. Family doctors must know how to design their clinics to enhance access and be familiar with ways to make system improvements. While the family doctor cannot always be present at the time and place of first presentation for care, they can learn to work effectively with other health care team members so that a patient can always access someone with basic training in primary care principles. If all members of the primary care team are properly trained in team-based health care, any team member providing initial care can then engage with the family doctor as needed to further address the patient's health needs and maximize application of the core principles of primary care.

Improving access through training can have meaningful results on outcomes.[32] The simple availability of primary care doctors, especially family doctors, has been shown to improve age-standardized mortality, infant mortality, and low birth weight percentage.[20-24] Greater access to primary care is known to lead to earlier detection of disease, a decrease in total mortality rates for a number of specific diseases, better overall health outcomes, and lower costs.[16,17,19,21-23]

Comprehensiveness

Comprehensiveness is an essential principle of family medicine, necessary for providing effective care at the point of first-contact. As already described, because of the undifferentiated nature of many problems and the need to see all people who present for care at the grassroots level, the family doctor must be prepared to deal with a wide variety of patients and illnesses and should be armed with a comprehensive set of clinical skills.

The family doctor should be able to:
➤ care for patients of all ages, genders, and cultures
➤ diagnose and manage a wide range of illness not limited by organ system
➤ recognize and be familiar with all local common diseases
➤ provide emergency services and surgical interventions consistent with their training, local need, and available resources

➤ promote family planning and deliver a full range of reproductive health services

➤ evaluate patients' risk for future illness and provide preventive services.

At first glance, it may seem difficult or even impossible for a single physician to be competent in providing such breadth of services. Certainly, it is impossible for any doctor to know the complete breadth and depth of any single subspecialty field of medicine, never mind the entirety. The family doctor can, however, become an expert in the common diseases seen frequently in their setting. In addition, they can seek basic competency in managing a larger range of illness.

Achieving competency in providing comprehensive care is possible for a number of reasons. First, a focus on common health conditions allows family doctors to target their in-depth skills. Additionally, there is a significant degree of overlap in overall health care principles between fields of medicine, allowing the trainee in family medicine to capitalize on lessons learned in one field while providing care related to another. Perhaps most interestingly, comprehensiveness of care is possible because the likelihood of serious illness is lower in primary care.[25] In the subspecialist clinic, patients are already pre-sorted, and so have an increased likelihood of having a disease related to the subspecialist's discipline and they are likely to have more severe disease as a result of both the sorting process and the time that lapses during that process.

In contrast, the job of the family doctor is first to determine if a patient is well or sick. The family doctor is expert at determining the presence, type and severity of disease in undifferentiated patients and in treating common conditions. In this setting, the priority does not need to be a comprehensive understanding of all diseases. Instead, another essential competency of the family doctor is to be able to recognize when there is an unfamiliar disease or presentation. In sum, family doctors need to know what they do not know. By knowing common diseases and typical presentations very well, the family doctor can quickly establish when an illness is unfamiliar or when disease is progressing in an unusual way. In these cases, family doctors can then determine if managing the problem is within their specific skill set or requires additional resources, such as referral to a subspecialist. As an expert in common disease, the family doctor can diagnose and treat a large number of presenting complaints. Coupled with the ability to expertly distinguish between typical and atypical presentations of disease, the family doctor is then capable of providing competent comprehensive care to everyone who presents for first-contact care.

It is also important to understand that while all of the principles of primary care are important for any family doctor, the degree to which any specific principle may be emphasized in a specific practice or care setting compared with another may vary depending on local need. Comprehensiveness can be a good example of this. The specific degree of comprehensiveness will be somewhat dependent on the local setting and resources. In a low resourced setting where a family doctor may be one of the only providers on staff in a local district hospital far from a source of referral care, the range of clinical skills needed will be very broad. The family doctor may need greater competency in emergent surgical procedures or managing trauma. Such family doctors may also be expected to stabilize and care for sick patients for a longer period or manage their illness to a greater degree of severity before seeking more advanced care services. In these settings, the balance of training may lend itself more toward increased attention to comprehensiveness, compared with other principles of primary care.

Teaching comprehensive care begins with didactic and clinical experiences to develop clinical skills across a number of different specialties, and at least some instruction is often led or augmented by subspecialists in these fields. As the experts in the most common and serious illnesses in their specific clinical area, they have valuable knowledge to impart, are typically the most skilled at teaching and assessing competency in related procedural skills, and often can offer clinical learning opportunities with more concentrated numbers of patients suffering from problems within their field compared with a primary care setting. It is not enough, however, to simply expose learners to a diversity of clinical topics. Instruction in these topics, including that from subspecialists, must be targeted at the special needs of the primary care doctor, with an emphasis on the type of care they are expected to provide in the first-contact setting. This means curricula from other specialties must be adapted to not simply replicate that taught to subspecialists in the field, but instead address the most core issues, such as how to recognize and diagnose the most common illnesses in a field, how to treat these illnesses, what can be managed safely at the primary care level, and when to refer to the subspecialist. In addition, the highest-severity illnesses in need of rapid intervention or referral must be identified, as well as strategies for dealing with those problems at the primary care level. Finally, the family doctor must understand a general approach to the subspecialty field for problems that fall outside these categories.

To truly teach comprehensiveness, however, learners must also be provided with opportunities to see and care for the types of undifferentiated patients that are typically seen at the point of first contact. Training programs utilizing clinical practice in grassroots settings allow learners to hone their skills in sorting wellness from sickness, increase their familiarity and expertise in managing the most common illnesses, recognize psychosocial problems that may present as physical symptoms, and build experience in determining when and how to effectively refer patients. In these training settings, it is usually best if a family doctor is the lead supervisor and teacher for primary care learners as she or he represents the most relevant specialist with targeted expertise in providing care in this setting.

Comprehensiveness as a principle, however, does also go beyond the ability to provide problem-based service delivery. It represents a philosophy of family medicine, in which the family doctor seeks to provide the maximum amount of health care for each patient to the upper limits of their ability and avoid unnecessary referrals to hospitals or subspecialists, improving care efficiency for both the patient and the entire health system. This approach reduces unnecessary testing and medical interventions, can reduce iatrogenic complications, and result in improved outcomes with lower costs. Instruction under the mentorship of an experience family doctor allows learners to develop this attitude.

Comprehensiveness as a philosophy of family medicine extends beyond the traditional reach of allopathic medicine as well, referring to a more comprehensive and holistic approach to care of patients. This approach takes into account the biological, clinical, social, and psychological needs of the patient as well as the family, community, and societal contexts impacting their health. The family doctor applies the biopsychosocial approach to address psychosocial factors that may influence health as much as biological factors.[33–35] The family doctor must learn to consider all these factors, integrate issues of family and community into their medical approach, and assist patients with strategies for navigating the challenging social determinants of health.[36]

Continuity of care

Continuity of care is a cornerstone principle of family medicine, and provides an essential tool for use by the family doctor in providing care. In most other medical disciplines, patients are seen for a disease-based complaint, and a health care provider only follows them on visits related to that specific complaint. In the case of family medicine, the family doctor seeks to establish a long-term relationship with each person, rather than simply focusing on a disease. This allows the family doctor to have a continuing impact on the health of each person, including monitoring of current problems and through multiple opportunities for prevention. This emphasis on continuity encourages each person to establish a usual source of care as their point of first contact with the health care system.

In teaching continuity of care, there are three levels of continuity to be considered: informational, longitudinal, and interpersonal.[37,38] Informational continuity relates to the collection, use, and access of medical information that can be used to inform and enhance care of the patient. An example would be the maintenance of a medical record, either in paper or electronic form. Longitudinal continuity can describe a place, such as a clinic, or alternatively a team of health care staff, that acts as a usual source of care for a patient. In some countries, this is referred to as a medical home, where a patient seeks to receive most of their health care in a familiar and accessible environment from an organized team of health care providers who accept responsibility for managing that patient's health over time.[37] As such, longitudinal continuity also relates to the process of care, describing a consistent and coherent approach to management of a patient's health care needs.[38] The third level of continuity, interpersonal continuity, represents the ongoing therapeutic relationship between a patient and their personal physician.

Family medicine as a discipline generally seeks to maximize all three levels of continuity. First, family doctors must understand principles of medical documentation and methods for completing and maintaining a medical record as part of informational continuity. This may include storage and retrieval processes for a paper-based medical record, or more advanced technological skills in utilizing an electronic health record, depending on the local setting.

For longitudinal continuity, family doctors need to be trained in how to work as part of an interprofessional team, as well as system-based care, health management, and quality improvement processes.

Enhancing the third level of interpersonal continuity requires both the provider and the patient to play an active role: the provider needs to be available to see the patient at each visit, and the patient needs to seek out the specific provider for each visit. This depends not only on the family doctor applying their skills in improving access, but they must also learn strategies for encouraging continuity-seeking behaviors from patients. Continuity can be influenced by the strength of the relationship and trust developed between provider and patient. If the relationship is weak or trust is low, a patient is more likely to see a different provider at each visit. In a primary care pediatric practice, availability of the provider (i.e., an adequate number of sessions in clinic), the parents' opinion of continuity, the family rating of the provider, the age of the child, the number of visits, and the length of time a patient has been going to a particular clinic have been shown to impact the degree of continuity.[39]

While there are a multitude of ways in which these different levels of continuity may be helpful in caring for patients, it is the specific and directed application of continuous care over time as a diagnostic and therapeutic tool that is so fundamental to family medicine. The passage of time allows the family doctor to observe a medical problem, especially if the symptoms are unclear, and monitor the patient to determine if a change in symptoms over time leads to a more precise diagnosis. Similarly, the passage of time allows the family doctor to monitor the success of a treatment plan, potentially confirming a diagnosis or suggesting a new plan of action is necessary – a process often referred to as "watchful waiting";[25] this is not just a happenstance occurrence, but instead a deliberate act on the part of the provider to allow a period of time to elapse as part of an active management plan. Utilization of this technique may also allow for less aggressive medical interventions, resulting in better care with lower expense and fewer iatrogenic complications. In order to learn the effective application of watchful waiting as a successful strategy for promoting health requires practice and experience with this technique. In practice, this means providing direct clinical care to a panel of patients at the first-contact point of care under the supervision and mentorship of an experienced primary care provider.

Repeated visits with the same source of care also offer other benefits. Family doctors learn to take advantage of an increased number of opportunities for preventive care. Continuity of care over time allows the family doctor to develop a deeper and more comprehensive understanding of a patient and their problems.[40] A variety of patient related factors have also been shown to be tied to patient interest in continuity, and these generally suggest that the most vulnerable patients are the ones who benefit most from a continuity relationship.[41,42] Continuity has been shown to improve patient and clinician satisfaction, compliance with treatment regimens, and patient outcomes, and these improvements may be greatest with interpersonal continuity.[40,43–46]

The only way to teach continuous health care over time is to provide opportunities to experience and practice health care with patients over time. For students this likely means a community-based experience over the course of at least a month where there is at least the possibility of seeing individual patients more than once. One example is the longitudinal integrated clerkship (*see* Box 4.3).[102] In a robust program, in order to maximize a continuity experience for medical students, each student is assigned to a carefully selected panel of patients chosen to represent a variety of medical fields based on their known ailments, and students are expected to follow them to all of their medical encounters.[47]

For in-service training, continuity of care is probably best taught by assigning responsibility for the first-contact care of a specific panel of patients. Throughout the period of their family medicine specialty training, providers are then expected to care for these patients in an ambulatory setting, developing strong patient-doctor relationships and learning to wield the tool of time under the tutelage of a family medicine educator.

Teaching continuity of care does, however, face certain challenges. First, by the very nature of time-limited training, a lack of sufficient extended time to build long-term relationships and monitor the progress of chronic disease can limit continuity opportunities and act as a significant barrier to learning effective continuity of care. As cited previously, local needs may also de-emphasize continuity of care in favor of maximizing training in other primary care principles. Some evidence suggests that maximizing access for patients to longitudinal continuity may have the tendency to reduce interpersonal continuity as patients opt for health care encounters that are more convenient over maintaining interpersonal continuity with their identified provider.[4]

BOX 4.3 Longitudinal integrated clerkships[102]

Longitudinal integrated clerkships are perhaps one of the more novel and innovative curricula for medical students developed in the last decade. They have been implemented by medical schools around the world in both rural and urban contexts.

While there is a wide range in the detailed structure of these different clerkships, programs are typically at least 6 months in duration, and a consensus definition suggests the following consistent components:

- students participate in the provision of comprehensive care of patients over time
- students participate in continuing learning relationships with the clinicians of these patients
- students meet the majority of the year's core clinical competencies across multiple disciplines simultaneously through these experiences.

This emphasis on continuity of care and comprehensive care is highly synergistic with principles of primary care. Academic and clinical results across a number of different programs suggest that students typically perform as well or better than their peers in traditional hospital-based curricula. The programs tend to be well liked by participating clinicians who greatly appreciate the continuity relationship with students, allowing them to make more meaningful contributions to a practice. There is also some limited evidence that these programs may influence student career choice, including a positive influence toward primary care.

In addition, in low-resourced settings where physicians are rarely employed in ambulatory clinic settings, there may be few opportunities for training family doctors in settings with interpersonal continuity. Often in these settings, physicians are a prized commodity asked to participate as one of very few providers in a district hospital remote from referral care. In these health systems, family medicine training may choose to emphasize a broad range of in-depth inpatient clinical skills in order to maximize comprehensiveness, at times at the expense of continuity of care. Training in continuity may also suffer in these locales from the lack of convenient access for patients. For instance, long travel distances may prevent multiple visits over time by patients. Nonetheless, even these health systems should consider working toward developing continuity-based care, and training in this principle offers a long-term investment in primary care system improvement.

Coordination

Family medicine is interdependent with the health system, its organization and resources. As health systems face multiple challenges, family doctors are frequently on the front lines advocating the best possible care for their patients and communities. Coordination of care is both a function and tool of family medicine for accomplishing this goal. The family doctor takes responsibility for managing the overall health of his or her patients over time, an important function of the family doctor within the health care system. As part of this task, coordinating care improves patient outcomes, making it a powerful tool for management and treatment of illness, especially chronic disease.[49,50]

Coordination includes diagnosing and treating many problems for a patient, managing multiple medical problems or diseases across multiple organ systems, and considering the impact of each on the other. It involves working with patients to determine how a diagnosis and treatment may impact their daily lives, and helping them to determine how they might overcome the many barriers in their lives to achieving good health. Good coordination by a family doctor will include considering what preventive measures are necessary and how to incorporate them into a patient's overall plan for health. Coordination by the family doctor includes actively working together with subspecialists, rather than simply transferring a patient to another clinic for care. If a single patient has many subspecialists involved with multiple diseases across several organ systems, it is the role of the family doctor to help the subspecialists coordinate their care and to advise the patient about how to integrate the different recommendations of various subspecialists.

To provide this type of coordination is not easy for a single physician, and outcomes seem to benefit with coordination of an entire primary care team and effective teamwork.[50-52] Primary care teams typically include a primary care physician, physician assistants, nurses, and nurse aides. Other members of the primary care team may include general clinic staff, pharmacists, midwives, and community health workers. For some tasks, nonphysician staff members may be more skilled or efficient than physicians at some coordinating functions. The family doctor, however, plays a key role as a lynchpin in guiding the primary care team in efficiently coordinating care for the patient and making it responsive to their needs. As such, the family doctor must be trained in ways counter to the traditional medical culture that often promotes hierarchical power structures along with isolation and autonomy as the practice of physicians.[53,54]

The family doctor, as a well-trained health care team member with advanced medical knowledge and training in comprehensive person-centered care, is in the best position to oversee coordination of care in the team model.[50] This is especially true when patients have several problems increasing the complexity of care and requiring integration and synthesis of recommendations from several different subspecialists or other health care providers. In some cases, recommendations may even conflict if the patient is seeing multiple subspecialists. The family doctor is ideally suited for distilling this information and providing clear direction to the other members of the health care team and simplifying the complexity when communicating with the patient and family.

It is important to realize that coordination of care does not happen without dedicated attention to the effort. Like the other principles of primary care, providers need to be educated in a variety of methods to facilitate their performance of this function. With guidance, students working in family practice settings can learn to think critically about health systems, and consider their roles in health system reform. Leadership and management curricula may be introduced to help learners envisage their roles as future health system leaders.

Those curricula may include the following components:
➤ history of health system developments and global and local trends
➤ government policies and regulations related to health care
➤ health care outcomes and areas in need of improvement
➤ patients' rights and health professionals' responsibilities
➤ quality improvement principles and methods
➤ how to serve as health activists for patients and for the community.

These materials come to life and have increased relevance when students can discuss case examples with practicing family doctors or participate actively in health system assessment and reform.

The family doctor needs to be highly skilled at thinking about systems, and how to impact these systems. In order to maximize coordination of care, the discipline of family medicine encourages the primary care provider to consider all systems that impact a patient's health, as well as to consider ways the provider might intervene in the system to facilitate improved health for the patient. For those systems directly influenced by or under the direct control of the primary care provider, family medicine encourages rational system design in order to enhance the overall care of the patient and build bridges to care between aspects of the health care system that might not otherwise work in collaboration with one another.

Practical training in coordination of care is an important method for learning this skill. The assignment of an ambulatory patient panel as suggested previously for promoting skills training in continuity of care offers similar benefits for learning coordination. In order to properly care for a panel of patients, many of the skills for coordination of care will be needed, ranging from effective communication skills to system-based practice and quality improvement. Practical training provides the opportunity for learners to experience systems of care first hand, and how they may facilitate or interfere with providing optimal care. This experience then drives educational processes for learning about the system-based provision of care and quality improvement.

It is worth recognizing, however, that the family doctor cannot provide coordination of care in a vacuum. Not only must the family doctor understand system-based care, but also the system itself must be designed to support primary care providers in order to maximize use of these skills. Utilizing referral systems is one highly effective system-based method for improving coordination and communication between the family doctor and subspecialist, so learning how to properly refer a patient within the local health system is of paramount importance. Ideally, use of such referral systems help streamline access for the patient to necessary subspecialists while also avoiding unnecessary visits to the subspecialist for less serious or complex problems. Clinical care is improved and physician satisfaction is increased when primary care providers effectively and reliably communicate information about patients they have referred to the subspecialist, and subspecialists send return information about their diagnosis and treatment plan to the primary care physician. Referral systems can then also help promote continuity of care by guiding the patient back to the family doctor after being seen by the subspecialist, and having the subspecialist provide the family doctor with information about how to manage the patient in their primary care clinic setting. While this coordination may seem simple enough, ensuring its success has largely become the province of the family doctor, and requires dedicated training in overcoming system barriers to be successful.

Coordination of care also may not be limited to the outpatient setting. Some studies have shown that effective coordination and development of good patient education and provider communication systems, including effective communication about aspects of a hospital stay with a patient's family doctor, can result in decreased rates of re-hospitalization after discharge.[50,55]

Family doctors who work in an inpatient setting can also be effective in promoting coordination of care. Given their detailed understanding of care in the outpatient setting and increased training in coordinating care, they can be especially effective as inpatient care providers in coordinating the consultations of many subspecialists. The family doctor working in an inpatient setting is also better trained in communicating with primary care providers based in outpatient settings, informing them of the patient's clinical course during hospitalization and providing them with information on how to best care for the patient in the future back in the community setting.

In sum, to effectively coordinate care, a family doctor needs good communication with specialists, referral systems for tracking patients, a method of recording the comprehensive medical history of a patient and tracking it over time, a strong understanding of how to work and mobilize change within health systems, and trained support staff who assist in the process of coordination. With these resources, the family doctor can be highly effective in assisting patients in navigating the challenging aspects of their health care system in order to access the essential care they need.

Prevention

Prevention is an important aspect of family doctors' care for individuals and communities, and is one of the most powerful tools in the family doctor's toolbox for promoting health. It is based on one simple concept: the avoidance of disease before it begins. While a simple concept, in practice it is much more difficult to implement.

Preventive care can involve primary, secondary, and tertiary prevention.[56]

➤ *Primary prevention*: action taken to avoid or remove the cause of a health problem in an individual or a population before it arises. Includes health promotion and specific protection (e.g., immunization).

➤ *Secondary prevention*: action taken to detect a health problem at an early stage in an individual or a population, thereby facilitating cure, or reducing or preventing it spreading or its long-term effects (e.g., methods, screening, case finding, and early diagnosis).

➤ *Tertiary prevention*: action taken to reduce the chronic effects of a health problem in an individual or a population by minimizing the functional impairment consequent to the acute or chronic health problem (e.g., prevent complications of diabetes). Includes rehabilitation.

In addition, the concept of quaternary prevention has been introduced, although there are competing definitions for the term.[57] While one definition tends to refer to the restoration of function in the severely ill, WONCA has also endorsed an alternative definition as the action taken to identify the risk of overmedicalization and protect a patient from additional medical invasions or interventions to the degree ethically acceptable.[56]

Prevention involves screening for disease and application of medical interventions such as vaccines coupled with counseling and patient education. The basics of prevention include:[58]

➤ understanding patterns of diseases
➤ assessing risk factors
➤ appropriate selection and use of screening tests
➤ understanding and applying age-specific and sex-specific prevention recommendations
➤ motivating patients to change their behavior.

The comprehensive nature of family doctors makes them ideally suited for carrying out such complex and multifactorial tasks, and the continuity relationship with patients places family doctors in the ideal situation of having multiple encounters in which to intervene with preventive services.

Medical students may learn the principles of prevention during the early years of medical school, and practice applying this knowledge in the care of individuals and communities in later clinical training. Many health problems are associated with lifestyle variables such as sexual behavior and use of tobacco, alcohol or other drugs. Students can learn to help patients avoid high-risk behaviors, and to motivate them to change these behaviors if they are established.[59,60]

Again the assignment of a panel of patients receiving continuity of care provides an ideal setting for training in prevention. Given responsibility for the overall health of a panel of patients, and not just the duty to treat a series of presenting medical problems, prevention takes on increased importance in training. Learners are taught to consider preventive interventions at every encounter, how to assess a patient's preventive health needs, and how to encourage a patient to accept and pursue such preventive measures. Application of these principles at the level of individual clinical service delivery helps extend the efforts of public health programs to the level of the individual patient.

Family orientation

Because family doctors need to provide comprehensive care for many members of the family, they must learn to routinely consider patients in the context of their families and, where appropriate, apply a family approach to patient care. This begins with understanding the role of families in health and illness behavior, the dynamics of family systems, and stages of the family life cycle. Involving family members in the birth of a child or in care at the end of life can improve both the quality of care and the adjustment of family members to changing circumstances.

A variety of skills must be learned for effective family-oriented care. Learners must practice taking family histories, beyond just medical information relevant to genetic burden of disease. Family doctors should learn how to draw a genogram, and the importance of tracking and maintaining such information as part of a patient's medical record. On this genogram should be included family relationships, both structural and emotional, as well as traditional genetic information. Family doctors should be skilled in leading family meetings to discuss important health issues, especially around transitions in health care and life in general. Family doctors must understand the importance of family dynamics and life cycle, and have basic skills in family counseling to help the families in their care navigate stressful situations impacting their health. Family doctors may also benefit from developing insight into their own family dynamics, and how this influences their perspective in working with their patients around these issues.

Many techniques can be applied to building these skills. Students may practice interviewing more than one family member, how to conduct a family meeting or conference, and how to establish a therapeutic alliance with the patient's family.[35,61] Students who have opportunities to experience and practice family-centered approaches will be able to work more effectively with families in their future practices.

A special issue related to family-orientation is women's health, family planning, and reproductive health services. While this might simply be considered as an important part of the clinical portfolio of care linked to the principle of comprehensiveness, it appears here as an essential skill set perhaps most closely allied with family-orientation. Effective family planning provides the foundation for creating healthy families, and thus the family doctor needs to be especially skilled in these areas. This not only involves timing of pregnancies and prevention of unwanted pregnancy, but should include active preconception counseling. It should include prenatal care, allowing the family doctor to maximize the opportunity for a healthy birth as well as take advantage of several health care encounters over time to assist families in preparing physically and emotionally for this powerful generative event in a family. Ideally, the family doctor will also be prepared to assist in the delivery of an infant, not only allowing them to effectively supervise midwives and other birth attendants and help manage obstetric complications, but at times being present to further enhance the bonding and interpersonal relationship between physician and family. A strong skill set in women's health permits the family doctor to provide these essential services while also maximizing the health of the mother who often drives a family's health care utilization.

Community orientation

Most family doctors are involved in the communities where they see patients, and they often perform important community health services. Community health activities may include a variety of educational, preventive or other interventions, such as school health programs, immunization clinics, or aged care homes for the elderly.

Such activities can be made even more effective as part of a deliberate strategy to provide community-oriented primary care. Community-oriented primary care provides a strategy for the family doctor to apply what they learn in their daily service delivery to the community health context.[25,62] Through the provision of individual clinical services, the observant family doctor recognizes this as a window into the overall health of the community. The diagnoses of the people who walk into a family doctor's clinic are a reflection of the health status of the community as a whole, as well as an indication of community-wide health stressors and promoters. In order to capitalize on this important feature of their primary care practice, family doctors need to be trained in how to act on their observations. The community-oriented primary care approach encourages providers to make these observations and then bring them to the community in a structured way in search of opportunities to identify and help meet local public health needs. Through this, the family doctor gains a greater appreciation of the social, environmental, and economic impacts of the broader community on the health of the individual patient.

Students can be introduced to the principles of epidemiology, population health, and community-oriented primary health care during their medical training. As part of practical skills building, learners can participate in assessing the health needs of communities, identifying health-related resources, selecting priorities for intervention, and assessing outcomes through working with trained family doctors in community settings.[63] When guided and supported by experienced health team members, learners can also serve as effective community health educators and role models for youth. In some schools, family doctors sponsor programs that engage medical students in community and school health education, providing opportunities for students to participate in community health early in their training. By working with family physicians who successfully integrate individual and community health activities, students learn to view these services as part of a continuum of comprehensive primary health care, rather than a series of disconnected elements.

One important issue to recognize in family medicine education is that while prevention and community-orientation are important parts of family medicine education, family medicine is not exclusively a public health discipline. A system of training providers exclusively in public health principles and programs focused on population-based care, such as for those who might lead community-based primary health care teams in providing preventive care at a population level, is not sufficient to provide competency in the practice of family medicine. On the contrary, family medicine is first and foremost a clinical discipline and its focus on preventive care and care of the community is necessarily grounded in the provision of direct person-focused clinical care, and so training programs must include this critical component. The family doctor, while not a replacement for the public health professional, is a critical contributor in a comprehensive public health delivery system targeted at promoting health for an entire community.

Patient-centeredness

Perhaps the most fundamental difference between family medicine and other medical disciplines is the overriding and core guiding principle of patient-centeredness. Patient-centeredness represents a shift in focus of clinical care from a curative disease-based approach to health to a more holistic and collaborative focus on the health of the entire person. While this principle of person-focused care might seem as if it should be core to all fields of medicine, family medicine takes on the principle as the driving force behind how all health care should be delivered.

Patient-centeredness as a driving principle of medical education may be quite different from the typical educational model in many systems. Traditionally, while communication skills and the patient-doctor relationship may have been important components, medical education has largely followed a disease-based approach relegating these other elements of care to a small and fragmented portion of the overall medical school curriculum. Certainly, decades of disease-oriented research has resulted in an explosion of medical knowledge in all fields of medicine. Such disease-oriented discovery, research, and clinical care have also provided scientifically proven and statistically significant quantitative improvements. Seeing this targeted success, health systems and various funders of health improvement have increased pressure for further rapid improvements in specific health indicators. There needs to be a balance and, for the family doctor, the ultimate goal is to keep each individual patient as well as the whole population as healthy as possible through the delivery of high-quality patient-centered primary care.

In family medicine, evidence-based medicine and the effort to effect improvements in population-based outcomes are important and essential to the daily work of the family doctor, and represent a core part of the principle toward provision of comprehensive care. The family doctor, however, also recognizes that each individual patient is an infinitely complex system that requires an expertise that goes beyond disease-based guidelines and population-based interventions. The health of an individual person is the result of a complicated set of interactions, affected not only by that person's behavior and genetics, but also by their family and community, and a group of specific comorbidities unique to that person. Furthermore, a person's personal life and health goals ultimately drive their health-seeking behaviors.

The discipline of family medicine has developed a variety of educational mechanisms for learning to build and optimize doctor-patient relationships. Doctor-patient communication is central to establishing therapeutic relationships with patients, and may be introduced early in medical education and refined in later clinical rotations.

There are many approaches to teaching patient-centered communication skills.[64–70] Box 4.4 lists essential elements of communication in medical encounters, summarized by teachers of communication skills.

Many family doctors use the patient-centered clinical method to teach and assess communication skills. Combining the essential elements of communication with the principles of family medicine, this method integrates communication regarding the patient's experience of illness with biomedical aspects of diagnosis and management.[71]

The patient-centered clinical method includes attention to six interrelated components of patient care:
1. exploring both the disease and illness experience
2. understanding the whole person
3. finding common ground regarding management
4. incorporating prevention and health promotion
5. enhancing the doctor-patient relationship
6. being realistic.

Family doctors may adapt these or other communication skill frameworks to model, teach, and evaluate each learner's communication skills as they progress through training. While excellent communication skills are important in all areas of medicine, family doctors are particularly well suited to model and teach

BOX 4.4 Essential elements of communication in medical encounters[103]

Open the discussion

- Allow the patient to complete his or her opening statement
- Elicit the patient's full set of concerns
- Establish/maintain a personal connection

Gather information

- Use open- and closed-ended questions appropriately
- Structure, clarify, and summarize information
- Actively listen using nonverbal (e.g., eye contact) and verbal (e.g., words of encouragement) techniques

Understand the patient's perspective

- Explore contextual factors (e.g., family, culture, sex, age, socioeconomic status, religion)
- Explore beliefs, concerns, and expectations about health and illness
- Acknowledge and respond to the patient's ideas, feelings, and values

Share information

- Use language the patient can understand
- Check for understanding
- Encourage questions

Reach agreement on problems and plans

- Encourage the patient to participate in and share decisions to the extent he or she desires
- Check the patient's willingness and ability to follow the plan
- Identify and enlist resources and supports

Provide closure

- Ask whether the patient wishes to bring up other issues or concerns
- Summarize and affirm agreement with the plan of action
- Discuss follow-up plans (e.g., next visit, plan for unexpected outcomes)

comprehensive communication skills, as they approach patients from a holistic perspective and must learn to foster meaningful relationships that persist over time. One specific technique, known as the Balint group, developed by a British general practitioner Michael Balint, is used widely as a reflective group-process and teaching method specifically for analyzing and improving the doctor-patient relationships of family doctors.[72] This method is utilized not just for trainees, but also for experienced family doctors as a way of continually improving their skills in managing the patient-doctor relationship.

A therapeutic patient-doctor relationship is also based on a strong ethical foundation.[73] This involves demonstrating:

➤ unconditional respect for the patient
➤ dedication to work in the patient's best interests
➤ commitment to do no harm
➤ maintenance of confidentiality
➤ respect for the wishes and autonomy of patients and their families.

While important in all areas of medicine, the principles of social justice and equity in health care are particularly relevant as family medicine strives to deal with the comprehensive health needs of individuals and communities. Family doctors are frequently on the front line of those providing primary care to disadvantaged populations. In such settings, family doctors often witness the inequities of society and health care systems and must learn mechanisms to effectively practice in these difficult settings. Working with family doctors who demonstrate unconditional regard and ethical behavior toward each of their patients regardless of circumstances helps learners to adopt similar values and attitudes. Clinical experiences that provide opportunities for reflection and discussion of ethical concerns allow teachers and learners to analyze the strengths and weaknesses of health systems, and may motivate students to work for changes in the medical school curriculum, in health care delivery and in their society (*see* Box 4.5).

Another important consideration to be taken into account in patient-centered care, which also impacts access to care, is the culture of local populations, especially multicultural ones. There are often local systems of treatments that are culturally sensitive and have been in place over many generations, and patients may remain very loyal to these alternative beliefs and systems of health care. Family doctors must learn to inquire about these complementary medical practices and how to incorporate them into their usual practice recommendations depending on the interest of the patient. The family doctor must learn to integrate a patient's cultural perception of their illness into acceptable management options.

To successfully maximize any individual patient's health, the family doctor must leverage all of the principles of primary care cited previously toward building a relationship founded on trust and understanding. As a specialist in these principles, the family doctor seeks to address the personal goals of the individual patient and thus maximize each individual patient's health to the degree the patient desires and will allow. For health systems and funders of global health improvement, the pressure to produce outcome improvements can be at odds with the interests of the individual patient and person-focused care. In fact, a patient's personal goals may run counter to the achievement of an objective maximized level of health, and as such be in opposition to those of public health efforts and the health system as a whole. The family doctor is trained to first consider the needs and desires of the individual sitting in front of them in the examination room and then apply other powerful disease-based tools in medicine. Family medicine as a specialty aims to reconcile these potentially oppositional forces by directly addressing the complexities of improving overall patient and population health at the level of the individual patient.

The role of the family doctor is also advancing the principle of patient-centeredness to become even more person-focused[105] through supporting the empowerment of individuals and communities though health education, improved access to information, promotion of self-care, and encouragement of shared decision making by patients and their doctors.

Bringing the eight core principles together

One can now see how the family doctor is uniquely situated to this task. Family doctors make themselves or members of their team optimally accessible to patients so they are positioned to intervene at a time the patient needs and desires. The family doctor is well trained in providing a comprehensive range of disease-based clinical services, and has familiarity with the complex tasks of treating and managing a variety of comorbidities across organ systems. The comprehensive approach of the family doctor, however, goes beyond disease-based care and includes specific expertise in communicating with patients and considering the many social determinants of their health. The family doctor develops a long-term and trusting relationship with a patient, providing an important perspective on the multifaceted interaction of a patient's health with their environment over time as well as the overall personal health goals of a patient.

Having developed this relationship and understanding of the patient, the family doctor then becomes a health advocate for the patient, not only providing direct clinical care but also coordinating the access and management of their overall health across a number of different health care venues. The family doctor looks for opportunities specific to this patient to prevent disease, and provides the relevant preventive services. The family doctor considers the influence of the patient's family, attempts to engage other family members when appropriate in an individual's care, and brings knowledge of the health of entire families to bear on addressing health issues within that family. The family doctor then seeks to look beyond the patient and family to the entire community, both in how the community may impact the health of the patient and how his or her experience with individual patients may inform what is happening in the health of the overall community. The family doctor then takes an approach to individual patients that will also help address the specific health needs of the community.

It is through the combined application of all of these principles that the family doctor can then bring the power of disease-based approaches to care in a synergistic way with a patient's individual health goals. A primary care provider trained in all of these principles will elicit the various problems and concerns of a patient, establish the findings within this patient pertinent to specific diagnoses and management plans, identify the influencing factors of particular comorbidities and in the patient's environment, counsel and educate the patient on relevant health issues, and then embark on a shared decision-making process to achieve the individual patient's personal health goals. By addressing the complex system of the individual patient and engaging in a joint effort to maximize the health of each patient by adapting disease-based approaches to reflect and respect an individual patient's specific needs, the family doctor can have the greatest impact on overall health outcomes.

4.3 HOW SHOULD FAMILY MEDICINE EDUCATION AND TRAINING BE IMPLEMENTED?

Understanding what is family medicine and how it is different from other types of training and medical specialties, one can now consider the mechanisms for implementing family medicine education and training programs. This section will not focus in great detail on general principles of medical education and curriculum development that should be common to all medical specialties and are better covered in resources dedicated to this purpose, nor will it delve too deeply into the specific details of any individual aspect of a family medicine curriculum or lesson plan. Rather, the emphasis of this section will be on a health system-based approach to implementation of family medicine education and training.

System-based implementation of family medicine education and training involves three core elements: building infrastructure, developing specific teaching programs, and evaluating providers and programs. This section starts with building infrastructure, for without a proper foundation, no comprehensive primary care training program is possible. Once an appropriate foundation is in place, it is possible to consider types of training programs and some commonalities to their development. With programs established, the process of evaluation and improvement can then begin.

Building family medicine infrastructure

Setting up a family medicine training program requires dedicated infrastructure, such as institutional commitment and the coordinated support of family medicine teaching faculty, specialty colleagues, health team members, program administrators, and staff. Training programs may be organized as part of, or independent from, academic departments of family medicine. When these programs are designed to benefit communities and health systems, they are more likely to be successful. Benefits include improving access, comprehensiveness and quality of care, providing hospital coverage, attracting patients, and recruiting high-quality trainees and teaching faculty. When local leaders and physicians understand the value of family medicine to communities and the health system, they are more likely to be supportive.

The fundamental infrastructure associated with developing a training program in family medicine is listed in Box 4.5. Elements may be developed simultaneously, or in a different order from that listed. There are several scenarios to consider. New programs will need to develop start-up and long-term plans. Recently established programs may review this list to identify areas for improvement. Well-established programs may wish to develop additional special areas of focus, expand research agendas, enter into partnership with newly developing programs in their own country or in other countries, or strengthen community health initiatives. Each area will be discussed in more detail but first we examine the three categories of infrastructure that are necessary to develop training: academic, human resource, and physical and financial.

Academic

The aim of specialty training in family medicine is to prepare family doctors to provide long-term, person-focused, comprehensive, high-quality care for individuals, families, and communities. This requires training that is specifically designed to convey the knowledge, attitudes, and skills that are necessary for their future practices. Successful systems for training family doctors vary from country to country.

Family doctors may be trained in a variety of educational and clinical settings. These usually include family practice teaching centers, hospitals, the practices of relevant specialty consultants, and other community health facilities. Content will depend on local needs and practice. Duration also varies with most specialty programs involving 2–5 years of full-time study after students have completed

BOX 4.5 Fundamental infrastructure in developing training programs in family medicine

Academic

- Establish and evaluate curriculum:
  - agree on the nature of family medicine
  - establish detailed learning objectives and expected competencies, based on community needs
  - develop core curriculum goals designed to facilitate achievement of these competencies
  - select best teaching methods and educational experiences to accomplish objectives
  - plan longitudinal curriculum
  - establish system for evaluation and feedback of learners
  - establish or meet criteria for program evaluation, recognition, and certification
- Establish a department or unit of family medicine
- Build relationships:
  - enter into partnership with hospitals and medical schools
  - affiliate with regional, national and international associations, such as WONCA

Human resource

- Recruit leaders, teachers, and staff
- Recruit patients
- Recruit trainees

Physical and financial

- Secure funding
- Organize family practice teaching centers
- Establish hospital, specialty, and community teaching sites

medical school, but the precise length of training necessary remains a matter of debate. The continued implementation of competency-based training may begin to shift the focus away from traditional time-based training programs toward a flexible model in which the time for any individual learner is based primarily on their achievement of competency.[106]

Family medicine has a core of knowledge that emphasizes breadth, and includes much of the same content as other disciplines such as internal medicine, pediatrics, obstetrics and gynecology, surgery, and psychiatry. Experiences in community and population health, practice management, and team approaches to health care allow the family doctor to serve as a bridge between individual and public health services and to contribute to the improvement of local health systems. However, family practice requires more than a series of disconnected training experiences. The family doctor learns to integrate and apply the knowledge and skills gained from other disciplines by providing comprehensive care to patients, families, and communities during their training.

BOX 4.6 Establishing family medicine training in the Eastern Mediterranean Region[107,108]

Family medicine activity began as early as 1961 in Turkey, followed by development of formal family medicine training programs in Bahrain in 1978 and Lebanon in 1979. Growth in the development of family medicine residency programs to other Arab countries steadily continued, with 31 programs in 12 countries graduating approximately 182 residents per year as of 2011, and another six new programs in development.

The Arab Board of Medical Specialties was established in 1978 to support improving health systems and residency training through establishment of regional standards. The Arab Board of Family and Community Medicine was later established and plays a strong role in setting standards for family medicine training and provides certification for graduates. While it is not required to have certification in order to be licensed, it is considered valuable often resulting in better job opportunities and compensation, and Arab Board certification is seen as a must in some academic settings.

Although the ratio of family physicians to the population in the region remains small, it is reassuring that most family medicine graduates work in the country in which they were training, and most are working in active clinical practice. Most work in government-run clinics, in solo private practice, or as academics. There are some concerns about limitations in the scope of practice, including a lack of obstetrics and inpatient care in some countries, although these generally remain in the scope of academic physicians due to the rotation requirements of the Arab Board.

The optimal skill mix for family doctors to address the primary health care needs of patients and communities will vary depending on local health system characteristics, disease patterns, practice location, resources available, and proximity to other health services. Nevertheless, as described in Chapter 3 and earlier in this chapter, there is a set of skills and competencies that characterize family doctors.[74] Although core curriculum guidelines have been established in many countries, family doctors are best prepared through training programs that tailor their educational goals to fit the needs and resources of local environments. At the core, the goals should reflect the regional job description of a first-contact primary care medical provider.

Human, physical, and financial resources are also required to establish a successful training program in family medicine. While these specific resources will be discussed elsewhere, these resources are usually organized through the academic systems in conjunction with a department or unit of family medicine.

Establish the core curriculum for family medicine

The building blocks of a family medicine training program include a core curriculum, organized around the foundational principles of family medicine and developed explicitly to meet the required competencies of its graduates. Through structured training, family doctors are prepared to manage a wide range of conditions in infants, children, adolescents, adults, pregnant women, and the elderly, to recognize patients with unusual diseases, and to stabilize and transfer patients with life-threatening emergencies to the most appropriate facility. In addition to providing comprehensive care, family doctors often serve as health coordinators and team leaders. The core content outlined in Box 4.7 serves as a starting point for program planning to achieve these competencies.

While all family medicine training programs share the goals of preparing family doctors to provide comprehensive primary health care, the details of family practice education will vary among programs. For instance, in some regions family doctors actively care for hospitalized patients; in others, family doctors restrict their activities to community and/or outpatient settings and refer patients who require hospital care to specialty colleagues. Agreement on the nature of family medicine and specific regional responsibilities of family doctors provides teachers and learners with a common understanding of the goals of training.

Once the broad goals of training are established, specific learning objectives and expected competencies are described. The curriculum is tailored to fit local needs by gathering information about prevalent conditions from epidemiological data, hospitals, clinics, practicing generalists and specialists. Lists of detailed learning objectives may be used to describe the expected competencies of family doctors to recognize, manage, or refer a wide range of patient problems. Tailored objectives guide learning activities. For example many family doctors provide prenatal care and recognize and refer patients with high-risk obstetric conditions, many family doctors attend routine obstetric deliveries, and some family doctors, especially if they work in areas where obstetricians are not available, perform caesarean deliveries. The obstetric training of family doctors, acquired in hospital and clinical settings, allows trainees to achieve the appropriate competencies.

BOX 4.7 Core content of family medicine includes …

Care for patients in specific groups
- Newborns
- Infants
- Children
- Adolescents
- Adults
- Pregnant women
- Elderly men and women

Integrate components of comprehensive care
- Understand primary care disease epidemiology
- Conduct appropriate history and physical examinations
- Understand differences in physiology and drug metabolism
- Interpret laboratory and radiological evaluations
- Conduct age-specific risk assessment
- Provide prevention, screening, nutritional guidance, and health education
- Understand normal developmental issues
- Provide behavioral or psychological counseling
- Refer patients appropriately when indicated
- Provide palliative, end-of-life care
- Consider ethical aspects of care
- Consider family, community, and cultural context

Manage prevalent problems
- Allergic disorders
- Anesthesia and pain management
- Cardiovascular disorders
- Dermatological disorders
- Eye, ear, nose, and throat disorders
- Emergencies and life-threatening conditions
- Gastrointestinal disorders
- Genitourinary disorders
- Gynecological disorders

- Infectious diseases
- Musculoskeletal disorders
- Neoplastic disorders
- Neurological disorders
- Obstetric problems
- Psychiatric and behavioral disorders
- Pulmonary disorders
- Renal disorders
- Surgical disorders
- Multimorbidity

Coordinate health services with …
- Families:
  - family assessment
  - conduct family meetings
  - family counseling and guidance
- Communities:
  - epidemiology and population health
  - community assessment
  - identification and use of community resources
  - community health education and prevention programs
  - political advocacy
  - health promotion intersectorial actions
- Health teams:
  - compose and mobilize teams
  - leadership skills
  - practice management skills

Learners achieve the required competencies through a structured curriculum process. For instance, the goal to provide comprehensive care for children includes the following competencies: provide preventive care, perform age-appropriate developmental assessments, and manage common disorders such as asthma, diarrhoea, and pneumonia. These objectives are linked to training processes so the learner participates in care of patients with these conditions and is assessed on his or her ability to do so. Trainees may learn to provide preventive care, counseling and management of prevalent childhood illnesses in the family practice training center, and management of emergencies and seriously ill children in hospital settings as well as in the community.

As an example, the minimum requirements for training family doctors in the United States[109] are outlined in Table 4.1. This training includes three interrelated components: (1) longitudinal experience in the family practice center that increases by year of training; (2) rotations in defined hospital and ambulatory specialty areas; and (3) lectures, seminars, and workshops to address specific content areas.

TABLE 4.1 Requirements for training family doctors in the United States[109]

Curriculum content	Minimum requirements
Family medicine core content	Defined longitudinal curriculum coupled with outpatient clinical care for a continuity panel of patients over the entire period of training
Human behavior and mental health	Defined longitudinal curriculum
Adult medicine	8 months (including at least 6 inpatient months, critical care and a range of medical subspecialties)
Maternity care	2 months plus elective opportunity (including 40 deliveries, and 10 from their continuity panel of patients)
Gynecological care	1 month
Care of the surgical patient	2 months (including general and surgical subspecialties such as urology; ear, nose, and throat; ophthalmology)
Musculoskeletal and sports medicine	2 months
Emergency care	2 months
Care of neonates, infants, children, and adolescents	4 months (including inpatient and outpatient care and care of the distressed neonate)
Community medicine	Structured curriculum including experiential components
Care of the elderly patient	Structured curriculum (including experience in hospital, family practice center, long-term facility and home)
Care of skin	Sufficient exposure
Diagnostic imaging	Structured curriculum
Teaching conferences	Defined longitudinal curriculum
Resident research and scholarship	Required participation
Management of health systems	1 month (or 100 hours longitudinally)
Electives	3–6 months
Total required curriculum	36 months

The structure of family medicine training programs varies between countries. Time in the family practice teaching center usually increases with year of training; in some countries, first-year trainees may spend one to two sessions (mornings or afternoons) per week in the family medicine training site, while third year trainees may spend most of their time in this facility. During this time the trainee works with a primary care team to provide continuous care for a specific panel of patients and families.

BOX 4.8 A new curriculum in family medicine in Austria

In 2002, a new curriculum was established in Austria at the Medical University Graz as part of an effort to make general and family practice an obligatory part of the education and training of future physicians. The curriculum follows a modular format of 30 modules in 5 years plus a clinical sixth year. General and family practitioners directly and actively participate in many aspects of the 6-year curriculum, including:

- introduction to the medical profession including observation of professionals in the work setting during the first year
- a communication skills track
- modules on "Health and Society," "Youth and Growing-up," and "Mental Health" in the third and fourth years
- an elective special module "General and Family Practice" in the fifth year
- a compulsory 5 weeks' practical training period in the sixth year in a general practice clinic, combined with a seminar.

General and family practitioners were eager to participate, and recruiting practices were simpler than expected. Engagement of general and family practitioners in the new program was evaluated highly, and opened up additional opportunities for further development of the discipline.

Source: Hellemann-Geschwinder I (personal communication).

The remainder of training time may be spent in hospital posts, selected specialty rotations, community health experience, quality improvement, or research activities and seminars and small group learning. Hospital rotations are designed to ensure that family doctors gain experience recognizing and managing conditions relevant to their future practice. Most programs provide a series of seminars to cover systematically the core curriculum through presentations, small group discussion, and skill-building sessions. Family doctor trainees may learn skills related to management, quality improvement, or skills related to community health by working with teams to complete health projects in the family practice center or community.

Establishing academic departments of family medicine

The establishment of a department or unit is an important confirmation of an institution's commitment to family medicine. Departments or units of family medicine can provide the leadership for establishing the discipline in the academic setting and organize the resources that are necessary to conduct teaching, patient care, and research programs. Establishing academic departments of family medicine requires participation of many leaders who understand and support the important functions and roles of family medicine. These leaders may include government authorities, medical association representatives, practicing family doctors in the community, staff from medical schools and teaching hospitals, public health officials, and members of the wider community who recognise the importance of family medicine.

Coalitions that support family medicine are sustained by commitment to shared goals, such as improving the education of students and serving the needs of communities. These goals may be established among medical school faculty by reviewing the medical school mission statement and emphasizing items relevant to meeting community health needs. From the beginning, a good rapport needs to be established with existing departments such as internal medicine and pediatrics that are likely to share common interests and may be willing to collaborate in teaching, clinical, and research projects. A dedicated effort may need to be made to educate subspecialist educators about family medicine, the added value for their own practice, and the benefits to the health care system. Specialist physicians are often supporters and teachers of family doctors, as many come to realize that they are more effective when they work in collaboration with well-trained primary care physicians. Academic medical centers are more likely to favor the development of family medicine as an academic discipline when the discipline is viewed as essential in enhancing the functions of others.

Departments of family medicine require human and physical resources to deliver the full spectrum of family medicine education, clinical services, and research programs. Human resources include faculty physicians and other staff with time available to teach and adequately supervise trainees, develop curricula, and conduct research. These faculty members may often include a combination of specialty trained family medicine physicians together with committed subspecialists. Practicing community-based family doctors may be recruited as full-time faculty or as part-time clinical supervisors or tutors. Physical resources include centers that integrate teaching and clinical services. In these centers, patient care is provided by teams that may include practicing physicians, family medicine trainees or medical students, along with nurses, social workers, and other health professionals. Family medicine teaching centers, which may be incorporated into community physicians' practices or community health centers, may also serve as important sites for primary care research.

Departments of family medicine often require governmental and institutional financial support. Once established, clinical revenues, research grants, hospitals, and governments may be important sources of finance for a substantial proportion of services. Departments usually begin with a small number of faculty and other staff members. As teaching, clinical, and research programs grow and resources increase, additional members may be recruited. Community or district hospitals are often important partners in the development and support of departments of family medicine. Faculty physicians and residents in training provide important clinical services for these institutions. A partnership approach ensures mutual benefits for the community, hospital, and department.

In some countries, academic departments of family medicine are well established and enjoy a reputation similar to that of any other department in their respective academic institutions. In other countries, where family medicine may not yet be fully recognized as a discipline or as a specialty, the establishment of an academic department may contribute to creating the momentum that will lead to full recognition and development of the profession. Other approaches are needed where countries cannot afford to establish academic departments because of lack of resources and expertise, or because policies have not yet been put into place to promote the concept of family medicine as a specialty requiring postgraduate education.

Planning an academic department of family medicine usually involves the following three steps.

First, form a small planning committee to consider desirability and feasibility, and to establish goals and a blueprint for development. This small group may enlist the support of a broader coalition that may include representatives of the government, universities, professional associations, health service organizations, and practicing physicians. These members usually become very knowledgeable and often serve as advocates if a decision is made to develop a department. They can help guide the fledgling department through political and economic challenges during its formative years.

Second, obtain on-site consultations from knowledgeable individuals. Sometimes, consultants – often from other countries – will be identified from past personal associations with members of the institution or the planning committee. Consultants with particular expertise can be identified through WONCA and its member national organizations in other countries, particularly those in similar economic and social circumstances or those with a family medicine organizational structure that is seen as being especially desirable.

Third, draw up a working plan for debate and discussion. This may include presentations to concerned organizations and individuals, as well as discussions with them about the financial implications and required educational resources. Inform citizens about the benefits to society from this initiative by enlisting the support of news media and prominent champions from the community.

Collaboration may take a variety of forms.

➤ Members of the steering committee may go on study tours to other countries to learn about the best way to set up a viable department as well as the pitfalls to avoid.

➤ A partnership may be formed with another institution that has already successfully established a department. Depending on the needs and available resources, faculty members may spend shorter or longer periods in departments in other countries. Some physicians may wish to participate in the full postgraduate training experience of another country before returning as faculty members to the new program. Partner programs may also send consultants to the new department for shorter or longer terms.

➤ International guidance can foster and support education and research projects. Membership of WONCA or organizations such as The Network: Towards Unity For Health will facilitate these efforts.

Boxes 4.9 and 4.10 outline some ways of establishing and strengthening an academic department of family medicine.

BOX 4.9 How to establish an academic department of family medicine

Form a steering committee involving the main stakeholders to:

- sponsor, promote, and support the establishment of a department
- develop short- and long-term goals and strategies
- seek financial, human, and physical resources
- cultivate relationships with existing departments and programs
- link planning to health reform processes, so as to ensure that well-trained generalist physicians will contribute to local, regional, and national goals
- educate and provide training-of-trainers for subspecialists who may be called upon to assist in teaching
- collaborate with other institutions or programs

BOX 4.10 How to strengthen an existing department of family medicine

In order to strengthen an existing department of family medicine, faculty members may:

- organize collaborative work and seminars with other departments within the home institution, focusing research on shared goals such as optimal training and health service delivery, efficient referral, and other issues important to primary care
- promote activities regarding health system development within the academic institution, such as improving the quality of primary health care and enhancing equity and cost-effectiveness
- develop and deliver masters and doctorate programs in primary care
- play a central role in establishing procedures for accrediting training for the entire profession, not just the discipline of family medicine
- contribute to local family medicine organizations and other medical organizations
- provide continuing professional development for practicing family doctors
- advocate for improving conditions for healthy communities
- assist academic, public, and private institutions in their efforts to become more socially accountable by regularly assessing community needs, developing programs to meet these needs, and assessing program outcomes
- share their knowledge and experience with others in their own country as well as internationally
- build relationships and seek opportunities to work on projects with local health care funders including government

---

Build relationships

Successful training programs in family medicine benefit from partnerships with hospitals and academic institutions. Community hospitals can provide intensive, inpatient learning experiences important in the education of family doctors. When hospital administrators understand the role and value of family doctors, they are often very supportive.

Family medicine faculty and trainees may provide important hospital services such as care of hospitalized adults and children, delivery of obstetric patients, and coverage of the emergency room. In turn, hospitals often provide financial support for facilities, teachers, and trainees. Negotiated contracts between these institutions and training programs in family medicine help to clarify expectations and responsibilities.

Medical schools are instrumental in the training of family doctors, providing a foundation for the continuum of family medicine education. Academic

---

BOX 4.11 Family medicine in Denmark

The health system in Denmark has been undergoing a series of reforms over the last decade. As part of these reforms, there has been an increasing effort in promoting primary care and general practice, including substantial improvements in specialist education of general practitioners (GPs). As part of these efforts since 2003, specialist education of GPs is now 5 years, similar to the length of training for all other medical specialties. In addition, there has been much emphasis on training of trainers in principles of family medicine.

As a result:

- prestige has risen considerably
- recruitment in many areas is now much easier (in some areas of Denmark it is far more difficult to get a training post in general practice than in many other specialties, such as surgery)
- quality of general practitioner training is rated very high not only by trainees, but also among educators in other specialties (average rating is around 7 in other specialties and 8.1 in GP, on a scale from 1 to 9).

Source: Maagaard R (personal communication with authors).

---

departments of family medicine may sponsor or affiliate with specialty training programs. Medical schools often place students in family practice teaching centers for their clinical experience, and may provide opportunities for faculty development. Family medicine teachers from medical schools and specialty training programs often collaborate to deliver the full spectrum of family medicine education.

Family practice training programs may gain valuable assistance through affiliation with other regional, national, and/or international programs. Curriculum goals, objectives, teaching and evaluation methods can be shared for mutual improvement. Information about resources or successful programs developed at one institution can be rapidly disseminated to others in a network. Computers and the Internet now serve as convenient instruments for sharing curricula, teaching methods, and evaluation tools. A wealth of curriculum materials is now available online. Consultants from other institutions may be invited to review program development and progress and provide suggestions for improvement. Participation in regional, national, and international professional meetings provides excellent opportunities for networking and sharing program developments.

Educational research and medical journals with a focus on family medicine and family medicine education provide additional opportunities for networking.

Human resource

Recruit leaders, teachers, and staff

Human resources are critical components of training programs in family medicine. They include educational leaders, teachers, support staff, patients, and trainees. Leaders establish the vision, develop the framework, determine needs, secure adequate resources, delineate roles and responsibilities, and measure progress. The program director often works with a team of faculty and other staff to develop plans and recruit additional teachers.

Family medicine teachers may be recruited from practicing family doctors, subspecialty consultants, and/or allied health professionals. Experienced family doctors may supervise learners in academic teaching centers or, alternatively, learners may work under direct supervision in the practices of community-based physicians.

Subspecialty consultants are important teachers of family medicine in hospital and clinical settings and these consultants are often eager to participate when they understand the benefits of well-trained family physicians. Support staff members are required for the smooth functioning of training programs. Other health professionals can also make valuable contributions to the education of family doctors and may include psychologists, social workers, nurses, medical anthropologists, educational consultants, and pharmacists, and they are recruited according to needs and resources. Many of these professionals also work as members of primary care teams.

Recruiting staff to be teachers in family medicine may require committed educational and advocacy efforts to promote the concepts and value of family medicine. In health systems without a tradition of strong primary care, it may be necessary to provide key leaders and educators with a structured experience in primary care education and delivery, such as a study tour in another country with established systems of family medicine training and clinical service delivery. Without any reference point, it may be difficult for subspecialty providers to conceive of the high-quality practice of primary care. Offering such a structured experience in conjunction with supportive colleagues from regions more developed in primary care can be a powerful and transformative intervention.

Recruiting patients

Patients, families, and communities are also important teachers of family doctors in training. It is difficult to conceive of person-centered training without participating patients. Patients are usually recruited through family medicine practices that are engaged in teaching. In some cases, a cohort of committed patients may be trained as standardized patients for participating in simulated teaching exercises and evaluation.

When patients and communities understand the dual educational and service goals and the structures and processes of the trainee's education, they are often eager to participate in teaching practices. Individuals and communities may be especially eager to assist in traditionally underserved areas in hopes of retaining trainees in the area as new local primary care physicians when they finish training.

Recruiting trainees

Family medicine trainees are usually recruited as recent medical school graduates or practicing physicians who have identified the need for additional training or who wish to change their specialty. The inclusion of family medicine in the medical school curriculum is essential as a mechanism for demonstrating to medical students how family medicine is a viable and desirable career path. In new programs, recruitment committees may emphasize the future benefits and potential opportunities associated with postgraduate training in family medicine. In established programs, enthusiastic trainees and successful graduates may contribute to recruiting subsequent cohorts of trainnes. Those health care systems with incentives designed to support and promote advanced training in primary care can be most successful in recruiting trainees.

Enhancing the skills of family medicine educators

In addition to excellent clinical skills, many effective teachers of family medicine also demonstrate expertise in education, administration, and research. Academic family doctors may acquire these skills through full-time fellowships, or through shorter, intensive training programs in local, national, or international locations. Networking and collaboration with experienced mentors and colleagues are additional mechanisms for improving the skills of new faculty members. The needs of the population, as well as the interests of the medical faculty and the needs of the program, are used to determine priorities for faculty improvement.

Faculty members may acquire specific teaching skills through academic fellowships or teacher training programs. There are also many online resources available, some of which are interactive. These programs emphasize basic educational principles, such as establishing educational goals, assessing learners' needs, developing specific learning objectives, designing appropriate teaching methods, and the use of evaluation tools to assess outcomes. Developing and organizing curricular programs, presentation skills, using audiovisual aids, and writing skills may be included in faculty development programs. Some programs focus on the use of specific teaching techniques, such as working effectively with small groups, problem-based learning, or the use of evidence-based or community-based teaching methods. Educational programs that deal with clinical teaching focus on organizing the teaching environment for optimal learning and patient care, and require attention to the needs of the patient and the learner. Clinical teaching strategies include regular observation and feedback, brief presentations and structured modeling.

Most important is the development of a cohort of committed educators with

---

BOX 4.12 EURACT: a regional academy for teachers of general practice and family medicine

The European Academy of Teachers in General Practice/Family Medicine (EURACT) was first established in 1992 following several earlier efforts to bring together European leaders in primary care education of physicians. EURACT consists of individual members and is intended to support educators in general practice/family medicine. EURACT published an educational agenda for general practice/family medicine in 2005, which included potential competency frameworks consisting of objectives, learning methods, and assessment tools based on the following consensus categories of competencies:

- primary care management
- person-centered care
- specific problem-solving skills
- comprehensive-approach
- community orientation
- holistic approach.

In 2010, EURACT also developed a framework for continuing professional development of trainers in general practice/family medicine, providing the basis for educational courses targeted at educators of three levels: competent educators, proficient educators, and educational experts. This framework led to the establishment of a European Network of General Practice/Family Medicine teachers and professional development programs supported by an innovative Internet-based educational platform hosted by EURACT on their website (www.euract.eu).

specific training and skills in the core principles of primary care, including both generalists and subspecialists. Generalists with this training become core faculty of a family medicine department, and the primary clinical supervisors of learners in the ambulatory setting. Subspecialists with this training develop skills to adapt their curricula and training methods to better match the needs of the primary care provider, incorporating elements of the primary care principles into their subspecialty training modules for their family medicine trainees.

There is a parallel process between providing patient-centered clinical care and learner-centered clinical teaching (*see* Table 4.2). While clinical practice begins with eliciting the needs of the patient, clinical tutoring begins with eliciting the needs or questions of the learner. Once information is gathered on the nature of the patient's problem, or student's question, the clinician helps the patient understand the diagnosis and management while the teacher helps the learner develop plans to provide optimal care for the patient. These sessions may be supplemented with brief presentations if the learner requires information, or through structured modelling so the learner may observe their teachers working as clinicians and gradually acquire specific skills. Effective clinical teachers make the best use of a rapid succession of brief teaching interactions to guide the development of the learner. Additional family medicine faculty skills include research, administration, and leadership and these are discussed in Chapters 3 and 5.

TABLE 4.2 Parallel processes of patient care and medical teaching

	Patient-centered care	**Learner-centered teaching**
Context	Family, cultural and socioeconomic factors	Background and stage of learner
Establish agenda	Identify reasons for visit	Solicit needs of learner
Gather information	History and physical examination	Observation of learner
Assessment	Provide diagnosis; education about problem(s)	Provide specific feedback
Plan	Outline management; negotiate follow-up	Identify strategies for improvement

Physical and financial

Secure funding

Financial resources provide competitive salaries to attract a director of an education program, qualified teachers and other staff, as well as residents, and teaching facilities and supplies. Financial support for part-time specialty consultants (both generalists and subspecialists) ensures their active participation in development and assessment of the curriculum. Funds are often acquired through a combination of educational, patient care, and hospital or government revenues. Faculty members may supplement their salaries through direct patient care.

Possible financial sources for family medicine training programs include:

➤ national, state, or local government educational training funds
➤ government or private foundation grants
➤ academic institutions
➤ community or public hospitals
➤ patient fees
➤ insurance schemes
➤ health maintenance organizations.

Organize family practice teaching centers

The distinguishing feature of family medicine training programs is that most education is provided in the ambulatory setting rather than the highly specialized hospital environment. Thus trainees are exposed to the types of patients and settings they will encounter in their future practices. This can be accomplished in a variety of ways. For instance, in the United Kingdom and Australia, exemplary community-based family doctors convert their offices into teaching practices. This approach is applicable to all countries and does not involve major capital investments.

Another approach is to utilize community health centers. Kahssay has pointed out that "Health centres in all their shapes and forms are the interface between communities and the health and development sectors. In most countries they are the most numerous and widespread structure for the delivery of health services."[75] These facilities are already available, are oriented to the needs of the community and involve a variety of like-minded professionals committed to comprehensive care of the population they serve.

In the United States and Canada, the predominant mode is to develop specific family medicine teaching centers to model and teach family medicine trainees. Efforts to utilize community health centers as training sites in the United States is gaining ground, however, due to recognition of their provision of high-quality primary care services to underserved populations and the synergistic benefits to both academic institutions and community health centers.[76]

In all of these circumstances the family medicine teaching center serves as the home for a learning community of trainees, teachers, and health team members who share continuous, comprehensive care for a group of patients.

Teaching centers serve the dual mission of patient care and education. The trainees integrate and apply the knowledge and skills gained from hospital and subspecialty settings as they provide continuity of care to their patients and work under the supervision of experienced family doctors. Supervision may include direct observation or, when resources permit, use of one-way mirrors, video or audio tape recorders.

Establish hospital, specialty, and community teaching sites

Hospital and other subspecialty rotations provide trainees with opportunities to develop skills in caring for patients with serious or unusual illnesses and to appreciate the natural history of some chronic diseases such as end-stage renal failure or cancer.

Through these rotations family medicine trainees develop skills for hospital practice and become familiar with conditions managed by other specialists. The time spent and skills learned in subspecialty rotations are determined by local needs. For instance, family doctors who plan to practice in remote or rural areas may need to acquire advanced surgical skills such as caesarean delivery for the management of obstructed labour, and the management of hospitalized patients. Those who practice in areas with a high prevalence of HIV/AIDS or tropical infectious diseases will need expertise in managing these illnesses. In the offices of subspecialty consultants, family doctors can gain experience in technical procedures such as the application of casts for fractures, or expertise in the care of patients with conditions such as heart failure.

Community-based health professionals, public health facilities, and other community programs also make important contributions to training family doctors. Family doctors who are familiar with community resources, aware of community health risks, and able to work in partnership with a wide array of community health-related groups are more effective in working with their local communities. Public health officials may provide important epidemiological information for the care of communities. Schools, religious groups, and civic organizations can provide information and resources pertaining to the health of the community. Participation in home visits helps family doctors understand the lives, conditions, and cultural context of individual patients and their families.

In some communities, family doctors work efficiently when teamed with medical assistants, nurse practitioners, community health workers, or other community health providers. Visiting nurses, community health workers, and social workers are familiar with local conditions and health risks, and are important allies in the delivery of coordinated care. In rural and urban settings, community health workers can serve as effective links between health centers and the community.[77] A partnership approach between family medicine training programs and community agencies increases the likelihood of sustainability.

4.4 FAMILY MEDICINE TEACHING PROGRAMS

In this section, specific issues related to pre-service versus in-service training will be considered. In discussing in-service training, this section will review the variety of programs that are helpful in developing a comprehensive primary care-based system of care, including traditional postgraduate training, retraining of practicing physicians, and continuing medical education.

Pre-service undergraduate medical education

Integrating family medicine into the basic curriculum

Family doctors, as comprehensive generalists, have much to contribute to teaching students the art and science of medical practice. Family medicine, with a dual emphasis on patient-centered and population-based health care, can add value to the medical school curriculum by providing all students with a solid foundation of generalist physician skills and appreciation of social accountability.

Caring for individuals, families, and communities is best learned from experienced family doctors who demonstrate these principles and skills through their daily clinical practice. Family doctors may serve as important teachers and role models, demonstrating how to integrate the disparate aspects of medical training as they provide long-term person-focused comprehensive care to patients within the context of each patient's family and community. These concepts are transmitted most effectively when taught throughout the medical school curriculum.

Medical school curricular priorities are most relevant when they emphasize the burden of disease and health needs of the population served rather than the latest technology or special interests of individual members of the teaching faculty. Traditionally, medical school instruction starts with basic science followed by clinical years that include a series of rotations in hospital and ambulatory settings. More recently, many medical schools have made efforts to integrate the clinical and basic sciences and in some medical schools, students are exposed to community health problems early and throughout their medical training.

In recent years, a number of institutions around the world have pursued the development of longitudinally integrated clerkships, designed to provide students with better continuity experiences and a more holistic understanding of the provision of medical care.[102] Medical schools should consider additional methods for demonstrating a commitment to their communities and an integration with their national health system through their training programs. Pre-service family medicine training programs for medical students involving regional networks of primary care clinics, community health centers, community hospitals, and tertiary care medical centers can begin to instill the importance of continuity and coordinated care with a community orientation and in the context of social accountability.[76,78] Later in-service programs for family medicine trainees would then be capable of training primary care physicians fully competent to work in and maintain these types of robust primary care-based health systems.

Medical students typically develop clinical skills in the management of prevalent conditions through a full-time rotation in family medicine. During the rotation, students see patients under the supervision of experienced family doctors and gradually assume more responsibility for patient care. Regular small group discussions led by experienced clinician teachers allow students to discuss the management of clinical situations in greater depth. Reading materials and interactive web-based exercises may be used to supplement clinical activities, and to ensure that all students have exposure to the same set of core problems.[79]

The majority of the clinical practice of family doctors is devoted to providing care to individuals with frequently occurring conditions. The best management of patients with these acute or chronic conditions, based on current evidence, should serve as the core curriculum for family medicine courses for medical students during the clinical years. The curriculum should be organized around the conditions that have the greatest impact on the morbidity and mortality in the population served. While managing patients with these conditions, medical students can apply their skills in communication, prevention, and community orientation. Through direct observation or review of video or audiotapes of student-patient encounters, experienced clinicians can provide specific feedback to improve student performance.

In family medicine settings, management of patients with acute problems includes evaluation and treatment of injuries, infectious diseases, and the initial manifestation of chronic diseases. Medical students can learn the optimal management of patients with chronic conditions such as diabetes, hypertension, cardiovascular, and pulmonary diseases, the complexity of managing multiple comorbidities, and the skills needed for efficient triage, recognition, and referral of patients who require hospitalization or subspecialty evaluation. Integrating prevention and addressing the community-wide implications of individual patient problems are special areas of the expertise of family doctors.

In addition to the core curriculum, family doctors may offer a range of elective experiences. Electives can provide opportunities for students to pursue special interests. Many family doctors participate in primary care research, and medical students can contribute to their research programs. Family physicians with special areas of expertise can share these skills with interested students. These special skills may include caring for rural populations, adolescents, people with substance use problems, athletes, prisoners, or people requiring palliative care at the end of life. Through elective opportunities, students may discover that they can effectively combine special interests with a career in family medicine.

Service learning programs that combine essential patient care services with opportunities for reflection and discussion allow medical students and faculty members to share in the development of projects that serve unmet community needs. When students voluntarily develop and participate in projects, such as free clinics for the poor or community health education programs, they are often inspired by such work and find ways to continue making valuable community service contributions throughout their careers.

The extent of family doctor involvement in the medical school curriculum depends on the institution's commitment and the availability of family medicine faculty members. Medical schools that wish to emphasize primary care engage family physicians and other primary care professionals in order to benefit from their experiences throughout the curriculum.

Enhancing the medical school curriculum with family medicine

Family doctors can contribute to the medical school curriculum in classroom or clinical settings by incorporating a variety of educational methods. In the classroom, family doctors can organize and teach introductory courses that include basic patient care skills, such as taking a history, conducting a focused or comprehensive physical examination, clinical reasoning, diagnosis and management, and medical ethics. Because family doctors emphasize comprehensive care, communication skills and the long term doctor-patient relationship, they can teach students to deal with relevant problems for the entire spectrum of patients from infants to the elderly, and how to approach patients from different ethnic backgrounds.

While basic medical skills are often introduced in classroom settings, they are effectively acquired through hands-on practice in small groups, followed by reinforcement and application in clinical settings. As learning is reinforced by doing, many medical schools now assign students to work with family doctors from the first weeks of their medical school training. Early clinical experiences may include weekly or monthly sessions in which students work with community-based family doctors. These sessions provide students with opportunities to observe and reflect on the work of the doctor in action, then to practice applying their new knowledge and skills in clinical situations. During the later years of medical school, intensive full-time clinical rotations in family medicine allow students to refine and integrate their skills in the comprehensive care of patients and communities.

Family doctors may provide care for patients in their homes, community clinics, outpatient teaching clinics, emergency rooms or hospitals, and employ their skills in comprehensive patient evaluations, or more commonly in problem-focused visits. The basic tools of family medicine include refined communication, examination and diagnostic skills. These skills may be demonstrated regardless of location or the nature of the individual patient's problem. When medical students participate in continuity of care and coordination of care, they experience the development of doctor-patient relationships and can observe the evolution of a patient's symptoms over the course of an illness. Students learn that the comprehensive health care needs of a patient are not necessarily met in a single visit, but may be effectively addressed over a series of encounters, often through teamwork involving other health professionals, and coordinated by the family doctor. As medical students work with experienced family doctors to care for patients with new, undifferentiated problems, or those with chronic diseases or terminal illnesses, they are able to cultivate these generalist skills.

BOX 4.13 How to enhance the medical school curriculum

- Discuss the contribution of family medicine with leaders of the medical school
- Secure funding to support family doctor participation in the medical school curriculum
- Involve family doctors with medical school curriculum committees to assess the relevance of the curriculum
- Recruit and support family doctors to serve as course directors for the introduction to clinical medicine and for clinical rotations in advanced family medicine
- Describe and agree on core competencies in primary care for all medical students
- Provide ambulatory educational experiences to involve students with community-based family doctors early and throughout their medical training
- Establish required rotations in family medicine with rigorous learning objectives, teaching and evaluation methods
- Develop extracurricular and elective programs in family medicine, such as community health, primary care research, or health care for disadvantaged members of the community
- Recruit family doctors to serve on medical school admissions committees to assist in the selection of students interested in primary health care

---

Family doctors may contribute to development of the basic medical education curriculum in a medical school by teaching any of the topics mentioned above. In addition, family doctors may enhance the medical school curriculum through the strategies outlined in Box 4.13. Priorities among these strategies will vary depending on the availability of faculty members, and the needs of the medical school and the communities served by its graduates.

Factors affecting the choices medical students make about their future careers

Medical student pre-service training is critical in the effort to recruit and train sufficient numbers of primary care providers for a health system. Medical schools act as the first point of entry into the medical education system for learners, and thus have great influence in the future careers of students. Medical schools can promote the perception of primary care as a respected and viable career choice, or devalue the specialty of family medicine and the critical function of primary care within a health system.

Medical students select specialty careers through a complex decision process influenced by numerous factors. These may include intrinsic factors such as personal attributes, interests, gender, age, and family background, as well as extrinsic factors that include the medical school environment, curricular and clinical experiences (such as having a good role model), perceived and actual employment opportunities, professional satisfaction, and earning potential.[80] While the relative impact of these factors will vary among students, prior studies have emphasized the importance of student selection and the medical school environment as the factors most under the control of medical schools.[81,82]

The admissions process plays an important role in selecting those students who are most likely to enter generalist or specialty careers. Students' personal characteristics and values have a significant impact on their subsequent choice of specialty and ultimate practice location. Students who value the opportunity to form long-term relationships with patients and those who enjoy providing care for a variety of patients and conditions are also more likely to seek primary care careers.[83,84] Many medical schools have increased the number of students who select primary care careers through changes in admissions policies.[85]

How to attract students to family medicine careers

When students interact with family doctors in classroom and clinical settings, and perceive family doctors as valued members of health teams, they are more likely to consider a career in family practice.[86,87] Enthusiastic family doctors who demonstrate humanistic values, and provide high-quality patient care and excellent teaching, serve as positive role models that many students will wish to emulate. Conversely, if students are not exposed to family medicine during their education, they may be unaware of the content and challenges associated with family practice and be less likely to select family medicine as a career.

Students need to see a future in family medicine as a personally satisfying and beneficial career choice. If primary care as a career means certain lifelong isolation in a remote practice setting without future opportunities for advanced study or career advancement, it is likely many quality students will not find family medicine an appealing specialty choice. This is compounded by the possibility of being sent to practice primary care in an underresourced setting without adequate clinical training specific to the performance context in which they are being asked to practice. Providers who feel unprepared and unskilled in caring for sick people who seek their aid, coupled with a sense of helplessness in an under-resourced practice setting, may be quick to pursue alternative career options.

In some countries, government policies regulate the number of specialty training positions for family medicine and other medical disciplines through financial incentives or legislation. If these policies are based on sound information regarding projected health workforce needs as well as learner and provider interests, incentives can be provided to influence students to select careers and future practice locations that match the care needed by the population.[88] Strategies to attract students to careers in family medicine are summarized in Box 4.14.

BOX 4.14 How to attract students to careers in family medicine

- Recruit and admit students to medical school who are interested in primary care and community service
- Emphasize primary care in the required curriculum
- Expose students to family doctor role models during training
- Provide specialty or focused training options within family medicine training
- Provide incentives to encourage selection of careers in family practice
- Offer a variety of career opportunities in family medicine
- Support family medicine graduates with competitive salaries after training

---

In-service vocational training

In this section, we review three types of in-service vocational training. First, we review traditional postgraduate specialty training, sometimes known as residency training. While this is perhaps more traditionally seen as an extension of the pre-service spectrum of training, we have chosen to discuss it here as the continuity-based model of training lends itself to a complex blend of clinical service provision, and the traditional family medicine model of postgraduate training typically places more direct responsibility for patient care in the hands of the trainee, compared with that of some other medical specialties.

Next, we will review the issue of re-training of physicians already in practice. This type of training is closely related to traditional postgraduate specialty training in family medicine due to the nature of its enhanced level of clinical responsibility, and is another reason for the inclusion of traditional postgraduate specialty training under the category of in-service training.

Finally, the issue of continuing medical education, also known as continuing professional development, in family medicine will be covered, recognizing family medicine's lead role in many countries in advocating for structured lifelong mechanisms for continuous learning.

Traditional postgraduate specialty training

Postgraduate specialty training is considered an essential component of all subspecialty medical disciplines in organized academic health systems throughout the world. While medical school graduates have developed competency in the most basic medical knowledge and general clinical skills, they typically lack an overall clinical competency in the complete practice of any field of medicine. No well-developed and sufficiently resourced health system would consider developing policies to have basic undergraduate medical school graduates perform complex surgeries or provide subspecialty referral care.

Yet many health systems throughout the world still engage these same recent medical graduates in one of the most complex medical activities of all: first-contact clinical care for undifferentiated patients with complex combinations of medical and social problems in loosely-supervised and minimally supported medical settings. As a result, patients in these countries often recognize the poor quality provided at their local community health clinic. They may instead seek care from a traditional healer, bypass the local health clinic in pursuit of self-directed hospital or subspecialty-based care, or simply prolong their time to presentation until symptoms are severe. Unfortunately, not every academic health system recognizes the degree of challenge involved in providing high-quality primary care services. Much like other clinical specialties, true competency in clinical service delivery of high-quality primary care requires additional time and skills training beyond the completion of medical school.

Postgraduate specialty training in family medicine is specifically designed for the purpose of helping providers achieve competency in a variety of vocational skills necessary to deliver adequate primary care within a national health system. Family medicine postgraduate training in these vocational skills is structured entirely around the core principles of primary care, to a degree and level of expertise unattainable through an undergraduate medical school curriculum. Many of the strategies and methods tied to advanced training in these specific principles of primary care and family medicine have already been outlined earlier in this chapter.

BOX 4.15 Renewing postgraduate family medicine education in Canada

In 2007, the College of Family Physicians of Canada appointed a working group to review the curriculum for postgraduate training. There are 17 residency programs in Canada, each within a university school of medicine. While there is considerable diversity in the settings for each, common accreditation standards and the requirement that graduates are fit to practice anywhere in Canada have ensured commonality in training.

Reasons for the renewal
- Greater emphasis on social accountability and the need to produce family physicians to meet the needs of the community
- Increasing movement of training into rural and community settings, away from academic centres
- New advances and evidence in medical education

Steps taken
- Working group on curriculum review has developed a competency framework (CanMEDS-Family Medicine) and made recommendations for curricular change to a competency based curriculum that is Comprehensive, focused on Continuity of education and patient care, and Centred in family medicine (The Triple C Curriculum). The process involved consultations with administrators, educational leaders and learners over 5–6 years, as well as reviews of literature, and curricula in other countries.
- Working group on certification process developed complimentary assessment tools.
- Implementation task force rolled out the new curriculum. Consultations with funders, university leaders, regulatory authorities and regular retreats with educational leaders were implemented.
- Initiatives to prepare teachers were developed at both the individual program level and nationally.
- New accreditation standards were developed to support the new curricular changes.

One core method of clinical teaching in family medicine and primary care, however, deserves further explanation. Unlike other disciplines, in many health systems throughout the world, a large percentage of postgraduate training in family medicine is delivered in ambulatory settings or outpatient clinics. Many health systems have no tradition of outpatient medical training, and educators can be perplexed as to how to apply their skills in medical education in the ambulatory setting.

Outpatient-based family medicine training benefits from a number of factors. Most importantly, it usually replicates the performance context and future practice setting of the family doctor. Vocational training that occurs within this environment is most likely to be directly applicable and relevant to the learner seeking specialty training in family medicine. Outpatient training benefits from a higher volume of patients than in the inpatient setting, and when coupled with practice providing continuity of care, it provides multiple opportunities to manage and experience particular medical problems over time. Outpatient training in a first-contact setting also increases the exposure of the trainee to undifferentiated patients, as well as the number and variety of medical illnesses and comorbidities seen in primary care, providing an ideal setting for building a comprehensive set of clinical skills. This training also allows experience with multiple members of a family and patients from within a single community.

In many of these outpatient-based family medicine training programs, trainees are assigned a specific panel of patients to care for, much as they would in a future community-based family practice. While long-term continuity with this population may be reduced by the time-limited nature of a postgraduate training program, it does simulate the nature of future practice. Learners are often expected to take responsibility for the overall health care of this panel of patients, and learn all aspects of coordination of care and illness prevention. They may be assigned activities to help them make linkages between their patient panel and the surrounding community through dedicated community-oriented primary care projects. To gain the full benefit of these educational settings, it is important that learners have sufficient clinical time committed to practice within the outpatient clinic. This expanded amount of outpatient clinical time should begin with the start of training in order to allow the immediate commencement of continuity of care and development of interpersonal patient-doctor relationships.

Clinical teaching techniques in the ambulatory setting may be somewhat different from those used in inpatient hospital-based care. Because of the limited time with individual patients in the outpatient clinic and the rapid turnover in patient visits, specific techniques have been developed to promote effective clinical teaching in the ambulatory setting. In undergraduate education, shadowing may be the predominant method of outpatient clinical teaching, but this offers limited ability for the postgraduate trainee to actually practice their skills and demonstrate competency. In postgraduate family medicine outpatient training, the most common and widely utilized teaching structure is the precepting model. In this model, a clinical supervisor, usually an experienced family medicine provider and educator, oversees a group of trainees during a session in the clinic as they provide clinical primary care services to their panel of patients. Learners present each of their patient cases to the supervising physician, who assesses the work of the trainee and offers clinical teaching and mentorship. The supervisor may directly see the patient and verify the findings and management plan of learner, or they may choose to only discuss the case and allow the trainee to complete the outpatient visit on their own, having determined the learner is competent in handling this particular case.

The supervising family doctor is able to make such a determination for several reasons. First, much as the family doctor develops a continuity relationship with his or her patients, they also develop continuity teaching relationships with their learners. They usually supervise the learners multiple times in the same clinic setting, and over time they build a better understanding of any specific trainee's competency in managing specific aspects of particular cases. This global assessment over time permits the family medicine teacher to develop a more comprehensive understanding of the strengths and weaknesses of the learner and their skills that may be applicable in a variety of cases.

In addition, a clinical teaching technique formally known as the clinical "microskills" technique, but sometimes referred to as the "1-minute preceptor," has been developed specifically for use in ambulatory teaching.[89] While the one-minute preceptor may be a bit of a misnomer, as it is difficult to adequately assess a trainee and offer relevant teaching in a single minute, it does speak to the time-limited nature of the clinical teaching technique and its ideal application to the clinic context.

The clinical microskills technique focuses on three educational tasks of the family medicine teacher while also maintaining quality care of the patient as paramount in any encounter. The clinical teacher first allows the learner to present a patient case, and uses the specific microskills to diagnose both the patient's particular medical problem and the learner's diagnostic reasoning and clinical management approach. Next, the supervising family doctor offers targeted teaching directed at the trainee's specific learning needs based on their assessment of the learner's reasoning and clinical approach. Finally, the family medicine educator provides clear and specific feedback to the learner so they might replicate the competent behaviors they exhibited in the encounter and avoid or modify any clinical mistakes.

The microskills take mere minutes to perform, and one can envision the broad range of clinical skills a trainee can develop over hundreds and potentially thousands of these encounters with patients and teachers. Other effective outpatient teaching frameworks also exist based on mnemonics such as SNAPPS and RIME.[90–92] Through a combination of inpatient-based subspecialty-supported hospital teaching programs, precepted outpatient clinical care, and a range of project activities and didactics, the family medicine postgraduate trainee is able to achieve complete competency in the full range of clinical skills and become solidly grounded in the core principles of primary care.

Retraining practicing physicians

In countries where family medicine is not yet established, retraining practicing physicians to become family doctors may improve health care and hasten development of the specialty. It takes several years to establish new training programs and graduate substantial numbers of family doctors. Retraining is an excellent option during the transitional period while family medicine is being established, although non-certification-based training is not a substitute for full-time specialty training in family medicine (*see* Box 4.16).

BOX 4.16 Two cases for retraining in family medicine in Southeast Asia

Both Vietnam and Laos have established formal family medicine postgraduate training programs with an intent toward primary care strengthening, and both have included retraining of physicians as an important part of their strategy. In both cases, there is a recognition that the typical doctor in practice at the first-contact level lacks complete competency in the skills needed for their role, and that retraining of these doctors will be necessary to effect meaningful system-wide change.

In the Socialist Republic of Vietnam, all postgraduate training in family medicine for the last ten years has focused on retraining of physicians with a 2-year formal certification program in family medicine, targeted primarily at those providing care in a commune health center – the unit for community-based ambulatory health care in the public sector. Most universities have offered a local program of this type, and in recent years, models have been developed where universities send faculty to remote districts to provide didactic training then coupled with practical skills training supervised by local hospital physicians. This model allows practicing physicians to continue to see patients in their home commune while training, and has been shown to result in physicians with increased knowledge and confidence,

---

as well as improvements in their skills related to the core principles of primary care. As part of an effort to continue to expand and nationalize the family medicine program, it is recognized that additional retraining programs are necessary, and options being considered include core curricular modules delivered through a continuing medical education format and short course offerings for private practice subspecialists already providing primary care services.

In the Lao People's Democratic Republic, while there has been a continuously developing family medicine training program for recent medical school graduates for some years now, only in recent years has a model been developed for retraining practicing physicians. In the Lao model, doctors from remote districts travel to a regional provincial hospital training center to study both didactic content and practical skills for three months at a time, followed by three months of work back in their home district hospital coupled with distance education assignments tied to topics such as family medicine management skills and community-oriented primary care. The entire program is three years in duration and provides a formal master degree in family medicine.

The Lao People's Democratic Republic has many fewer health human resources than Vietnam with very few physicians working in outpatient clinics, so the focus for training is on physicians providing first-contact care as one of very few physicians in a rural district hospital rather than in a more traditional ambulatory setting. Nonetheless, the training curriculum remains targeted at the core principles of primary care, albeit with a shift in emphasis based on the local need. Trainees in this program report they have increased medical knowledge, improved clinical skills and greater confidence in their care resulting in fewer patient transfers over long distances to a higher level of care. They demonstrate vastly improved technological skills in analyzing and presenting community-based data as well as in providing team-based educational programs for local nursing staff to disseminate important lessons learned in their training.

Through retraining programs, practicing generalists may acquire the knowledge, attitudes, and skills necessary for comprehensive family practice more rapidly than in a full-time specialty training program. Generalists who have not completed specialty training often recognize their lack of core competency in delivering primary care and the need for additional skills. Incentives for retraining may include improving skills to deliver high-quality health care, joining a newly developing specialty, advanced career opportunities, and increased financial rewards. Family physicians who complete retraining should, during the transition period, have the same certification and career opportunities as specialty-trained family doctors entering programs directly from medical school. These practicing physicians, who enter retraining with considerable practice experience, often become leaders and teachers of the next generation of family doctors.

Successful retraining programs have been developed in countries as diverse as Bulgaria, Croatia, the Czech Republic, Estonia, Hungary, Israel, Kyrgyzstan, Laos, Latvia, Lithuania, Poland, Portugal, the Republic of Korea, Romania, the Russian Federation, Sri Lanka, Turkey, and Vietnam. These programs are usually offered by academic departments or units of family medicine, and often focus on specific practice objectives. The trainees' basic medical education and practice experience influence their educational needs. For instance, prerequisites for retraining may include a minimum number of years in practice. In 1995, a WHO meeting of the Expert Network on Family Practice Development for the European Region concluded that retraining is both feasible and appropriate, but stressed the importance of well-designed, achievable educational objectives, outcome indicators and changes in the health system to accommodate the retrained family doctors.[93] Some countries also retrain practicing specialists such as those in pediatrics and internal medicine to become family doctors.

Flexible and part-time retraining programs are more convenient for practicing physicians. Many programs allow physicians to continue their regular practices by providing weekend, afternoon, evening, or block rotations over a period of months or years. Many programs use the physician's ongoing practice as a source of learning and as a site to apply new skills. Strategies to address the challenges of retraining are listed in Table 4.3.

TABLE 4.3 Retraining family physicians

Challenges	Strategies
Lack of clarity or agreement around required competencies	Determine job requirements with local stakeholders and review relevant existing resources
Absence of core curriculum	Establish core curriculum linked to local needs
Limited motivation	Provide incentives
Limited understanding of specialty and goals of retraining	Educate regarding identity, skills, and need for well-trained family doctors
No career opportunities or incentives	Provide career opportunities and rewards
Busy practitioners have little time for retraining	Develop flexible training options, self study, and computer-based learning
Hard to break old habits	Document practice through self-assessment/survey/quality instruments
Skills needed vary depending on background of trainee	Conduct a thorough needs assessment and design programs accordingly

Continuing professional development and medical education

Continuing medical education (CME) serves to refine the skills of family doctors throughout their careers. The field of family medicine has traditionally been a pioneer in CME, recognizing both the difficulty and importance of maintaining competency in a wide range of clinical skills. There are many options for continuing education including periodic conferences, independent self-study using journals or written materials, review of audiocassettes or videotapes, computer-based interactive programs, group seminars, or hands-on workshops. More than any other type of training program, CME is undergoing an expansion of e-learning offerings and educational programs. Effective continuing education is based on the needs of doctors with predetermined objectives for desired clinical competence, and assumes the prior achievement of a baseline level of clinical competence within one's clinical specialty.[94,95] Those practicing physicians without formal postgraduate training are likely to need a more robust and time-intensive clinical training program than usual models of CME can provide.[96]

There is a movement toward critical assessment of different dimensions of medical education, such as quality, relevance, and utility, with the goal of applying the best evidence-based medical education whenever possible.[97–99] This is a laudable and necessary goal for CME, but it is also necessary to recognize that a regionally and culturally appropriate evidence base may often be lacking for the specific settings, wide range of problems, and complex comorbidities and social influences in primary care. As such, application of evidence-based training programs should proceed with caution so as not to promote unhelpful, or worse, harmful medical practices for a particular locale. Also, an ongoing process of self-assessment and participation in continuing education can help physicians to maintain high-quality standards and up-to-date practice. Recognizing the importance of this process, some specialty societies require family doctors to complete a specific number of continuing medical education hours per year to maintain their specialty certification, and some health systems require a certain amount of CME in order to maintain a medical license to practice.

Active learning, in which learners discuss, apply or practice the use of information and skills, is more likely to result in physician behavior change.

While lectures may effectively transmit knowledge, improving physician practice often requires more complex skills. Physicians are faced with many competing priorities as they strive to incorporate recommendations systematically and efficiently into their busy practice environments. Educational programs that provide family doctors with new information that is relevant to the needs of their patients, encourage motivation for change, and provide opportunities to practice and receive feedback and reinforcement from peers, are more likely to result in long-term improvements in practice. With the expansion in e-learning programs that at times tend to lend themselves toward more traditional didactic medical education, it is especially important to consider ways for the learner to apply the skills taught and actively demonstrate competency within their existing practice. Box 4.17 provides suggestions for effective continuing medical education consistent with the principles of adult education.

BOX 4.17 How to provide effective continuing medical education

- Assess participants' needs, outline objectives, select appropriate methods
- Balance lectures with active learning methods to engage learners
- Precede small group activities with adequate preparation and specific tasks
- Limit small groups to no more than 12 participants to facilitate interaction and discussion
- Bring cases or encourage participants to bring their own for discussion
- Allow participants to practise skills and receive feedback
- Provide exercises to directly apply new skills to the active clinical setting
- Use family physicians as teachers when appropriate
- Identify challenges and discuss strategies for applying new skills
- Include methods of evaluation sufficient for determining competency
- Gather feedback from participants to improve future sessions

Source: adapted from Davis et al.[110]

BOX 4.18 Bringing together all the components of family medicine training in Sri Lanka

Undergraduate education in family medicine

Family medicine was formally accepted as an academic discipline in 1994 through joint departments of Community and Family Medicine in the Universities of Kelaniya and Sri Jayawardnenepura. Later both universities established separate departments of family medicine. The six remaining medical schools teach family medicine to varying extents.

Postgraduate education in family medicine

There has been an ongoing 1-year Postgraduate Diploma course in family medicine by the Postgraduate Institute of Medicine in Sri Lanka since 1981. Those who aspire for Board certification as specialists in family medicine can enroll in a 3-year MD training program in family medicine or can carry out a research project and submission of a thesis. To enable full-time private sector general practitioners to pursue further training, a Diploma in Family Medicine distance education program was launched in 2007 and is presently being delivered in the online mode (at pgim.nodes.lk). This has enabled learning to be flexible and has also helped doctors in remote areas to pursue higher education in family medicine.

The College of General Practitioners of Sri Lanka has been conducting a course leading to Membership of the College (MCGP) since 2003. In 2012 there was a major revision in the course to a two-year diploma program with classroom teaching on weekends and hospital rotations and general practice sessions during the week. A portfolio for recording learning activities and reflective writing allows for formative and summative assessment. The portfolio includes workplace-based assessments at the point of delivery of care and is a new addition to the program, along with a mentorship program to support learners. The MCGP of the College of General Practitioners of Sri Lanka has been recognized by the Sri Lanka Medical Council for registration as a postgraduate qualification, and is the first professional medical body in Sri Lanka to achieve this goal.

Continuing medical education and continuing professional development
The College of General Practitioners of Sri Lanka conducts continuing medical education through monthly lectures and workshops and through well-attended Annual Academic Sessions. The Open University of Sri Lanka started conducting continuing medical education courses for general practitioners through the online mode of delivery in 2008.

Source: Nandani de Silva (personal communication with authors, 2012).

Learner and program evaluation

In order to prepare family doctors with the necessary range of skills, the educational process is coordinated so knowledge and skills are developed sequentially and progressively, and evaluation is conducted at regular intervals. Learners master basic skills in the first years of training, and build on these to accomplish more complex skills in later years.

Evaluation and feedback are used to improve the performance of the learner, the teacher, and the educational process. Comprehensive evaluation includes attention to cognitive, psychomotor, and attitudinal skills, including the humanistic qualities of the trainee. Both formative and summative evaluation processes are important. Formative evaluation is the process of ongoing evaluation of learners as they progress through training and provides learners with regular, specific feedback as they master basic skills, become more efficient, and progress to caring for patients with more complex problems. Formative evaluation allows teachers to identify learners who may benefit from additional instruction to master specific skills prior to the completion of training and provides learners with the tools for guided self-assessment of their journey to attain the required competencies. Summative evaluation is used to assess a learner's overall performance at specific end points in a training program, such as at the end of a block rotation, the end of each year or prior to graduation. Strategies to select the best

---

BOX 4.19 Checklist for family medicine experiences

A Delphi process was initiated in 2006 toward developing a global consensus on what medical students should experience during a placement in family medicine, with responses from 15 countries on five continents. Developed with the WONCA Working Party on Education for the International Federation of Medical Student Associations to guide student exchanges in family medicine, the following checklist can be used in any context to help set a family medicine curriculum for medical students or to guide an evaluation of their experiences:

- Describe the health care system and the position and impact of primary care.
- Describe which conditions are handled by primary care and which by other levels of care.
- Select differences in diagnostic procedures and treatments related to incidence and prevalence in primary care, as compared to secondary and tertiary care.
- Discuss the doctor-patient relationship unique to family practice.
- Explain differences between illness and disease, using the patient-centered clinical approach.
- Perform and explain a patient-centred consultation.
- Provide care to patients over time (same patient, several visits).
- Evaluate and manage patients with chronic diseases over time.
- Evaluate, diagnose, and propose initial management for patients with common acute presentations.
- Deal with situations of clinical uncertainty.
- Discuss ethical aspects in family practice.
- Demonstrate respect for patients' culture and sensitivity to their own beliefs and assumptions.
- Provide health promotion and disease prevention counseling.

It may be helpful to consider these items in the context of occurring with observation only (beginner), with assistance from a supervisor present (intermediate), or performed independently with advice (advanced).

method of evaluation to assess different competencies have been summarized by the Accreditation Council for Graduate Medical Education (ACGME) in the United States. Certification assures overall competence and is discussed in Chapter 5. The ACGME is now in the process of moving toward a model of continuous assessment.[100] The ACGME is also developing international accreditation standards for a variety of specialty training programs (www.acgme-i.org).

The family medicine curriculum is updated and regularly improved through a cycle of continuous feedback and assessment. Each educational goal is accomplished through a process of developing objectives, methods, evaluation, and feedback for improvement. The synthesis and integration of family doctors' knowledge and skills is achieved by providing comprehensive care to a panel of patients in the family practice center. Required competencies and educational goals are periodically reviewed and revised to assure that they are relevant to current conditions. The quality of the curriculum is assessed by regularly reviewing learner outcomes and the satisfaction of learners, teachers, and patients.

To provide relevant and up-to-date education, teachers of family medicine also need to regularly assess the needs of the patients, communities, learners, and institutions they serve. Needs assessment is a fundamental component of patient-centered medical care, learner-centered teaching, community-oriented primary care, and socially accountable medical education. Such assessment requires an attitude of curiosity and willingness to ask questions such as the following:

➤ Are the clinical services, or teaching programs, meeting the most important needs of the communities or learners?
➤ Are learners satisfied with their education, or do they identify additional skills necessary for high-quality practice?
➤ How can the quality of services or teaching be improved?
➤ Is there new information suggesting different ways to deliver the services for lower costs?
➤ Are the benefits of the services fairly distributed?
➤ Do graduates have satisfactory options to provide services where they are needed?
➤ Are patients satisfied with the care provided by family doctors?

In educational programs, these questions are not only important for the present, but for planning adaptations for changing future conditions.

Change involves people with processes. The people are both the change agents and the constituents who may be affected by change. Planning for change may include analyzing the context, setting directions, planning, implementing, sustaining, and finally assessing the impacts of change.[101] Steps for achieving such change are outlined in Box 4.20.

BOX 4.20 Protocol for change in medical education[111]

In 1992, international leaders of medical education met at the University of Washington in Seattle to discuss strategies for changing medical education to meet the needs of society. They outlined a stepwise protocol for change that included the elements listed here.

Phase 1: Steps for getting started
- Develop a mission statement
- Work with other concerned parties
- Plan the curriculum according to health needs
- Develop the profile of the "future doctor"
- Assess the usefulness of the present curriculum
- Assess the student evaluation system
- Assess the faculty and staff
- Assess the organizational structure
- Assess the reward system
- Estimate the chances for successful change
- Prepare appropriate leaders

Phase 2: Steps to initiate implementation
- Seek financial support
- Gather materials to develop a new curriculum
- Develop organizational plan
- Maintain communication
- Solidify a positive image for change
- Deal with barriers to change

Phase 3: Steps for full implementation
- Develop a curriculum schedule
- Establish an appropriate curriculum governance structure
- Establish ongoing short-term and long-term evaluation plans
- Participate in community health programs and health service research

---

4.5 TRANSITIONING FROM EDUCATION TO PRACTICE

This chapter outlined what family medicine education is, why it is different from education and training for other medical specialties, and how family medicine education and training can be successfully implemented.

BOX 4.21 Applying international standards to family medicine

In 1998, the World Federation for Medical Education (WFME) launched a program on international standards in medical education. The purpose was to provide a mechanism for quality improvement in medical education, in a global context, to be applied by institutions responsible for medical education, and in programs throughout the continuum of medical education. Medical educators from around the globe developed WFME global standards for basic medical education, postgraduate medical education, and continuing professional development, all published in 2003 with support from the World Health Organization and the World Medical Association.

WONCA has been developing standards for family doctors in training, based on the two level framework of the WFME international standards: *Basic* for programs in an early stage of development, and *Quality Development* for programs which are more mature and long standing. This is a useful concept, given the diversity of family medicine resources and educational settings.

In development, a variety of issues are being addressed, including:
- relevance of such standards to a wide variety of contexts
- additional areas specific to family medicine
- utility of these standards to educational programs across the globe
- value of developing accompanying international accreditation standards.

In summary, family medicine is the specialty field of medicine dedicated specifically to the provision of primary care, and family medicine education and training programs are exclusive in their focus on teaching in all of the core principles of primary care. Undergraduate medical students are typically exposed to the basics of primary care through a dedicated rotation in the undergraduate curriculum. Because of the inability to achieve adequate competency in the complex skills of primary care during the basic medical school years, family medicine specialty training is offered for learners to develop complete competency. Postgraduate vocational training programs typically involve a mix of didactic, hospital, and outpatient teaching, with a special emphasis on training in the ambulatory care setting. This outpatient training is enhanced through special teaching techniques designed especially for the busy family medicine clinic. Retraining specialty programs in family medicine are similar to traditional postgraduate programs with modifications to accommodate practicing physicians who have to achieve a basic competency in primary care, and these programs are a crucial part of helping health systems rapidly build a base of well-trained primary care providers where none exist currently. Continuing medical education is an important in-service training mechanism often championed by the specialty of family medicine for assisting the practicing family doctor in maintaining a minimum level of competency in clinical care. Evaluation based on competency-based training is essential in assuring provider competency in primary care and improving educational programs in the specialty.

While education and professional development are essential for high-quality family practice, a supportive environment is also necessary. As family medicine trainees transition from learner to independent provider, they quickly seek the system supports to be able to practice their new specialty field to the upper limits of their improved abilities. The development of a large cohort of family doctors within a health system will be of limited benefit if they are not provided with the systems and resources to maximize use of their skills in principles such as comprehensive and coordinated care. To accomplish improved population-based outcomes resulting from a strong foundation in primary care, health systems must continue their investment in primary care system strengthening beyond just training and the development of these human resources. Components of this environment are reviewed in the next chapter.

REFERENCES

1. Dewey J, Archambault RD. *John Dewey on Education: selected writings.* New York: Modern Library. 1964.
2. Maritain J. *Education at the Crossroads.* New Haven, CT: Yale University Press, 1943.
3. Hutchins RM. *The Conflict in Education in a Democratic Society.* 1st ed. New York: Harper, 1953: 67–76.
4. McGuire C. *An Overview of Medical Education in the Late 20th Century. International handbook of medical education.* Westport, CT: Greenwood Press, 1994.
5. Boelen C. Medical education reform: the need for global action. *Academic Medicine.* 1992; **67**(11): 745–9.
6. Boelen C, Heck JE. *Defining and Measuring the Social Accountability of Medical Schools.* Geneva: World Health Organization, Division of Development of Human Resources for Health; 1995.
7. Lipkin M. *Toward the Education of Doctors who Care for the Needs of People: innovative approaches in medical education. New directions for medical education: problem-based learning and community-oriented medical education.* New York: Springer-Verlag, 1989.
8. Golden A, Carlson D, Hagen J. *A Definition of Primary Care for Educational Purposes. The art of teaching primary care.* New York: Springer 1982.
9. Gabriel BA. Beyond hospital walls: teaching students about social determinants of health.

AAMC Reporter [Internet] 2012. Available from: www.aamc.org/newsroom/reporter/sept2012/303664/hospital-walls.html

10. Moore MG, Kearsley G. *Distance Education: a systems view of online learning.* 3rd ed. Belmont, CA: Wadsworth Cengage Learning, 2012.

11. NextGenU: NextGenU.org 2012. Available at: www.nextgenu.org

12. Lewin T. Harvard and M.I.T. team up to offer free online courses. *New York Times*, 2012, May 2.

13. De Silva N. Development of the Postgraduate Diploma in Family Medicine by distance education. The Sri Lankan experience. *Medicine Today.* 2008; **6**(2): 173–7. Available at: pgim.nodes.lk

14. Starfield B, Shi L, Grover A, et al. The effects of specialist supply on populations' health: assessing the evidence. *Health Affairs (Millwood).* 2005 Jan-Jun; Suppl Web Exclusives: W5-97-W5-107.

15. Gulliford MC. Availability of primary care doctors and population health in England: is there an association? *Journal of Public Health Medicine.* 2002; **24**(4): 252–4.

16. Campbell RJ, Ramirez AM, Perez K, et al. Cervical cancer rates and the supply of primary care physicians in Florida. *Family Medicine.* 2003; **35**(1): 60–4.

17. Ferrante JM, Gonzalez EC, Pal N, et al. Effects of physician supply on early detection of breast cancer. *Journal of the American Board of Family Practice.* 2000; **13**(6): 408–14.

18. Lee J, Park S, Choi K, et al. The association between the supply of primary care physicians and population health outcomes in Korea. *Family Medicine.* 2010; **42**(9): 628–35.

19. Roetzheim RG, Pal N, van Durme DJ, et al. Increasing supplies of dermatologists and family physicians are associated with earlier stage of melanoma detection. *Journal of the American Academy of Dermatology.* 2000; **43**(2 Pt. 1): 211–18.

20. Shi L, Macinko J, Starfield B, et al. The relationship between primary care, income inequality, and mortality in US States, 1980–1995. *Journal of the American Board of Family Practice.* 2003; **16**(5): 412–22.

21. Franks P, Fiscella K. Primary care physicians and specialists as personal physicians. Health care expenditures and mortality experience. *Journal of Family Practice.* 1998; **47**(2): 105–9.

22. Roetzheim RG, Pal N, Gonzalez EC, Fet al. The effects of physician supply on the early detection of colorectal cancer. *Journal of Family Practice.* 1999; **48**(11): 850–8.

23. Shi L, Macinko J, Starfield B, et al. Primary care, income inequality, and stroke mortality in the United States: a longitudinal analysis, 1985–1995. *Stroke.* 2003; **34**(8): 1958–64.

24. Shi L, Macinko J, Starfield B, et al. Primary care, infant mortality, and low birth weight in the states of the USA. *Journal of Epidemiology and Community Health.* 2004; **58**(5): 374–80.

25. Starfield B. *Primary Care: balancing health needs, services, and technology.* Rev. ed. New York: Oxford University Press, 1998; ix: 438.

26. *Training of the Physician for Family Practice: eleventh report of the Expert Committee on Professional and Technical Education of Medical and Auxiliary Personnel.* Geneva: World Health Organization 1963.

27. Haq C, Ventres W, Hunt V, et al. Where there is no family doctor: the development of family practice around the world. *Academic Medicine.* 1995; **70**(5): 370–80.

28. Hansen MF. An educational program for primary care. *Journal of Medical Education.* 1970; **45**(12): 1001–15.

29. *Making Medical Practice and Education More Relevant to People's Needs: the contribution of the family doctor.* Geneva: World Health Organization, 1994.

30. *The World Health Report 2008: Primary health care – now more than ever.* Geneva: World Health Organization, 2008.

31. *World Medical Association Statement on the Global Burden of Chronic Disease.* World Medical Association, 2011.

32. Montegut AJ. To achieve "health for all" we must shift the world's paradigm to "primary care access for all". *Journal of the American Board Family Medicine.* 2007; **20**(6): 514–17.

33. Ershler I. Comprehensive primary health care. A letter to a medical student. *Archives of Internal Medicine.* 1989; **149**(11): 2404–6.

34. Golinkoff M. Managed care best practices: the road from diagnosis to recovery: access to appropriate care. *Journal of Managed Care Pharmacy.* 2007; **13**(9 Suppl A): S23–7.

35. McDaniel SH, McDaniel SH. *Family-Oriented Primary Care.* 2nd ed. New York: Springer, 2005; xix: 477.

36. Global learning device on social determinants of health and public policy formulation. Pan American Health Organization, World Health Organization; 2011.

37. Saultz JW. Defining and measuring interpersonal continuity of care. *Annals of Family Medicine.* 2003; **1**(3): 134–43.

38. Haggerty JL, Reid RJ, Freeman GK, et al. Continuity of care: a multidisciplinary review. *British Medical Journal.* 2003; **327**(7425): 1219–21.

39. Christakis DA, Kazak AE, Wright JA, et al. What factors are associated with achieving high continuity of care? *Family Medicine.* 2004; **36**(1): 55–60.

40. Becker MH, Drachman RH, Kirscht JP. A field experiment to evaluate various outcomes of continuity of physician care. *American Journal of Public Health.* 1974; **64**(11): 1062–70.

41. Nutting PA, Goodwin MA, Flocke SA, et al. Continuity of primary care: to whom does it matter and when? *Annals of Family Medicine.* 2003; **1**(3): 149–55.

42. Thompson M, Nussbaum R. Asking women to see nurses or unfamiliar physicians as part of primary care redesign. *American Journal of Managed Care.* 2000; **6**(2): 187–99.

43. Bodenheimer T. *Building Teams in Primary Care: case studies.* Oakland, CA: California HealthCare Foundation 2007.

44. Menec VH, Sirski M, Attawar D, et al. Does continuity of care with a family physician reduce hospitalizations among older adults? *Journal of Health Services Research and Policy.* 2006; **11**(4): 196–201.

45. Sperl-Hillen JM, Solberg LI, Hroscikoski MC, et al. The effect of advanced access implementation on quality of diabetes care. *Preventing Chronic Disease.* 2008; **5**(1): A16.

46. Wolinsky FD, Bentler SE, Liu L, et al. Continuity of care with a primary care physician and mortality in older adults. *Journals of Gerontology Series A, Biological Sciences and Medical Sciences.* 2010; **65**(4): 421–8.

47. Ogur B, Hirsh D, Krupat E, et al. The Harvard Medical School-Cambridge integrated clerkship: an innovative model of clinical education. *Academic Medicine.* 2007; **82**(4): 397–404.

48. Phan K, Brown SR. Decreased continuity in a residency clinic: a consequence of open access scheduling. *Family Medicine.* 2009; **41**(1): 46–50.

49. Powell Davies G, Williams AM, Larsen K, Pet al. Coordinating primary health care: an analysis of the outcomes of a systematic review. *Medical Journal of Australia.* 2008; **188**(8 Suppl.): S65–8.

50. Stille CJ, Jerant A, Bell D, Meltzer D, Elmore JG. Coordinating care across diseases, settings, and clinicians: a key role for the generalist in practice. *Annals of Internal Medicine.* 2005; **142**(8): 700–8.

51. Grumbach K, Bodenheimer T. Can health care teams improve primary care practice? *Journal of the American Medical Association..* 2004; **291**(10): 1246–51.

52. De Maeseneer J, van Weel C, Roberts R. Family medicine's commitment to the MDGs. *Lancet.* 2010; **375**(9726): 1588–9.

53. Mills P, Neily J, Dunn E. Teamwork and communication in surgical teams: implications for patient safety. *Journal of the American College of Surgeons.* 2008; **206**(1): 107–12.

54. Nandiwada DR, Dang-Vu C. Transdisciplinary health care education: training team players. *Journal of Health Care for the Poor and Underserved.* 2010; **21**(1): 26–34.

55. Jack B, Greenwald J, Forsythe S, et al. Developing the Tools to Administer a Comprehensive Hospital Discharge Program: The ReEngineered Discharge (RED) Program (Vol. 3: Performance and Tools) 2008.

56. *Wonca International Dictionary.* Copenhagen: Wonca International Classification Committee, 2003.

57. Starfield B, Hyde J, Gervas J, et al. The concept of prevention: a good idea gone astray? *Journal of Epidemiology and Community Health.* 2008; **62**(7): 580–3.

58. United States Department of Health and Human Services. *Clinician's Handbook of Preventative Services.* 2nd ed. McLean, VA: International Medical Publishing 1997.

59. Prochaska J, DiClemente C. In search of the structure of behaviour change. In: Y Klar, J. D. Fisher, J. M. Chinsky, et al (eds). *Self-Change: social, psychological and clinical perspectives.* New York: Springer-Verlag, 1992.

60. Rollnick S, Mason P, Butler C. *Health Behavior Change: a guide for practitioners.* Edinburgh: Churchill Livingstone, 1999.

61. Christie-Seely J (ed). *Working With the Family in Primary Care: a systems approach to health and illness.* Westport, CT: Praeger Publishers 1984.

62. Kark SL. *The Practice of Community-oriented Primary Health Care.* New York: Appleton-Century-Crofts, 1981.

63. Rhyne R. *Community Oriented Primary Care: health care for the 21st century.* Washington DC: American Public Health Association 1998.

64. Lipkin M, Putnam SM, Lazare A. *The Medical Interview: clinical care, education, and research.* New York: Springer-Verlag 1995; 22: 643.

65. Stuart MR, Lieberman JA. *The Fifteen Minute Hour: practical therapeutic interventions in primary care.* 3rd ed. Philadelphia: Saunders, 2002.

66. Brown J, Stewart M, McCracken E, et al. The patient-centred clinical method. 2. Definition and application. *Family Practice.* 1986; **3**(2): 75–9.

67. Coulehan JL, Block MR. *The Medical Interview: mastering skills for clinical practice.* 5th ed. Philadelphia: F.A. Davis Co., 2006.

68. Levenstein JH, McCracken EC, McWhinney IR, et al. The patient-centred clinical method. 1. A model for the doctor-patient interaction in family medicine. *Family Practice.* 1986; **3**(1): 24–30.

69. Mengel M, Holleman W (eds). *Fundamentals of Clinical Practice. A textbook on the patient, doctor and society.* New York: Plenum Medical Book Company 1997.

70. Stewart M, Brown J, Levenstein J, et al. The patient-centred clinical method. 3. Changes in residents' performance over two months of training. *Family Practice.* 1986; **3**(3): 164–7.

71. Stewart M, Brown JB, Weston WW, et al. *Patient-Centred Medicine: transforming the clinical method.* 2nd ed. Stewart M, Brown JB, Freeman TR (eds). United Kingdom: Radcliffe Medical Press, 2003.

72. The American Balint Society. Available from: www.americanbalintsociety.org

73. Pellegrino E, Thomasma D. *For the Patient's Good: the restoration of beneficence in health care.* Oxford: Oxford University Press 1988.

74. Rivo ML, Saultz JW, Wartman SA, et al. Defining the generalist physician's training. *Journal of the American Medical Association..* 1994; **271**(19): 1499–504.

75. Kahssay HM. Health centres: the future of health depends on them. *World Health Forum.* 1998; **19**(4): 341–7, discussion 8–60.

76. Markuns JF, Culpepper L, Halpin WJ Jr. Commentary: a need for leadership in primary health care for the underserved: a call to action. *Academic Medicine.* 2009; **84**(10): 1325–7.

77. Kahssay H, Taylor M, Berman P. *Community Health Workers: the way forward.* Geneva: World Health Organization, 1998.

78. Demarzo MM. Transforming health professionals' education. *Lancet.* 2011; **377**(9773): 1235, author reply 8–9.

79. Sloane PD. *Essentials of Family Medicine.* 6th ed. Philadelphia: Wolters Kluwer Health/ Lippincott Williams & Wilkins, 2012.

80. Scott I, Gowans M, Wright B, et al. Determinants of choosing a career in family medicine. *Canadian Medical Association Journal.* 2011; **183**(1): E1–8.

81. Bland CJ, Meurer LN, Maldonado G. Determinants of primary care specialty choice: a non-statistical meta-analysis of the literature. *Academic Medicine.* 1995; **70**(7): 620–41.

82. West CP, Dupras DM. General medicine vs subspecialty career plans among internal medicine residents. *Journal of the American Medical Association..* 2012; **308**(21): 2241–7.

83. Sinclair HK, Ritchie LD, Lee AJ. A future career in general practice? A longitudinal study of medical students and pre-registration house officers. *European Journal of General Practice.* 2006; **12**(3): 120–7.

84. Tolhurst H, Stewart M. Becoming a GP-a qualitative study of the career interests of medical students. *Australian Family Physician.* 2005; **34**(3): 204–6.

85. Pathman DE, Steiner BD, Jones BD, et al. Preparing and retaining rural physicians through medical education. *Academic Medicine.* 1999; **74**(7): 810–20.

86. Campos-Outcalt D, Senf J, Watkins AJ, et al. The effects of medical school curricula, faculty role models, and biomedical research support on choice of generalist physician careers: a review and quality assessment of the literature. *Academic Medicine.* 1995; **70**(7): 611–19.

87. Kamien BA, Bassiri M, Kamien M. Doctors badmouthing each other. Does it affect medical students' career choices? *Australian Family Physician.* 1999; **28**(6): 576–9.

88. Vujicic M, Alfano M, Shengelia B, et al. *Attracting Doctors and Medical Students to Rural Vietnam: insights from a discrete choice experiment.* The World Bank, 2010.

89. Neher JO, Gordon KC, Meyer B, et al. A five-step "microskills" model of clinical teaching. *Journal of the American Board of Family Practice.* 1992; **5**(4): 419–24.

90. Pangaro L. A new vocabulary and other innovations for improving descriptive in-training evaluations. *Academic Medicine.* 1999; **74**(11): 1203–7.

91. Wolpaw TM, Wolpaw DR, Papp KK. SNAPPS: a learner-centered model for outpatient education. *Academic Medicine.* 2003; **78**(9): 893–8.

92. Wolpaw T, Papp KK, Bordage G. Using SNAPPS to facilitate the expression of clinical reasoning and uncertainties: a randomized comparison group trial. *Academic Medicine.* 2009; **84**(4): 517–24.

93. *Family Practice Development Strategies: report on the second World Health Organization meeting of the Expert Network.* Warsaw, Poland: World Health Organization Regional Office for Europe 1995.

94. Mazmanian PE, Davis DA. Continuing medical education and the physician as a learner: guide to the evidence. *Journal of the American Medical Association..* 2002; **288**(9): 1057–60.

95. Fabb W, Janssens H. Continuing education. In: Fry J (ed). *Primary Care.* London: William Heinemen Medical Books, 1980: 473.

96. Hauer KE, Ciccone A, Henzel TR, et al. Remediation of the deficiencies of physicians

across the continuum from medical school to practice: a thematic review of the literature. *Academic Medicine.* 2009; **84**(12): 1822–32.

97. Harden RM, Grant J, Buckley G, et al. Best evidence medical education. *Advances in Health Sciences Education: Theory and Practice.* 2000; **5**(1): 71–90.

98. Hart I. Best evidence medical education (BEME). *Medical Teacher.* 1999; **21**(5): 453–4.

99. Stewart M, Mennin P, McGrew M. Scholarship in teaching and best evidence medical education: synergy for teaching and learning. *Medical Teacher.* 2000; **22**(5): 468–70.

100. Nasca TJ, Philibert I, Brigham T, et al. The next GME accreditation system – rationale and benefits. *New England Journal of Medicine.* 2012; **366**(11): 1051–6.

101. Neufeld V. *Leadership for Change in the Education of Health Professionals.* Maastrict: Network Publications, 1995.

102. Walters L, Greenhill J, Richards J, et al. Outcomes of longitudinal integrated clinical placements for students, clinicians and society. *Medical Education.* 2012; **46**(11): 1028–41.

103. Makoul G. Essential elements of communication in medical encounters: the Kalamazoo consensus statement. *Academic Medicine.* 2001; **76**: 390–3.

104. *The World Health Report 2008: Primary health care – now more than ever.* Geneva: World Health Organization 2008. Available at: www.who.int/whr/2008/whr08_en.pdf

105. Starfield B. Is patient-centred care the same as person-focused care? *Permanente Journal.* 2011; **15**(2): 63–9.

106. Kidd MR, Beilby JJ, Farmer EA, et al. General practice education and training: past experiences, current issues and future challenges. *Medical Journal of Australia.* 2011; **194**(11): S53–4.

107. Osman H, Romani M, Hlais S. Family medicine in Arab countries. *Family Medicine.* 2011; **43**: 37–42.

108. Abyad A, Al-Baho AK, Unluoglu I, et al. Development of family medicine in the Middle East. *Family Medicine.* 2007; **39**: 736–41.

109. Accreditation Council for Graduate Medical Education (ACGME) Program Requirements for Graduate Medical Education in Family Medicine, 2007, United States of America.

110. Davis D, O'Brien MA, Freemantle N, et al. Impact of formal continuing medical education. Do conferences, workshops, rounds and other traditional continuing education activities change physician behavior or health outcomes? *Journal of the American Medical Association..* 1999; 282: 867–74.

111. Boelen C, Des Marchais JE, Dohner CW, et al. *Developing Protocols for Change in Medical Education. Report of an informal consultation, Seattle, Washington, USA, 11–14 August 1992.* Geneva: World Health Organization. 1995. (WHO/HRH/95.5)

112. Boelen C. A new paradigm for medical schools a century after Flexner's report. *Bulletin of the World Health Organization.* 2002; 80.

113. *The Global Consensus for Social Accountability of Medical Schools, 2010.* Available at: www. healthsocialaccountability.org

114. Frehywot S, Vovides Y, Talib Z, et al. E-learning in medical education in resource constrained low- and middle-income countries. *Human Resources for Health.* 2013; **11**: 4. Available at: www.human-resources-health.com/content/pdf/1478-4491-11-4.pdf.

CHAPTER 5

Creating a supportive environment for optimal family practice

Family doctors need supportive environments to enable them to care for individuals, families, and communities. Many conditions are necessary for the success of family practice (*see* Table 5.1). Necessary education and training prepares family doctors, while effective health systems and collaborative teams provide the organizational structure necessary for the delivery of efficient health services. Supportive environments make it possible for family doctors to provide the highest-quality health care with available resources.

TABLE 5.1 Key conditions for optimal family practice

Component	Examples
Relationships	Effective communication and collaboration with patients, families, communities, health teams, specialty colleagues, medical schools and academic medical centers, government and public health authorities, and professional associations
Education	High-quality education provided through medical school, specialty training, and continuing education
Health teams and systems	Primary care teams provided with adequate resources, sufficient numbers of health professionals, and collaborative practice models
Professional associations	Standards established for high-quality family medicine, needs assessments conducted, examination and certification in place, adequate resources secured, public educated about the role and value of family doctors, productive collaboration with national and international organizations
Primary care research	Sufficient funding provided for family medicine researchers to generate new knowledge, knowledge applied to improve the quality and assess outcomes of care
Quality improvement	Family doctors possess knowledge and skills to assess quality and to improve clinical processes and outcomes
Policy and financing	Incentives provided to support high-quality primary care for the entire population

This chapter covers components of supportive environments necessary for high-quality family practice. These include promoting positive relationships; developing professional organizations; financing and rewarding optimal practice; improving access; supporting primary care research; enhancing the quality and outcomes of practice; and strategic planning for family medicine development. Each of these interrelated components contributes to supportive family practice environments.

5.1 PROMOTING POSITIVE RELATIONSHIPS

While the components listed in Table 5.1 contribute to conditions for optimal practice, the well-regarded image of a well-trained family doctor results from positive relationships developed over time with patients and the public, health professional colleagues, academic facilities, and health authorities. Relationships with these health system stakeholders are based on family doctors' provision of high-quality patient care, effective collaboration with primary care team members and other specialty colleagues, and dedicated service to communities. Promoting such positive relationships begins by understanding and addressing the needs and the potential underlying resistance of each stakeholder.

Relationships with individuals and the community

Relationships between family doctors and their patients, colleagues, and the community affect the climate for continued growth and development of family medicine as a discipline. As an example, the Canadian health system has undergone transformation to strengthen primary care delivery in the past decade, with encouragement, engagement, and collaboration with all stakeholders including patients, providers, and policy makers, as an essential part of the reforms.[1]

In another example, in 2010, the president of the United States signed into law that country's most comprehensive health reform package since 1965. The Patient Protection and Affordable Care Act (ACA) will assure health insurance coverage to more than 30 million previously uninsured Americans. The ACA and the Congressional testimony that underpinned it, focus heavily on primary care as being essential and important to reducing costs. This law should help bring family physicians closer to more members of the population of the United States.[2]

When introducing family medicine in a country, the public may first need to be educated about the role of the family doctor in the health care system. In some countries in which general practitioners are inadequately trained, overworked, and under-rewarded, the public may have a negative opinion about the family doctor as personal physician.[3] In this situation, it may be essential for governments or the private sector to fund family medicine development and support model practices to demonstrate to the public that well-trained family doctors can provide high-quality care with high patient satisfaction.[4]

In situations where family physicians have substantial control over referral to other medical specialist services, and are pressured by their employers or the government to restrict such access, patients and the public may voice unhappiness with restricted access. Such a situation already exists, for example in the United Kingdom, where proposed reforms would move toward a more market-driven system with general practitioners acting as payers for specialist care and controlling 70% of the National Health Service budget.[5] These situations require careful monitoring to ensure that family doctors are able to continue to serve as effective patient advocates.

In reality, the public is often quite appreciative of the primary care services provided by family doctors.[4] Treating patients promptly and courteously enhances public acceptance. When individuals find they can depend on their family doctor and local health team to serve as competent providers and advocates, family doctors and members of the entire primary care team become highly regarded members of the community. In addition, if family doctors work collaboratively with others on community health improvement projects, either as paid or as volunteer contributors, they are perceived as willing to work for the well-being of the entire community. As a result, they may be invited to act as community health advocates and leaders to contribute to other health-related programs such as planning for economic development, education, or safety. Such leadership roles enhance the value of family doctors to the whole community.

Family physicians can engage in a strategy of community-oriented primary health care (COPC) (*see* Chapter 2, Section 2.7). Starting from experiences in daily practice, complemented by epidemiological data, the primary care team, together with the local community, can formulate a "Community Diagnosis," and start action to address the causes that lead to ill health.[66]

Family doctors can contribute to public health education. Activities may include writing newspaper columns, participating in radio talk shows, and providing televised updates on current health topics. To enhance their image, family doctors and their representative organizations can develop successful public education campaigns using advertisements, posters, and brochures to promote the perception of the family doctor as a personal and caring doctor. Such campaigns can emphasize the advantages of having one doctor to provide comprehensive health care to individuals and families and to coordinate all health care needs. Raising awareness of the characteristics and functions of family medicine instills public confidence in the quality of care provided. Strategies to promote positive relationships with local communities are listed in Box 5.1.

BOX 5.1 How family doctors can promote positive relationships with the community

Family doctors may:
- provide high-quality, accessible, comprehensive health care services
- provide continuity of care
- provide people-centered care
- treat patients and families promptly, courteously, and with sensitivity to their health care needs and concerns
- act as patient advocates
- engage with community leaders and health advocates to the benefit of their communities
- participate in community health improvement programs
- participate in volunteer services
- deliver public health education
- develop public information materials

Relationships with colleagues

Positive relationships between family doctors, health team members, and colleagues provide a foundation for effective partnerships. A number of groups of health professionals may be affected by the development of family medicine. These groups may include practicing generalist physicians who were not trained as family doctors, other specialists, and allied health professionals. Many of these professionals may be involved in primary care delivery and share the goals of family doctors. Some may question the need for family doctors or fear for their own survival.[6]

Addressing these concerns, negotiating the complementary roles of family doctors and other health professionals, and inviting others to participate in the development of family medicine will help build alliances to deliver effective primary care. Strategies may include retraining practicing specialist physicians who wish to become family doctors, or developing new practice models that integrate family doctors with other health professionals.

In coordinated health systems, the roles of family doctors and other health professionals are complementary; each enables the other to be optimally effective.[7] Family doctors may rely on primary care team members to provide services such as screening, health education, and treatment of chronic conditions.

Reciprocal, supportive relationships among primary care team members enhance the effectiveness of the entire team.

Where family doctors assume greater responsibilities for the community or for public health, especially when they coordinate services for a given target population, they are even more dependent on a variety of allied health professionals. While trained family doctors are able to handle the majority of individual health problems in a community, they are also aware of their limitations, and know when and how to ask for help from other specialist colleagues.

When specialty physicians are appropriately consulted and share in the care of patients with complex needs, they come to understand and respect the value of the family doctor in patient care. Appropriate consultation includes providing the consultant with important background information about the patient, outlining the problems for the consultant to address, and determining the roles of the family doctor and the consultant in the continuing care of the patient.

Coordination of care is especially important when a patient is hospitalized. Some family doctors provide hospital care. Even if another physician is responsible for hospital care, the family doctor is responsible for referral and follow-up of the hospitalized patient.

Such recognition, discussion, and negotiation of the complementary roles of family doctors and other health professionals in the care of patients minimizes competition and promotes collaboration. Other specialists who work collaboratively with family doctors may become important allies in the development of the specialty. Strategies to promote positive relationships with colleagues are listed in Box 5.2.

BOX 5.2 How family doctors can promote positive relationships with colleagues

Family doctors may:

- serve as collaborative team members
- communicate directly and effectively with consultant specialists
- share information to better address priority health needs
- coordinate the admission, care, and discharge of hospitalized patients
- identify problems and develop strategies to improve coordination of care
- provide continuing education programs for allied health professionals
- invite specialty colleagues to participate in teaching and continuing education programs

Relationships with medical schools

Many medical schools have discovered that family medicine departments play important roles in their school and local academic medical centers in the areas of teaching, research, and clinical care. Initially, however, some faculty or departments may resist the introduction of family medicine.[8]

Visits and presentations by faculty and heads of departments from places where family medicine is well established and respected may lend a more favourable attitude toward the specialty. Often, a medical school dean or respected head of department of another specialty may be a key ally in establishing family medicine in an academic medical center or medical school.

Community-based family doctors can enhance their relationships with academic medical centers and medical schools by serving as valuable clinicians, teachers, and role models for medical students and doctors in specialty training. Community-based learning experiences provide benefits for students, doctors-in-training, and the supervising doctors. When learners work under the supervision of community-based family doctors, they are able to appreciate the value and complexity of high quality, comprehensive primary care. Community-based family doctors who serve as teachers are generally motivated to deliver high-quality services, and are stimulated by interactions with eager learners. The quality of patient care is improved when family doctors participate in primary care research efforts and in continuing education to keep up to date and further improve their teaching skills. When family doctors are recognized and rewarded as teachers, their image is enhanced. Considerations for improving family doctors' relationships with medical schools and academic medical centers are listed in Box 5.3.

> **BOX 5.3** How family doctors can promote positive relationships with medical schools and academic medical centers
>
> Family doctors may:
> - serve as full-time faculty in medical school departments of family medicine
> - serve on medical school admissions committees
> - help teach family medicine to medical students
> - serve as clinician teachers to doctors in training
> - teach or participate in continuing education programs
> - engage in primary care research
> - enhance the social accountability of academic institutions

Relationships with health authorities

Supportive relationships with government authorities responsible for planning and financing health care will enhance the abilities of family doctors to serve communities and the potential for family medicine to become a driving force in health reform processes. Among the factors influencing the development of family medicine, ideological and financial support from government is the most

---

BOX 5.4 Partnerships between the government and family medicine in the Philippines

The Philippine Academy of Family Physicians (PAFP), the Philippine Society of Teachers of Family Medicine and the Department of Family and Community Medicine at the University of the Philippines have collaborated with the national government and its implementation arm, the Philippine Health Insurance Corporation, on a variety of projects designed to enhance family medicine and improve quality of care.

The National Health Insurance Law, enacted in 1994, helped to formalize the role of the family doctor. Key components of this law include:

- universal access for both ambulatory care and hospitalizations
- classification of family doctors as specialists with corresponding payment for their services
- specialty referrals through family doctors
- provision for quality assurance programs to improve practice.

Projects included joint workshops on competencies, development of evidence-based clinical practice guidelines for commonly encountered conditions in primary care, research to improve access and quality of care, and pilot projects dealing with the delivery of hospice care, family wellness, and care of the disadvantaged.

Continuing medical education is required by the Professional Regulations Commission in order for family doctors to renew their licences and maintain their practicing status. The PAFP now requires participation in quality assurance activities in order for family doctors to maintain active membership. Quality improvement has also been enhanced by assistance from the World Organization of Family Doctors Working Party on Quality in Family Medicine.

Thus a mutually beneficial relationship continues to evolve. With the assistance of government support and stature, family doctors have pursued a variety of measures that assure society of the quality of their care.

Source: Leopando Z, Siao W (personal communication).

important. History shows that once this is obtained, progress is usually rapid. Governments and health authorities need to be provided with the accumulating evidence that enhancing the contribution of family medicine will help health systems provide high-quality, equitable, cost-effective care. Government health officials may be able to provide valuable information for health planning efforts, and often welcome partnerships with local physicians (*see* Box 5.4).

Collaborative relationships between family doctors and local public health officials provide opportunities to strengthen the links between clinical medicine and community health. Strategies to promote positive relationships with health authorities are listed in Box 5.5.

BOX 5.5 How family doctors can promote positive relationships with government health authorities

Family doctors:

- engage in dialogue about options for health sector reform
- participate in government health planning to improve primary health care
- communicate with health authorities to share health information for local, regional or national planning
- participate in disease surveillance and community prevention efforts
- serve as district medical officers, public health officials or public service officers
- work with professional associations to advocate optimal conditions for family practice

---

While each of these relationships forms an essential foundation for high-quality family practice, many other conditions contribute to the professional development of family doctors. Boxes 5.6, 5.7, 5.8, 5.9, and 5.10 list initiatives from different countries that have supported the development of positive relationships.

BOX 5.6 How New Zealand provides a central government-driven, tax-funded health system with the government as dominant payer and with support provided by network organizations[10]

Networks provide:

- administration
- budget holding
- incentivized programs
- data feedback
- peer review

- education
- human relations
- health information technology support and resources.

Networks are similarly important in many other countries and are an important way of providing a supportive environment for practicing family medicine, with a team-based and patient-centered approach

---

BOX 5.7 How primary health care in Australia has been reformed by the establishment of local primary health care organizations[11]

These organizations have supported the further development of the Australian primary health care system by:
- supporting the roll-out of initiatives including national practice accreditation
- a focus on quality improvement
- expansion of multidisciplinary teams into general practice
- regional integration
- information technology adoption
- improved access to care

BOX 5.8 General practice is the cornerstone of Danish primary health care[12]

It is characterized by five key components:
1. a list system, with an average of close to 1600 persons on the list of a typical general practitioner (GP)
2. the GP as gatekeeper and first-line provider in the sense that a referral from a GP is required for most office-based specialists and always for inpatient and outpatient hospital treatment
3. an after-hours system staffed by GPs on a rota basis
4. a mixed capitation and fee-for-service system
5. GPs are self-employed, working on contract for the public funder based on a national agreement that details not only services and reimbursement but also opening hours and required postgraduate education

BOX 5.9 Canadian provincial and territorial health systems have taken diverse approaches to strengthening primary care delivery[1]

The range of primary care reform initiatives implemented across Canada target:

- organizational infrastructure
- provider payment
- health care workforce
- quality and safety.

Primary care teams and networks in which multiple physicians work in concert with other providers have become widespread in some provinces. They vary on a number of dimensions, including:

- physician payment
- incorporation of other providers
- formal enrolment of patients.

Family medicine is attracting more recent medical school graduates, a trend likely affected by new physician payment models, increases in the number of primary care providers, and efforts to better integrate non-physician providers into clinical practice.

BOX 5.10 Recent innovations in Dutch health care reforms[13]

- Introduction of private insurance based on the principles of primary care-led health care and including all citizens irrespective of their financial, employment, or health status
- Introduction of primary care collaboratives for out-of-hour services and chronic disease management
- Primary care team building, including practice nurses.

These innovations were introduced on top of a strong primary care tradition of family practices with defined populations based on patient panels, practice-based research, evidence-based medicine, large-scale computerization, and strong primary care health informatics.

Since 1948 health care in the United Kingdom has been centrally funded through the National Health Service which provides both primary and specialist health care which is largely free at the point of delivery. Family practitioners are responsible for registered populations of patients and typically work in groups of four to six self-employed physicians. They hire nurses and a range of other ancillary staff, and act as gatekeepers to specialist care. Recent reforms include a wide range of national quality improvement initiatives and a pay for performance scheme that now accounts for around 25% of family practitioner incomes.[14]

5.2 ESTABLISHING PROFESSIONAL ORGANIZATIONS FOR FAMILY DOCTORS

In most countries where family medicine has developed, a professional organization has been established by family doctors for family doctors. This section explores how professional organizations are established and why they are important for the development of family medicine.

What kind of professional organization?

Professional organizations of family doctors are called by different names in different countries and may serve different functions. They may be known as societies, associations, colleges, or academies. What matters is not the name, but the function performed by the organization. There are many different sorts of family medicine organizations and they may serve different functions within a country, for example political roles such as unionizing and networking.

Colleges should be standard setting, with accreditation to Fellowship through assessment, and providing reaccreditation in line with colleges of other medical specialties. Without this, family medicine cannot be viewed as a specialty alongside other medical specialties. Usually the accrediting college needs to be recognised by the medical council of that country.

National or regional organizations of family doctors often begin as a means of networking, organizing and facilitating communication among family doctors in a geographic area. Some countries organize all of their functions under one unifying organization. Others have several organizations that may serve distinct and complementary functions. For example, in the United Kingdom, the political, certifying, and academic functions are all roles of the Royal College of General Practitioners. In contrast, the United States has several organizations, including the American Academy of Family Physicians, the American Board of Family Practice, and the Society of Teachers of Family Medicine, each with defined roles.

Why establish a professional organization?

Organizations of family medicine exist to raise the standards of care for patients and communities. This is their unifying theme and their greatest success has been when responsibility to patients and to the community has been their paramount concern. For example, the mission of the Royal College of General Practitioners is "to encourage, foster and maintain the highest possible standards of general medical practice."

Another important goal of a professional organization is to establish family medicine as an independent discipline of equal importance and standing to other specialist medical disciplines – in other words, as an independent academic discipline in its own right. This includes facilitating the development of academic departments and faculties of family medicine in medical schools and recognition by the nation's medical specialty accreditation authority. The professional organization can play a central role in establishing positive relationships with politicians, health authorities, professional colleagues, medical schools, and the public. The professional association can also help provide the rationale and public support to obtain funding to establish academic departments in medical schools, faculty training programs, and model family practices in the community.

Family practice associations provide a rich array of expertise and resources to assist in the development of the specialty. They provide opportunities for family doctors to locate colleagues with shared interests and to collaborate on joint community and research projects. Family medicine networks at the local, regional, national, and international levels allow colleagues to develop specific aspects of the specialty, such as teaching, research, or quality improvement.

Another important activity of professional organizations is training new doctors in their chosen discipline and certifying that they are properly trained. Until national standards are established and widely disseminated, there will be confusion regarding the identity and skills of family doctors. National organizations can exert considerable influence on training programs by establishing minimum training requirements and core competencies for certification.[15]

Professional family medicine associations may supervise the process of certification or certifying bodies may be organized independently. There are a variety of approaches to certification.[16] These tend to fall into two categories: (1) meeting defined standards of professional performance in the setting of the family practice or (2) passing an examination. For example, the Royal New Zealand College of General Practitioners and the Royal Australian College of General Practitioners both provide options for candidates to qualify for specialty certification through clinical training and examinations or through practice eligibility routes.

In some countries, the standards for training and recertification of family doctors are more stringent than for some other medical specialties. The certification process for family doctors may include methods such as assessments of consultation and communication skills, practice management skills, ethical standards, patient satisfaction, and medical chart audits. In many countries, family doctors are required to complete a minimum number of hours of continuing medical education annually in order to maintain their certification. In the United States, the American Board of Family Practice was the first specialty society to require members to pass a recertification examination every 7 years.

Providing appropriate, continuing medical education for family doctors is another important service of national associations. This includes conducting educational programs as well as certifying that educational activities are well designed and appropriate for improving the skills of family doctors. The latter function is important because inappropriate educational activities may be intended to persuade family doctors to use specific products or unnecessarily refer patients to other sources of care.

When should a professional organization be established?

Forming an organization for family medicine depends on the development of a critical mass of enthusiastic family doctors. When family doctors are able to work together, share common goals, and have a clear idea that family medicine is an internationally recognized discipline that can play an important role in their country, they are often ready to form effective organizations.

It is not necessary to have large numbers of general practitioners to form an organization. The Royal College of General Practitioners, for example, was formed in 1952 by a steering committee of only 16 members.[15,17] To be productive, however, there needs to be a body of subscribing members who can, through their subscriptions, finance a fledgling organization. This will usually mean at least a few hundred members. The Royal College of General Practitioners got off to a good start when Foundation Membership was offered to established general practitioners who satisfied defined criteria, with 1655 doctors joining in the first 6 weeks.

It is not necessary for all who are eligible to become members. Some organizations have nearly all eligible doctors in their countries as subscribing members, while others may have only one third to one half of all eligible doctors as members. This also depends on the type of organization; for example, in a college accrediting to Fellowship status and also offering reaccredition, it may be necessary for all full members to be qualified family medicine specialists.

Who can become a member of a family medicine organization?

A major question is who should be the members and who should be the leaders of a family medicine organization. Such organizations are more likely to have an impact on family practice when they include and represent practicing family doctors in the country concerned.

A matter that frequently arises in the early phase of forming an organization is that of the qualifying credentials for membership. Most new colleges, associations or societies start by accepting any family doctor who is prepared to make a commitment and pay the initial subscription. As the specialty matures, more rigorous standards are often introduced and membership may be restricted to certified or recognized family doctors.

As primary care becomes increasingly multi-professional, some colleges and associations of family doctors may accept primary care nurses and other primary care health professionals as members. One of the first organizations to do this is in Hungary.[18] The Society of Teachers of Family Medicine in the United States accepts any teacher of family medicine, including nurses, psychologists, and anthropologists.

How to form a family medicine organization

How do family medicine organizations get started? The leadership of general practice organizations has to be drawn from family doctors themselves, both to demonstrate professional independence and also to create a cadre of family medicine leaders who may serve as role models. Typically, the leadership of family medicine organizations is assumed by charismatic, service-oriented family doctors with a clear vision and a strong sense of purpose. Such individuals usually have the ability to make things happen locally and a track record of success. They may or may not have established academic careers. The core characteristics of leadership in professional bodies are vision, the ability to speak and write well, good organizational skills, and dedication to the cause.

In some countries, the emerging professional organization may require the involvement or assistance of the government. The nation's chief doctor or minister of health may be particularly helpful. Every organization will operate within the culture and political system of its country, but it is desirable in the long term for these organizations to become fully independent of government. An example of the establishment of the College of Family Physicians in Poland and how this development has strengthened and enhanced family medicine and health care in that country is in Box 5.11.

One question to consider is whether or not the emerging family medicine organization should be an independent body or should begin as a branch of a specialist organization. Each choice has advantages and disadvantages. Becoming a branch of a well-established specialist organization has the advantage of an easier beginning, and immediate access to staff such as managers, public relations officers, and finance officers. It often means avoiding costs, such as those arising from setting up headquarters in an expensive building in a capital city. However, sometimes such organizations have not felt as independent as they would wish.

On the other hand, starting a new organization means a lot of work: setting up new systems for everything, usually renting premises, later fundraising to buy premises, and challenges in funding traveling expenses and staff, particularly in the early years. However, the advantages are self-government, real independence, and, in the long term, the likelihood of greater influence.

Where should a professional organization be based?

Professional organizations are mostly based and work within an individual country.

In smaller countries, it can be valuable to combine resources and have a college that spans more than one country – for example, the Caribbean College of Family Physicians (www.caribgp.org).

Most family medicine organizations have found it necessary to set up an office in the capital city of the country concerned. This is because political power tends to be located in the capital, and access to government ministers, civil servants, and leaders of other specialty groups provides an opportunity to influence policy.

BOX 5.11 Enhancement of family medicine and health care in Poland

A family doctor task force was established in Poland in 1991, with the aim of enhancing family medicine to improve the quality and efficiency of primary care. The group, which was based in the School of Public Health in Cracow, but working for the Ministry of Health, reviewed the job descriptions and responsibilities of family doctors in other countries and prepared a draft document on the responsibility of Polish family physicians. The draft was made available for review by the public, and a final version was presented to the national College of Family Physicians and the Ministry of Health for approval. The document defines areas of competence of a family practitioner in relation to prevention, diagnosis, treatment, and rehabilitation, separating the responsibilities of a family physician from those of other specialists. The document constitutes the official basis for family medicine and for determining the scope of educational programs.

The College of Family Physicians was established in Poland in 1992 by 34 people, including members of parliament, health care administrators, academics, community leaders and practicing doctors. According to its statutes, the College accepts as new members only physicians holding a diploma in family medicine. A strategic plan was developed to establish family medicine departments and residency training programs, and to enhance the practice of family medicine.

Success built during the first few years led to further enhancements in family medicine. The first educational journal for Polish family physicians, *Lekarz Rodzinny*, was started in 1996 as a tool for continuous medical education and a forum for discussion and exchange of experiences. The journal is published monthly, has over 6000 subscribers and is widely read by family doctors.

Today, over 5000 physicians hold a diploma in family medicine and over 25% of Polish inhabitants are served by family physicians. Over 80% of trained family physicians are members of the College of Family Physicians – an organization that plays a leading role in the implementation of family medicine and in health system reform.

The European Union provided US$14 million to support the establishment of nine university departments as regional training units for family physicians, as well as to provide initial training of consultative family medicine teaching staff in Western Europe. Three additional departments and 600 practices were financed by a World Bank loan. Modern family practices started work at the end of 1995 and by the end of the first year it was clear that they were more effective and efficient than the old model. Studies showed that they enjoyed a high level of acceptance by patients.

Family medicine was recognized as an independent medical specialty in Poland in 1996, not only by the government but also by the autonomous university, which established family medicine as a subject taught during basic medical education.

Source: Windak A (personal communication).

5.3 FINANCING PRIMARY HEALTH CARE SERVICES AND FAMILY DOCTORS

It can be assumed that implementation of government health policies and health initiatives will only succeed when health systems are rationally funded to achieve priority objectives. A priority goal of primary health care is to provide easy access to essential health services for all, with as few financial barriers as possible. A number of physician payment options may exist in any country or health care system. Payment options include fee for service, salaries, capitation payments, integrated capitation, and combination payment systems. While the advantages and disadvantages of each option may vary depending on considerations particular to a given country, some generalizations about the main systems of payment can be made.

Fee-for-service

In fee-for-service systems doctors are paid an amount of money for each service or activity they provide.[19] Fee-for-service systems are organized around fee schedules that classify physicians' activities with varying degrees of precision.[20] Using this system, medical practice can be influenced by selectively adjusting the fee schedule so physicians are only paid or paid relatively more for services considered to be effective. For example, payments for screening procedures or preventive services can be increased to stimulate these services.[21] Fee-for-service payment allows physicians to respond in a flexible manner to patients' perceived needs and connects financial payment directly with these activities. Some health systems that principally use fee-for-service payment have experienced spiraling costs resulting from the unrestrained incentive to pay for any service provided.

A recent study has found that newly practicing physicians in British Columbia, Canada, prefer alternatives to fee-for-service payment models. These models are perceived as contributing to fewer frustrations with billing systems, improved quality of work life, and better quality of patient care.[22]

In health systems financed by fee-for-service payments, patients may or may not be registered with specific primary care doctors. In addition, fee-for service payments may be associated with relatively higher payments for diagnostic studies and medical procedures, but relatively lower reimbursement for "cognitive" services, such as counseling and education, which are usually a feature of the practices of family doctors. As a consequence, the financing system may not reinforce the functions of the family doctor to provide continuous, coordinated, and comprehensive care.[23]

Despite several shortcomings, fee-for-service is still considered and retained as a remuneration model for many physician services.[24]

Salary

A salary system pays doctors a contractually agreed sum of money for a specified amount of time worked or patients treated. Salaried family doctors are able to combine many primary care roles with other administrative and public health duties.[25] Patients may or may not be registered with individual family doctors. If the level of remuneration is relatively low, morale may be adversely affected. Furthermore, in a fixed salary system, family doctors do not receive additional payment for exceeding the required patient load. This can undermine the efficiency and functioning of the system, particularly if the physician has the capacity to earn more in the private sector.[23]

Capitation payments

In a capitation-based financing system the health care professional is paid a specific sum of money for providing continuous care for a person or group of people for a particular period, however much or little the service is used.[21,28] For primary care, the system depends on patients being registered with a family doctor or group of family doctors that the patient is normally able to choose. The sum payable is usually fixed on a regular basis, often monthly and in advance of the period covered. This sum represents an estimate of how much it will cost to provide the patient's entire health care needs over that time period.[26]

There are several benefits of capitation payment systems for family doctors. This method of funding requires registration of patients with a specific family doctor or group. As a consequence, patient registries associated with capitation systems give family doctors a central role in caring for the patient's common health problems and in coordinating secondary and tertiary care. Capitation systems provide a fixed budget for family doctors to hire staff and buy equipment, and eliminate the administrative burden of sending bills and tracking payments for each service provided. Capitation systems encourage the development of partnerships for financial risk sharing. In the United Kingdom, where capitation payments comprise the major component of family doctor incomes, very few family doctors work in solo practice.[27] It is common for groups of doctors to organize after hours coverage for their patients by grouping together in cooperatives or working with commercial services.[28]

Capitation payment systems pay family doctors a fixed payment whether or not they see the patient and no more if they provide more costly services. This can be a disincentive to family doctors who wish to expand their scope of practice. Few if any systems rely solely on capitation payments to pay family doctors.[23]

In a study carried out on people with hypertension in Ontario, Canada, it was found there were differences in treatment and control rates, with capitation physicians having the best treatment and control rates in comparison with those on salary or fee-for-service model.[29]

Integrated capitation

In an integrated capitation system, payments made for services delivered by different providers or at different levels of care are incorporated into a defined sum of money. Integrated capitation differs from simple capitation by incorporating payments to cover specific additional expenditures such as drugs, diagnostics and some areas of secondary health care.[30] Hospital-based care may be included in an integrated capitation contract and provided by a larger group, such as the health maintenance organizations in the United States,[31] or may be purchased directly by family doctors. Integrated capitation facilitates continuity of care, interdisciplinary coordination, preventive services, and care for patients with chronic diseases, while permitting cost containment.[23]

In Belgium, a study by the Federal Knowledge Center on Health Care, revealed that compared to fee-for-service-financed practices, community health centers financed with integrated capitation were more accessible, especially for socially vulnerable groups of people. There were no indications for risk-selection. Moreover, in terms of quality, the performance of the family physicians in the capitated system was at least equal to the performance in the fee-for-service-system, and where differences appeared, the better quality was in the capitation system: better performance in prescription of antibiotics, better preventive services, more cost-effective drug prescription.[67]

Integrated capitation depends upon a list of patients registered with a family doctor. It exerts considerable pressure on family doctors to reduce patient access to costly investigations and referral to the secondary and tertiary care sectors.[23] This system may favor the selection of patients with low health risks and the rejection of those with high risks. Continuity of care and interdisciplinary coordination may be enhanced because there are incentives provided to physicians for disease management beyond the boundaries of primary care.

Combination payment systems

Each health care payment system has some disadvantages, so more countries are using a mixture of payment systems (*see* Box 5.12). Composite systems frequently include a basic payment, usually capitation or salary, with additional incentive payments or allowances to encourage selected clinical activities. Target payments may be used as incentives to provide certain types of service, such as immunization, or more frequent visits for people with chronic conditions such as diabetes. Additional payments may be given to reward family doctors or family practices that provide extra services over and above the normal contract or outside the usual working hours, such as being open in the evenings and weekends, conducting health education groups or providing services for the disadvantaged.

Pay-for-performance

In some countries, health care providers may be paid in relation to performance. In the United Kingdom, different domains of the Quality and Outcomes

BOX 5.12 Bamako Initiative[32]

In some communities, local people have assumed greater responsibility for health system guidance and financing. Through the Bamako Initiative launched in 1987, many African nations found that a combination of user fees and public funds could be used to improve the quality of primary care services. Follow-up revealed that, in some cases, the initiative generated additional funds, and increased quality and utilization of services, even among the very poor. However, for some groups, even minimal charges created obstacles and required further solutions to ensure equity. The 2010 World Health Report of the World Health Organization has recommended lowering out-of-pocket payments as the optimal way to ensure universal access to health care services.[33]

Framework have contributed to this payment system, and indicators have been created in order to assess the degree of clinician and practice "performance." Evaluation has shown that the quality of care, for those conditions included in the program, improved during the first year at a faster rate than the pre-intervention trend and subsequently returned to prior rates of improvement. There were modest cost-effective reductions in mortality and hospital admissions in some domains. Differences in performance narrowed in deprived areas compared with non-deprived areas. Doctors and nurses believe that the person-centeredness of consultations and continuity of care were negatively affected by this system of payment. Patients' satisfaction with continuity of care declined, with little change in other domains of patient experience. Observed improvements in quality of care for chronic diseases were modest. Health care organizations should remain cautious about the benefits of similar schemes.[68]

Finding the best way

There is no ideal single method for remunerating family doctors to encourage the provision of every facet of continuing, high-quality primary care. The advantages and disadvantages of each method of payment were analyzed by a group of 57 delegates from 56 countries,[34] who found that there was little valid literature available but concluded that a mixed payment system may be the most effective.

Family doctors may be best funded when they are supported as a component of comprehensive primary health care services, and through a combination of capitation or salaried payment plus targeted payments to encourage specific services. Equity is achieved when primary care systems are funded so that the entire population has ready access to services, with limited financial barriers for essential care. Box 5.13 lists financing strategies that are likely to improve the quality and comprehensiveness of primary care services.

BOX 5.13 Financing strategies to improve primary health care services

- Provide sufficient funding to support a strong primary care infrastructure
- Minimize financial barriers for people to access essential health services
- Provide financial and other incentives to attract family doctors to areas of greatest need
- Use a combination of payment methods to support and reward high-quality, comprehensive, equitable primary care services
- Measure performance and provide incentives for targeted services such as preventive health care

---

5.4 IMPROVING ACCESS TO PRIMARY CARE

The goal of providing equitable health care for all has implications for health workforce policies and the recruitment and training of family doctors. In general, if health professionals are allowed to select their practice locations, they tend to choose environments with which they are familiar, where they have family or friends, or where there are good social, cultural, economic, and educational opportunities. Preparing and recruiting family doctors and other health professionals to provide care for the disadvantaged – those who lack access to essential health care services because of financial, geographical, ethnic, racial, or other barriers – presents special challenges.

Difficult working conditions including poverty, limited educational and employment opportunities, and high crime rates frequently characterize disadvantaged rural and urban communities. Because the disadvantaged are frequently poor, and poverty is a risk factor for poor health outcomes, the disadvantaged often suffer disproportionately from increased morbidity and premature mortality.

Much of the world's population lives in rural areas and people in rural and remote communities universally have poorer health than urban people. Often the health status of special needs groups, such as women or elderly or indigenous people, is worse in rural areas than in metropolitan areas. Despite this, rural health services command proportionately fewer resources and staff than urban health services in almost every country in the world. The worldwide shortage of rural health professionals results in those working in rural areas often becoming overworked and isolated, compounding the problems of recruitment and retention.

Because family doctors are trained to provide comprehensive health care services and can work as coordinators and leaders in primary care, their presence ensures that a comprehensive array of health services is provided. In areas where other health professionals provide the majority of primary care, integrating family doctors into the teams will enhance the scope and quality of health services provided at the local level. Focused strategies and incentives are necessary to recruit family doctors and other health professionals to disadvantaged areas to attain the goal of universal access by all people to primary care.

Recruiting family doctors to work in disadvantaged areas

Targeted recruitment programs may be necessary to identify and prepare the health care workforce needed for disadvantaged communities. Medical students who come from disadvantaged populations, or who have spent considerable time living and working in areas with such populations, are more likely to ultimately practice in these areas. Since areas with disadvantaged populations may not offer students the same educational opportunities, special programs may be required to attract youth from these areas to careers in the health professions, and to prepare them for the rigors of medical education. Another way of drawing health professionals toward practice in disadvantaged areas is to ensure that they spend time training in such areas. If students and trainees find these experiences stimulating and rewarding, they are more likely to consider such areas for their future practice, particularly when incentives are provided.

The Training in Health Equity Network (www.thenetcommunity.org) brings together medical schools that make a special effort to recruit medical students from remote and underserved areas, in order to better respond to the needs of those communities. This is an example of the increasing emphasis on the need for social accountability by those institutions responsible for the education of medical and other health professionals.[69]

Providing incentives or requirements for work in disadvantaged areas

Financial incentives and educational or service requirements are common strategies to increase the numbers of health professionals in disadvantaged areas. In some countries service requirements are imposed on the entire medical student population. Graduates who are required to complete a period of practice in disadvantaged areas, unless appropriately trained and adequately supported to function as generalist physicians, may deliver low-quality care and be likely to leave the area as soon as their term of compulsory service has ended.

One strategy to recruit family doctors to disadvantaged areas is to increase reimbursement rates or salaries for providing care in such communities. In countries where physicians have to borrow money to finance their training, loan repayment programs are often used to encourage practice in disadvantaged areas. Such loan repayments are often provided in proportion to the number of years the physician practices in an area of need. Once health professionals begin to practice in such areas they often find the work rewarding and are willing to make long-term commitments. Such financial strategies and educational or service requirements are most effective when integrated with overall systems of financing health care services for poor and vulnerable populations.

Supporting family doctors to practice in disadvantaged areas

Family doctors who work with rural and remote populations often need additional skills to be able to manage patients with surgical or other life-threatening emergencies or to provide culturally sensitive care to special populations. They may require protocols for remote consultation with other specialist doctors, specific language or cultural training, or an understanding of the local particularities of team management. Efficient systems of continuing and remote medical education are especially important for health professionals who practice in relative isolation. When family doctors have the opportunity to gain and maintain special skills, and are exposed to the realities of practice among disadvantaged groups during their specialty training, they are better prepared to meet community health needs, more confident of their abilities, and more likely to remain in disadvantaged areas.

Associations and networks of health professionals practicing in disadvantaged areas provide additional support. When resources are available, air transport has the potential to reduce isolation and speed the transfer of emergency patients from rural areas. Modern communication tools such as the Internet and satellite-based telephones may be used to provide rapid consultation and reduce the isolation of rural health professionals anywhere in the world. Professional associations offer opportunities for education, networking, problem solving, recognition, and other important social benefits. Box 5.14 lists some ways of attracting family doctors to work in disadvantaged areas.

No single strategy is likely to be effective in addressing the health needs of disadvantaged groups of people. Multiple strategies involving the health system, financing, policy development, and educational programs can prepare, recruit, and support family doctors to provide optimal care in areas where high-quality primary care is so desperately needed.

A well-planned and evidence-based approach is the only way forward to ensure universal access to primary care for all populations. Access to people-centered care is essential and provision of health services through a well-defined health system with a prime focus on a primary care model delivered by trained family doctors is the single most appropriate step to achieve health for all.[35]

BOX 5.14 How to encourage family doctors to work in medically disadvantaged areas

- Promote health policy and financing mechanisms that support primary care and the equitable distribution of health resources
- Recruit and select health professional students from disadvantaged areas
- Ensure that medical training includes experience providing health care to members of disadvantaged populations
- Provide doctors with the skills needed to practice in disadvantaged areas
- Require all new graduates to undertake a period of service in disadvantaged areas
- Enhance infrastructure and support networks
- Provide financial and other incentives to encourage and support family doctors working in disadvantaged areas
- Work with local communities on strategies to enhance recruitment and retention of family doctors

---

5.5 SUPPORTING PRIMARY CARE RESEARCH

Research conducted in the context of primary care is broadly divided into five categories as listed in Box 5.15.

BOX 5.15 Primary care research categories[36]

1. *Basic research*: to develop research methods in the discipline
2. *Clinical research*: to inform clinical practice
3. *Health services research*: to improve health service delivery
4. *Health systems research*: to improve health systems and policies
5. *Educational research*: to improve education for primary care clinicians

---

Consistent with the breadth of primary health care, related research encompasses a broad range of topics including producing evidence to guide the treatment of people with diseases, not just diseases in isolation.[37]

Examples of research that can best be done in primary care settings include:
➤ epidemiology and natural history of common primary care problems
➤ effectiveness of diagnosis and treatment of health problems in primary care

➤ methods to improve the process of primary care, including team development

➤ methods to improve the integration of community primary care with secondary and tertiary care

➤ the relevance of evidence-based medicine and treatment guidelines for patients seen in primary care with multiple problems or for people seen in different care settings

➤ methods to integrate preventive services with ongoing illness-oriented care

➤ reduction in errors and increase in patient safety in primary care

➤ determinants of patient and doctor satisfaction in primary care

➤ methods to improve education and research in primary care settings.

There is a particular need for effectiveness research – a continuing assessment of how one can, or when one should, translate health care research results into practice. There is also a need for research that defines the process and activities of primary care practice,[38] to help understand how to better apply clinical knowledge from other settings to community practice, to guide future research about patient care, and to inform policy makers and educators.

Five decades ago, most medical research was conducted in hospitals or academic medical centers and with a reductionist, biomedical model to make technical advances to patient care. This has changed in the last 2 decades and a substantial amount of primary care research is being conducted in primary care settings. It is important to ask research questions in a variety of settings outside the hospital, as populations, disease patterns, and care systems differ, not only between countries but also in various regions of the same country. The focus on biomedical research and its application in hospital settings leaves many questions of importance to family medicine and wider primary care unasked and unanswered, and deprives the discipline of the robust research needed to improve practice and gain academic credibility.[39] A new domain for challenge in research for family medicine and primary health care is the approach to multimorbidity, and the question how to make a paradigm-shift from "problem-oriented" to "goal-oriented" care.[70]

Many important research questions can only be answered by physicians in community practice settings.[40] For example, a study of an intervention for alcohol abuse showed that brief advice by the primary physician is effective in reducing the rate of problem drinking for up to 1 year following the intervention.[41] Another study showed the effectiveness of aspirin and the lack of effectiveness of vitamin E for reducing coronary morbidity in people seen in primary care practices.[42]

To increase the relevance of research to community-based practice, family doctors need to be involved in defining goals, questions, and methods of this research. For example, much of the interest in the problem of medical errors has focused on errors that occur in hospitals.[43] This problem needs to be addressed in community practice as well, with the collaboration of community physicians.[44]

An important benefit of primary care research is that it provides a venue for collaboration with specialists in other areas. Such collaboration enhances the intellectual richness of family medicine in both clinical and research areas. This in turn promotes family medicine as part of the academic and clinical mainstream. Being part of the mainstream is essential to the recruitment of excellent research students and academic staff members. Finally, and perhaps most important, research activities help to establish a scholarly role and a critical thinking mind set among family doctors that can lead to improvements in their quality of practice.

Challenges for research in family medicine

Research in family medicine draws on the strengths of a variety of available patient populations, problems, and practice settings that can serve as natural laboratories. Yet the lack of experienced researchers in family practice limits the amount, scope, and quality of research that can be conducted. Family doctors and other health professionals with interest and expertise in primary care are often underrepresented on grant development and grant review panels, which is likely to restrict the quantity and quality of projects in primary care research. Similarly, family doctors find it difficult to invest the time and money required to apply successfully for research project funding.[45,46] As a result, despite recognition of the need for primary care research,[47,48] government and philanthropic funding remains insufficient, especially for needed infrastructure such as equipment and research staff.

Strategies to enhance research in family medicine

Building a robust research enterprise comparable with that of other medical specialties requires contributions from busy individual family doctors. It also requires reallocation of funds, time, and resources within academic institutions, and support from national and other funding agencies to ensure that a significant portion of each nation's health and medical research focuses on the health problems most of the people have most of the time.[49]

A renewed commitment to the role of research will be necessary in many countries, even those with well-developed academic family medicine departments and active professional societies. To achieve this goal, family doctors and their academic organizations may need to move on several fronts simultaneously.

It will be necessary for family physicians in community and academic settings to devote significant time and effort to designing and conducting worthwhile research projects, and writing applications to obtain funding. When successful with grant applications, family medicine researchers are then likely to be invited to participate in grant review panels and thereby begin to change the reductionist mindset typical of such panels. The research efforts of family doctors and group practices can also be enhanced through support, incentives, and grants from academic and practice organizations.

Individual family doctors, academic departments, and professional societies can work to raise the awareness among governmental and philanthropic donor agencies of the importance of funding primary care research. Most donor agencies are likely to support research for specific diseases, and individual bequests are usually made to foundations that fund research on a specific disease or group of diseases, such as cancer, rather than to support research on the comprehensive care that sustained the patient over many years. Agencies and benefactors need to be convinced of the importance of funding basic infrastructure for primary care research as well as for research into specific diseases.

In order to mature as a specialty, family medicine needs experienced researchers. In many countries leaders of the new discipline lack formal research training or skills, are busy establishing vocational training and medical student programs, and deal with a host of educational, political, administrative, and funding matters that preclude an emphasis on research. Most academic departments of family medicine, however, have at best a very small number of experienced researchers. A growing number of family medicine organizations are starting to provide primary care research training programs. Some university departments of family medicine are making efforts to involve students in research activities and to encourage them to enter the discipline.

One solution to the lack of available mentorship is to establish close working relations with skilled researchers in other disciplines who can mentor new family physician researchers. Beyond mentorship, there are other reasons for collaborating with researchers in different fields of study, including other medical specialties, nursing, pharmacology, engineering, and anthropology, to name a few. The dialogue between disciplines provides the family physician researcher with expertise in different topics and methodologies, while helping other researchers understand the importance of primary care. This collaboration can also help family doctors learn how to tailor their funding applications to the interests of funding agencies. It is also possible to receive funding for participation in research projects originating in other fields.

Clinical family medicine and primary care networks provide an important means of supporting practice-based research.[45,50–52,65] Effective networks can increase the productivity of research efforts.[50,53,54] Practice-based research networks can stimulate research interest among community-based clinicians and make possible the participation of family doctors in all phases of project development and execution.

They can serve as a focal point for research activities by sponsoring meetings and workshops, and form a bridge between academic institutions and the community. Virtually all successful networks are partnerships between academic institutions and groups of community-based physicians. They are often housed in academic institutions and include an academic family doctor who is funded to provide time, support, and expertise.

Primary care research may be promoted through international collaboration. In many countries, organizations of family doctors face challenges of limited resources as they work to identify and address specific research needs. The potential for fruitful international collaboration, as primary care researchers share questions, methods, and new information for practice, continues to grow.[53,55,56]

BOX 5.16 How to promote primary care research (World Organization of Family Doctors Kingston conference recommendations)[57]

1. World Organization of Family Doctors (WONCA) must develop a strategy to display research achievements in family medicine to policy makers, health (insurance) authorities and academic leaders.
2. WONCA should seek the development in all its member countries of sentinel practices to provide surveillance reports on illness and diseases that have the greatest impact on patients' health and wellness in the community.
3. WONCA should organize a clearinghouse for research expertise, training and mentoring.
4. WONCA should stimulate the development of national research institutes and university departments of Family Medicine with a research mission.
5. WONCA should organize an expert group to provide advice for the development of practice based research networks around the world.
6. WONCA should promote research journals, conferences and websites for the international dissemination of research findings.
7. WONCA should facilitate funding of international collaborative research.
8. WONCA should organize international ethical standards for international research cooperation and develop an international ethical review process.
9. WONCA should address in any recommendations for family medicine research the specific needs and implications for developing countries.

The World Organization of Family Doctors (WONCA) held a meeting in Kingston, Canada, of leading primary care researchers from across the globe. It came up with nine recommendations to promote primary care research (*see* Box 5.16).[57]

Researchers may collaborate through groups such as WONCA, the North American Primary Care Research Group, and the European General Practice Research Network. Such groups of primary care researchers share ideas, and organizational and methodological expertise, to sustain and encourage one another in uniting practice and research to improve patient care (*see* Box 5.17).

BOX 5.17 Ways to promote primary care research

- Promote commitment to primary care research among:
  - family doctors
  - professional societies
  - academic institutions
  - government
  - philanthropic agencies
  - the public
- Develop research projects
- Improve research methodologies
- Train more primary care researchers
- Solicit a larger base of donors and other funders for primary care research projects
- Develop and participate in primary care research networks

5.6 ENHANCING QUALITY OF CARE AND OUTCOMES

There are wide variations in medical practice patterns and outcomes both within and between countries, and many opportunities to improve the quality, efficiency, and effectiveness of health care delivery. If family medicine is to fulfill its potential to meet the needs of patients and communities, delivering the highest possible quality of care is of critical importance. The complexity and scope of family practice, as well as its interface with many other aspects of the health system, make this goal particularly challenging.

Goals and definitions

Quality in health care encompasses many complex and interrelated characteristics (*see* Table 5.2). It may also be viewed from a variety of perspectives. Patients, health care professionals, researchers, educators, public health officials, health system funding agencies, politicians, and others may each legitimately consider different aspects of health care as the most important. Ultimately, it is the totality of a health care experience that influences the patient's perception of quality. One negative incident, such as rude behavior from a staff member, may substantially diminish a person's perception of the quality of the entire experience.

Quality in health care may apply to the structure, process, or outcomes of care. Structure includes personnel, facilities, equipment, organization, and coverage arrangements. Process includes activities involved in providing or receiving care, and attributes such as timeliness and continuity. Outcomes may include morbidity and mortality data, as well as quality of life and patient satisfaction.

TABLE 5.2 Dimensions of quality in health care[58,59]

Dimension	Characteristics
Equity	Services are provided to all who require them
Accessibility	Ready access to services is ensured
Acceptability	Care meets the expectations of those who use the services
Appropriateness	Required care is provided; unnecessary or harmful care is avoided
Comprehensiveness	Care provision covers all aspects of disease management from prevention to rehabilitation; psychosocial aspects of care are considered
Effectiveness/Efficiency	Care produces positive change in the health status or quality of life of the patient; high-quality care is provided at the lowest possible cost
Safety	Avoidance or reduction to acceptable limits of actual or potential harm from health care management or the environment in which health care is delivered

Achieving high-quality health care is not a one-time effort; it requires continuous attention. Responding to new information and developments in medicine means ceaseless efforts to ensure that family doctors deliver high-quality services based on the best current evidence for practice. The WONCA Working Party on Quality in Family Medicine (Box 5.18) defines high-quality health care as: "the best health outcomes that are possible, given available resources, and that are consistent with patient values and preferences."

Professional perspectives of quality

For health care professionals, quality of care has often focused on providing competent, effective and safe care that contributes to health and well-being. Clinical performance can be assessed by measuring the extent to which the services

> **BOX 5.18** Mission of the World Organization of Family Doctors Working Party on Quality in Family Medicine[60]
>
> The mission of the World Organization of Family Doctors Working Party on Quality in Family Medicine is to support family doctors around the world in their efforts to review systematically and improve continuously the quality of health care they provide.
>
> This mission is based on the following principles.
>
> - To improve the quality of care, family doctors strive for the best structure, process, and outcomes of health care consistent with patient values and preferences, consistent with professional knowledge of appropriate and effective care, and given available resources.
> - Quality efforts should promote accountability, and reflect a partnership between patients and health care professionals.
> - Quality efforts should be explicit, systematic, a routine of daily practice, an integral aspect of basic and continuing medical education, consistent with the special role and setting of the family doctor, and applied in a positive, not punitive, manner.

delivered are consistent with the current state of knowledge and provided in a timely manner.

One approach is to measure quality against standards for good practice. Evidence-based practice guidelines, usually developed through a process of group consensus, compile findings from multiple sources and outline the best recommendations for managing frequently occurring problems. Their usefulness is enhanced by flexibility (enabling them to be modified according to local circumstances), conciseness, reminder systems, and educational activities that support implementation.[61]

Family doctors also recognize and value the humanistic and qualitative aspects of patient care, such as establishing therapeutic relationships, providing respect and empathy, addressing patient fears and sharing decision-making with patients and families. Health system managers and funders often emphasize such important aspects of quality as efficiency, logistics, available supplies, accurate record keeping, and cost-effectiveness. Public health officials often focus on measurable indicators and outcomes, such as achieving specific immunization rates or reducing age-specific mortality rates. Academics and health system managers view educational scholarship and research as tools to assess and improve quality.

Traditional quality indicators commonly address the accuracy of the diagnostic process and the appropriateness of the therapy for particular diagnoses. Although these are critical considerations, they provide an incomplete reflection of the complexity, richness, and depth of patient-doctor interactions. Thus efforts have been made to supplement conventional indicators with approaches more focused on patients' problems, their functional health status, their ability to perform activities of daily living and their health-related quality of life, including estimates of the years they would be expected to live in good health. These indicators improve capacity to assess the overall health of a population, judge the efficacy of interventions, and make comparisons across populations.

Patient satisfaction

People often evaluate quality based on whether their expectations are met in their interactions with health professionals. Patient expectation and patient satisfaction surveys are very useful tools to monitor and improve quality in family practice.[62]

Patient satisfaction may be measured and regularly reassessed, such as the time a patient spends waiting for a visit, the patient's confidence in the competence of the treating doctor and other members of the primary care team, the patient's perception of being understood and respected, and the patient's assessment of their doctor's communication skills and the friendliness and helpfulness of the office staff. Several patient survey tools are available and offer the means to incorporate into clinical practice the opportunity to monitor and improve patient satisfaction (aafp.mydocsurvey.com).

Assessment of quality in health systems

Health care quality may be influenced at many levels and by many components of the health care system. At the level of the individual health care professional, quality is determined by interactions between the patient and doctor. At the level of the practice, quality is affected by the patient's interactions with their family doctor, receptionists, clinical staff, nurses, and ancillary services. At the local level, groups of doctors, clusters of practices, and the availability of resources and facilities will have an impact on quality. At regional and national levels, health care policies, financing, allocation of resources, information gathering, and standards of education and certification can influence quality and structures of care throughout the health system. Information derived from each level of the health system may be used to assess different aspects of quality (*see* Table 5.3).

TABLE 5.3 Sources of data to assess quality of health care

Level of care	Examples of data sources
Individual family doctor	Patient satisfaction surveys
	Medical record reviews
Family practices and other community-based health centers	Aggregate patient satisfaction surveys
	Group record audits
Local health system	Hospital records
	Pharmacy data
	Local public health data (e.g., birth and death certificates)
	Financial data
Regional or national	Morbidity/mortality rates across health system
	Expenditures

Planning to improve the quality of family medicine

Given the broad scope of family practice, growing expectations for health care, limited resources, and rapid developments in medical information, achieving the best quality presents special challenges for family doctors. Additionally, as family doctors often work in health care teams, systematic team efforts are necessary to improve the quality of care.

Each level of the health system provides opportunities to enhance the quality of care. At the level of the individual family doctor, their abilities, interests, training, certification, and participation in continuing education influence competency and quality. While each physician is responsible for maintaining professional skills and knowing her or his own limitations, requirements for professional certification and incentives for quality performance will influence the physician's motivation.

At the practice level, quality can be enhanced when teams work collectively toward shared goals. In these settings, small practice groups or clinical networks may select specific areas for quality improvement, such as increasing immunization rates or improving blood pressure control. Increasingly, doctors and other health professionals pool their efforts to develop formal or informal practice networks, to critically examine current medical studies, and to develop evidence-based guidelines for high-quality care.

At the national level, government or professional associations can require regular review and certification of doctors and their practices. These standards often include requirements for training, examination, continuing education, and practice audits. Many countries have found that investments to improve quality result in better health outcomes, reduce costs, and enhance effectiveness.

Quality improvement efforts also occur at an international level. The European working party on Quality in Family Practice (EquiP) includes more than 30 countries that meet regularly to undertake collaborative quality improvement projects. Such groups work together to develop international guidelines and standards for performance. However, universal guidelines require adaptation and consideration of resources and cultural factors for successful implementation at the local level.

The process of quality improvement

Improving the quality of health care, regardless of the level of care, involves teams of individuals who collaborate to achieve shared goals. The planning process usually begins with an analysis of the current situation. For example, a small group may meet to analyze and identify the group's strengths, weaknesses, opportunities, and threats (SWOT). A SWOT analysis or similar procedure allows the group to identify and celebrate strengths, and to consider any identified weaknesses as opportunities for future growth and development.

After considering the potential opportunities, the group may then select a priority for quality improvement. This allows the group to focus their efforts, consider needs for funding and other resources, and anticipate potential problems. Selecting a specific problem that is feasible given available resources increases the chances of success. Involving key individuals who will participate in quality improvement efforts increases their motivation to participate in subsequent actions and analyses. Ideally, both those who will implement and those who will be affected by the changes should be consulted to obtain their advice and commitment to participate, and to establish realistic goals.

Many potential areas for improvement exist in a typical family practice, but they cannot all be dealt with at once. It is more effective to start by selecting one important problem area for improvement, collecting baseline information, implementing changes, and evaluating the impact. After completing an initial, successful quality improvement project, the practice team is usually enthusiastic about participating in subsequent projects.

Often, groups find the stepwise quality cycle a useful framework for improvement efforts. Many possible variations to this cycle exist, and the steps need not be completed in the order listed in Box 5.19.

Teaching to improve quality

While most health professionals understand the importance of quality improvement in health care, many are less knowledgeable about how to initiate and manage systematic quality improvement.

Quality improvement skills may be introduced early in the medical school

---

BOX 5.19 How to improve health care quality

- Select a topic or problem for quality improvement
- Form a team to address the topic
- Collect baseline data
- Reflect on current practices
- Plan changes
- Change work processes
- Collect data to assess the impact of changes
- Reflect on results
- Adjust process further if needed
- Measure again the impact of changes

---

curriculum, further developed through vocational training, and enhanced through lifelong, continuing medical education. Education can provide trainees with the attitudes, knowledge, and skills to critically evaluate medical literature and to participate in research to generate knowledge when the literature cannot provide answers. When integrated into the continuum of family medicine education, skills for quality improvement may be developed at all levels of training.

Students can be introduced to quality improvement concepts and tools in medical school. The curriculum should include an introduction to the various aspects of quality, methods for measurement, and the steps necessary to complete the project. Problem-based learning techniques may be used to engage small groups of students in the development of a quality improvement project. Case reviews will allow students to understand the processes and potential pitfalls associated with improvement efforts. Small groups of students can be given the task of assessing aspects of quality and completing projects.

Specialty training provides opportunities to infuse trainees with the attitudes, knowledge, and skills for lifelong quality improvement. The curriculum can introduce trainees to the fundamentals of quality, while clinical experience will provide ample material for projects. Although the fundamentals of quality improvement can be introduced in classroom settings, the application of knowledge and skills to clinical problems allows trainees to experience the complexity and satisfaction of a real project and is likely to instill confidence and enthusiasm for participation in future quality improvement efforts (*see* Box 5.20). Not all quality improvement projects are successful, and teams sometimes become disheartened. Guidance from experienced mentors can steer early learners toward projects that are more likely to result in substantial quality improvement.

BOX 5.20 Family medicine trainees improving quality of care in South Africa[60]

Medunsa University in South Africa provides opportunities for physicians in government clinics and hospitals or private practice to complete family medicine specialty training through distance learning. Participants complete 12 learning tasks related to their clinical practice, a master's dissertation, and a final examination. One of the learning tasks is to complete a quality improvement project. Trainees are expected to find and weigh clinical evidence, to measure, analyze, reflect, and change a specific practice.

Through one such project, a trainee and his local health team identified a problem of high mortality rates during weekend and night shifts in a rural community hospital. By developing new on-call and reporting arrangements, mortality was reduced by nearly 20% over a period of 4 months. The trainee not only learned important lessons about quality improvement but also contributed to improvements in patient care.

Continuing medical education

While quality training may begin in medical school and be further developed during specialty training in family medicine, ongoing professional training and support allow family doctors to maintain high-quality care throughout a lifetime of practice. Continuing education is most useful to practicing physicians when it employs the principles of adult self-directed learning, is based on experience and related to current practice, and allows opportunities for discussion and reflection among supportive groups of colleagues.

As many practicing physicians have not received formal training in quality improvement, an understanding of the concepts and skills is also important. These physicians will benefit from targeted instruction that addresses the following knowledge and skills:

➤ dimensions of quality in health care
➤ the process of quality improvement and how to select and complete a project
➤ how to select target groups that will benefit from the quality improvement activity
➤ assessing the process, structures, and outcomes of family medicine and its relationship to the health and social systems
➤ assessing the costs, benefits, and effectiveness of quality improvement methods
➤ understanding variations of performance in processes and systems

➤ understanding how to develop new, locally useful knowledge through research.

When family doctors learn to apply these skills in their practices, and receive feedback and support from colleagues, they are able to lead and participate in ongoing quality initiatives in a variety of clinical settings.

How to assist family doctors to improve quality

While teaching the principles and processes of quality improvements are important, knowledge and skills are not sufficient to assure that quality efforts are routinely included in family practice. Resources, incentives, and support systems can assist efforts to make the achievement of high-quality patient care a priority in family medicine. Some useful strategies are listed in Box 5.21.

BOX 5.21 Strategies to support quality improvement efforts

- Engage leaders, stakeholders, and participants in understanding and supporting quality-improvement efforts
- Gain commitment to quality at local, regional, and national levels
- Allocate financial and human resources to quality improvement as a routine part of clinical services
- Provide incentives to assess and improve quality
- Consider the social, economic, and cultural context to select realistic priorities
- Establish standards and enforce regulations to identify and improve substandard services
- Consider certification, recertification, or accreditation to ensure that family doctors develop and maintain appropriate skills
- Establish or join quality improvement networks

This brief introduction is provided as a starting point for those interested in improving the quality of health care through family medicine. A number of international and national organizations, many as members of WONCA, are networking to establish consortia to share findings and strategies. In particular, the resources *Family Doctors' Journey to Quality*[60] and *Tools and Methods for Quality Improvement* compiled by EquiP[63] provide many instruments that may be adapted for local use.

Continuing efforts to improve the quality of family medicine will enhance the effectiveness of family doctors in improving the health of their patients and their communities.

5.7 MOVING AHEAD

Family medicine is most likely to improve health system performance when based on careful consideration of local conditions. Countries in political transition face challenges as they attempt to forge a consensus in the direction that health care should take. Countries with large financial debts may have insufficient resources to make needed changes. Countries attempting to reform their health systems may face challenges in mobilizing groups of private practitioners toward supporting the broader societal goals of equity and access to essential services for the poor and other vulnerable groups of people. Family medicine will evolve differently in these different environments.

The future roles of family doctors should be considered in the wider context of health system improvements. Family doctors' contributions will be enhanced when they are integrated into effective primary health care delivery systems. Therefore, planning for the development or expansion of family medicine includes developing a vision, collaborating with key stakeholders, determining short- and long-term goals, and improving health service delivery. When planners agree that health systems should be established on the values of equity, quality, relevance, and cost-effectiveness, these values will guide program development.

Collaborative efforts among citizens, communities, health system leaders, health professionals, academics, and government authorities have considerable potential to create the conditions necessary for change, particularly when these groups establish sustainable partnerships. It is the implementation of collaborative, intersectoral programs at the local level that presents the greatest challenges and holds the greatest promise for meaningful improvements in health systems,[64] primary health care, and family medicine. Box 5.22 lists some of the essential elements to be considered in planning a family medicine program.

BOX 5.22 Elements of family medicine program planning

- Delineate the ideal profile and desired competencies of family doctors
- Enlist support from key stakeholders
- Determine plans for education, accreditation, and certification
- Develop specific training programs
- Determine short- and long-term needs
- Collaborate with stakeholders including other health professionals
- Develop integrated practice models
- Establish budget and acquire financial resources
- Assess costs, benefits, and areas for improvement
- Describe career paths and professional opportunities for family doctors

---

This guidebook provides a compass, map, and directions to assist in the never-ending journey toward improving health systems. Even when well planned, journeys are often full of unexpected twists and turns. A guidebook cannot prepare travelers for all conditions. Readers who continue the journey of improving health systems with family medicine are invited to share your ideas, feedback, progress reports, and updates with WONCA. Your contributions will be reviewed, compiled, and used to assist future travelers.

For family medicine to serve as the backbone of an equitable, high-quality, comprehensive, primary care delivery system, many complex and interrelated issues need to be considered. The evidence is clear that family medicine has the potential to assist health systems to provide comprehensive, high-quality, and affordable health care for all. The ability of family doctors to fulfill this potential will depend on the decisions, resources, and capacities of the health systems in which they will function.

This guidebook aims to provide health system decision makers with relevant knowledge and tools to facilitate the process of improving health systems to better meet the health care needs of all people in the world.

REFERENCES

1. Strumpf E, Levesque JF, Coyle N, et al. Innovative and diverse strategies toward primary health care reform: lessons learned from the Canadian experience. *Journal of the American Board of Family Medicine.* 2012; **25**(Suppl. 1): S27–33.
2. Phillips RL. International learning on increasing the value and effectiveness of primary care (I LIVE PC). *Journal of the American Board of Family Medicine.* 2012; **25**(Suppl 1): S2–5.
3. Qidwai W, Khoja TAM, Inem V, et al. Strategies to improve status of family physicians: a perspective from an international collaboration. *Middle East Journal of Family Medicine.* 2008; **6**(6); 12–19.
4. Qidwai W, Samani ZAA, Huda SA. Perceptions about family physicians: results of a patient survey in Karachi, Pakistan. *Journal of Liaquat University of Medicine and Health Sciences.* 2004; **3**(2): 74–8.
5. Roland, Guthrie B, Thome DC. Primary medical care in the United Kingdom. *Journal of the American Board of Family Medicine.* 2012; **25**(supp 1): S6–S11.
6. Qidwai W, Beasley JW, Francisco JGC, et al. The present status and future role of family doctors: a perspective from International Federation of Primary Care Research Networks. *Primary Health Care Research and Development.* 2008; **9**: 172–82.
7. Heath I. Boundaries: complementarity and co-operation. The pivotal role of the general practitioner in relation to primary and secondary care. In: Scott Brown S (ed). *Physician Funding and Health Care Systems: an international perspective.* London: Royal College of General Practitioners, 1999.
8. Haight KR. Family medicine in the undergraduate curriculum: differing views on where from here? *Canadian Family Physician.* 1987; **33**: 2792–4.
9. www.chanrobles.com/legal4nhia.htm
10. Goodyear-Smith F, Gauld R, Cumming J, et al. International learning on increasing

the value and effectiveness of primary care (I LIVE PC) in New Zealand. *Journal of the American Board of Family Medicine.* 2012; **25**(Suppl. 1): S39–44.

11. Nicholson C, Jackson CL, Marley JE, et al. The Australian experiment: how primary health care organizations supported the evolution of a primary health care system. *Journal of the American Board of Family Medicine.* 2012; **25**(Suppl. 1): S18–26.

12. Pedersen KM, Andersen JS, Sondergaard J. General practice and primary health care in Denmark. *Journal of the American Board of Family Medicine.* 2012; **25**(Suppl. 1): S34–8.

13. Van Weel C, Schers H, Timmermans A. Health care in the Netherlands. *Journal of the American Board of Family Medicine.* 2012; **25**(Suppl. 1): S12–17.

14. Roland M, Guthrie B, Thome DC. Primary medical care in the United Kingdom. *Journal of the American Board of Family Medicine.* 2012; **25**(Suppl. 1): S6–11.

15. Pereira Gray DJ. History of the Royal College of General Practitioners -the first 40 years. *British Journal of General Practice.* 1992; **42**: 29–35.

16. Royal College of General Practitioners. *Fellowship by Assessment.* London: Royal College of General Practitioners 1995 (Occasional Paper 50, 2nd ed.).

17. Fry J, Lord Hunt of Fawley, Pinsent RJFH. *A History of the Royal College of General Practitioners: the first 25 years.* Lancaster: MTP, 1983.

18. Steele RJF. *Can Educational Methods Developed for Training General Practitioners in the UK be Taught to Doctors and Nurses Working in Primary Health Care in Hungary?* Exeter: University of Exeter, 2000 (MPhil thesis).

19. Rice T. Physicians' payment policies: impacts and implications. *Annual Review of Public Health.* 1997; **18**: 549–65.

20. Safran D, Tarlov A, Rogers W. Primary care performance in fee-for-service and prepaid health care systems – results from the medial outcomes study. *Journal of the American Medical Association.* 1994; **271**(20): 1579–86.

21. Vayda E. Physicians in health care management 5: Payment of physicians and organisation of medical services. *Canadian Medical Association Journal.* 1994; **150**(10): 1583–7.

22. Brcic V, McGregor MJ, Kaczorowski J, et al. Practice and payment preferences of newly practicing family physicians in British Columbia. *Canadian Family Physician.* 2012; **58**(5): e275–81.

23. Brown JS (ed). *Physician Funding and Health Care Systems: an international perspective.* London: The Royal College of General Practitioners, 1999.

24. Ginsburg PB. Fee-for-service will remain a feature of major payment reforms, requiring more changes in medicare physician payment. *Health Affairs (Millwood).* 2012; **31**(9): 1977–83.

25. World Health Organization Regional Office for Europe. *European Health Care Reforms. Analysis of current strategies.* Copenhagen: World Health Organization Regional Office for Europe, 1996 (document ICP/CARE 94 01/CN01).

26. Berwick DM. Quality of health care. Part 5: Payment by capitation and the quality of care. The *New England Journal of Medicine.* 1996; **335**(16): 1227–30.

27. Groenewegen P, van der Zee J, van Haafden R. *Remunerating General Practitioners in Western Europe.* Aldershot: Avebury, 1991.

28. Abel-Smith B. *An Introduction to Health Policy, Planning and Financing.* New York: Longman Group, 1994.

29. Tu K, Cauch-Dudek K, Chen Z. Comparison of primary care physician payment models in the management of hypertension. *Canadian Family Physician.* 2009; **55**(7): 719–27.

30. Donaldson C, Gerard K. Paying general practitioners: shedding light on the review of health services. *Journal of the Royal College of General Practitioners.* 1989; **39**(320): 114–17.

31. Stearns SC, Wolfe BL, Kindig D. Physician responses to fee-for-service and capitation payment. *Inquiry.* 1992; **229**(4): 416–25.
32. McPake B, Hanson K, Mills A. Community financing of health care in Africa: an evaluation of the Bamako Initiative. *Social Science and Medicine.* 1993; **36**(11): 1383–95.
33. World Health Organization. *World Health Report 2010 – Health systems financing: the path to universal coverage.* Available at: www.who.int/whr/2010/en/index.html
34. World Health Organization. *Physician Funding and Health Care Systems – international perspective.* Geneva: World Health Organization, 1999.
35. Qidwai W, Ashfaq T, Khoja TAM, et al. Access to person-centered care: a perspective on status, barriers, opportunities and challenges from the Eastern Mediterranean Region. *Middle East Journal of Family Medicine.* 2012; **10**(6): 4–13.
36. Beasley JW, Starfield B, van Weel C, et al. Global health and primary care research. *Journal of the American Board of Family Medicine.* 2007; **20**(6): 518–26.
37. Van Weel C, Knottnerus JA. Evidence-based interventions and comprehensive treatment. *Lancet.* 1999; **353**: 916–18.
38. The DOPC Writing Group. Conducting the direct observation of primary care study. *Journal of Family Practice.* 2001; **50**: 345–52.
39. Stange KC, Miller WL, McWhinney I. Developing the knowledge base of family practice. *Family Medicine.* 2001; **33**: 286–97.
40. Ceitlin J. Primary care research in Latin America, Portugal and Spain. *Family Practice.* 1991; **8**: 161–7.
41. Fleming MF, Balousek SL, Grossberg PM, et al. Brief physician advice for problem alcohol drinkers: a randomized controlled trial in community primary care practices. *Journal of the American Medical Association.* 1997; **277**: 1039–45.
42. Collaborative Group of the Primary Prevention Project (PPP). Low-dose aspirin and vitamin E in people at cardiovascular risk: a randomized trial in general practice. *Lancet.* 2001; **357**: 89–95.
43. Kohn LT, Corrigan JM, Donaldson MS (eds). *To Err is Human: building a safer health system.* Washington DC: Institute of Medicine and National Academy Press, 2000.
44. Makeham MAB, Kidd MR, Saltman DC, et al. The incidence of errors reported in general practice. *Medical Journal of Australia.* 2006; **185**(2): 95–8.
45. Beasley JW. Practice-based research in the United States. *Primary Health Care Research and Development.* 2000; **1**: 135–7.
46. Stange KC. Primary care research: barriers and opportunities. *Journal of Family Practice.* 1996; **42**: 196–8.
47. Donaldson MS, Yordy KD, Lohr KN, et al. (eds). Primary care: America's health in a new era. Washington DC: Institute of Medicine, National Academy Press, 1996.
48. Mant D. *R&D in Primary Care: national working group report.* Wetherby: NHS Executive 1997.
49. Nutting PA, Green LA. Practice-based research networks: reuniting practice and research about the problems most of the people have most of the time. *Journal of Family Practice.* 1994; **38**: 335–6.
50. Nutting PA, Beasley JW, Werner JJ. Asking and answering questions in practice: practice-based research networks build the science base of family practice. *Journal of the American Medical Association.* 1999; **28**(8): 686–8.
51. Van Weel C, Smith H, Beasley JW. Family practice research networks: experiences from 3 countries. *Journal of Family Practice.* 2000; **49**: 938–943.

52. Thomas P, Griffith F, Kai J, et al. Networks for research in primary health care. *British Medical Journal.* 2001; **322**: 588–90.

53. Meyers D. Introduction from the Agency for Healthcare Research and Quality. *Journal of the American Board of Family Medicine.* 2012; **25**(supp 1): S1.

54. American Academy of Family Physicians. *Practice-based Research Networks in the 21st Century: the pearls of research.* Washington DC: MFP, 1998.

55. Beasley JW. Lessons from the International Primary Care Network. *Journal of the American Board of Family Practice.* 1993; **6**: 419–420.

56. Global Forum for Health Research. *The 10/90 Report on Health Research.* World Health Organization: Geneva, 1999.

57. Van Weel C, Rosser WW. Improving health care globally: a critical review of the necessity of family medicine research and recommendations to build research capacity. *Annals of Family Medicine.* 2004; **2**(Suppl. 2): S5–16.

58. Australian Institute of Health and Welfare. Definitions of safety and quality of health care 2012. Available at: www.aihw.gov.au/sqhc-definitions

59. Woodward CA. *Strategies for Assisting Health Workers to Modify and Improve Skills – developing quality health care: a process of change.* Geneva: World Health Organization 2000 (Issues in Health Services Delivery Discussion Paper No.1, Improving provider skills; document WHO/EIP/OSD/OO.1).

60. Makela M, Booth B, Roberts R, eds. Family doctors' journey to quality. Helsinki: Stakes National Research and Development Centre for Welfare and Health, 2001.

61. Davis D, O'Brien MAT, Freemantle N, et al. Impact of formal continuing medical education. Do conferences, workshops, rounds and other traditional continuing education activities change physician behavior or health outcomes? *Journal of the American Medical Association.* 1999; 282: 867–74.

62. Qidwai W, Dhanani RH, Khan FM. Implications for the practice of a Patient Expectation and Satisfaction Survey, at a teaching hospital in Karachi, Pakistan. *Journal of the Pakistan Medical Association.* 2003; **53**(3): 122–5.

63. Alles V, Makela M, Persson L, et al. *Tools and Methods for Quality Improvement in General Practice.* Helsinki: Stakes, 1998.

64. Kahssay HM. Health Centres – the future of health depends on them. *World Health Forum.* 1998; **19**: 341–60.

65. Beasley JW, Hahn DL, Wiesen P, et al. The cost of primary care research. *Journal of Family Practice.* 2000; **49**: 985–9.

66. Rhyne R, Bogue R, Kukulka G, et al. *Community-oriented Primary Care: health care for the 21st century.* Washington: American Association for Public Health, 1998.

67. KCE. *Comparison of Cost and Quality of Two Financing Systems for Primary Health Care in Belgium.* KCE Report 85A. Available at: kce.fgov.be/sites/default/files/page_documents/d20081027349_0.pdf

68. Gillam S J, Siriwardena AN, Steel N. Pay-for-performance in the United Kingdom: impact of the Quality and Outcomes Framework – A Systematic Review. *Annals of Family Medicine.* 2012; **10**(5): 461–8.

69. The Global Consensus for Social Accountability of Medical Schools, 2010. Available at: www.healthsocialaccountability.org

70. De Maeseneer J, Boeckxstaens P. James MacKenzie Lecture 2011: multimorbidity, goal-oriented care, and equity. *British Journal of General Practice.* 2012; **62**: e522–4.

CHAPTER 6

Family medicine in lower- and upper-middle income countries[*]

The path to universal health coverage draws attention to various barriers in access to health services linked to significant shortages in resources, fragmentation of health care systems, and lack of people-centeredness. Worldwide, it is estimated that over one billion people lack access to essential health services. In many low- and middle-income countries health services can be too costly for a population (affordability barrier), or too far away (accessibility barrier), or poorly staffed with long waiting hours (availability barrier), or do not conform to people's cultural and gender preferences (acceptability barrier). The way people perceive their need for health care, beyond the biological dimension of their concerns, is usually only of marginal concern for service providers. Even when people do access services, those are often of poor quality and, in some cases, even harmful. In addition, services tend to be fragmented, curative, hospital-based, and disease-oriented, all of which further hampers access to comprehensive and quality care services.

These issues are long-standing and pervasive in many countries and need a comprehensive and coherent solution. To improve health and social outcomes, health systems must "put people first." They must respond to people's needs and expectations. Health care should focus on the whole person, adjusting its response to the specificities of his or her local community, family, and individual life course context. To become more relevant, services also have to do more to meet the needs of the entire population, while at the same time addressing the specific needs of some population subgroups.

Since the Declaration of Alma-Ata of 1978, primary health care has been recognized as one of the key components of an effective health system and a fundamental strategy to achieve health for all. Health systems based on a strong primary health care orientation have better and more equitable health outcomes, are more efficient, have lower health care costs, and can achieve higher user satisfaction than those whose health systems have only a weak primary health care orientation. Experiences in more-developed and less-developed countries alike have demonstrated that primary health care can be adapted and interpreted to suit a wide variety of political, social, and cultural contexts.[1]

There is growing consensus worldwide on the areas in which health systems must be transformed. The World Health Organization (WHO) World Health Report 2008 suggests four sets of policy directions that will reorient health systems toward a primary health care approach. Along with moving toward universal coverage, health in all policies and more inclusive governance, the WHO recommends reorganizing health services around people's needs and expectations.[2] In 2009, the World Health Assembly adopted a resolution on primary health care, urging countries to

> put people at the center of health care by adopting ... delivery models focused on the local and district levels that provide comprehensive primary health care services, including health promotion, disease prevention, curative care and palliative care, that are integrated with other levels of care and coordinated according to need.[3]

More recently in the year 2011, the World Health Assembly Resolution WHA64.9 affirmed that universal health coverage cannot be achieved without addressing the barriers to high-quality, people-centered service delivery in countries.[4]

The fundamental characteristics of family medicine and their derivative attributes allow family doctors to contribute substantially to the goal of universal health coverage through primary care services that are family and community oriented. This is because the essential attributes of family practice are completely aligned with people-centeredness and include attributes such as generalism; comprehensive, coordinated, and continuous care; collaborative work; and family and community orientation, among others.

It is in this context that WHO is contributing to this guidebook with a special chapter dedicated to family medicine in lower- and upper-middle income countries, building on the experiences of Brazil, China, the Eastern Mediterranean Region, and Thailand. It is hoped that the lessons learned from these countries will help build the case for the need and feasibility of introducing family medicine even in medium- and low-resource settings. Each case study presented addresses general information about the country and its main health system challenges; an explanation of the primary care reforms undertaken by the country, including an analysis of trends, the main drivers of change, and the pathway chosen to move forward; key lessons learned throughout the implementation process, including obstacles and facilitators; and the main results and impact of the reforms.

The wide range of countries presented demonstrates that family medicine, or its local adaptations, can improve population satisfaction as well as clinical and population health outcomes in middle-income countries and low-resource settings, especially when embedded in wider sector reforms. Strong examples of this can be seen in Brazil, China, Thailand, and some countries in the Eastern Mediterranean Region, even if the specific modalities of family medicine and family oriented models of care differ across these countries. The degree of success of family medicine, or its local adaptations, in lower-middle income countries is less clear, given the limited number of countries studied that belong to this income group.

Brazil's case is a clear testimony for the pivotal role of community-based family care teams in primary health care reform. The Brazilian National Health System is based on universal and comprehensive access, monitored by the community and organized on a decentralized, line-managed, and regionalized basis. The National Primary Health Care Policy was launched in 2006, based on the earlier successes in the 1990s of the community health worker program and family health program. The program aims at building an inclusive system around the family health strategy. Central to this model are the multidisciplinary teams working in a coordinated manner to deliver effectively the services that people actually need. The family physicians have a pivotal role within this team and are supported by community health workers. In spite of continuing challenges, such as the limited number of qualified family health workers, the reform is considered a big success, with a clear and positive impact on key health and socioeconomic indicators.

In China, the former community-based primary health care system founded on the "barefoot doctor" concept was replaced by a hospital-centered health care system after the Cultural Revolution and economic reforms of 1978. Early attempts at introducing general practice and the family medicine specialization had some successes but remained underdeveloped due to little recognition and a lack of funding. It was only with the health system reform in 2006 that the objective of universal primary health services and the promotion of general practice took root in China. Critical factors for this success were the introduction of a universal health insurance system, strong investments in training for family physicians and advocacy by experts, academics, and grassroots health workers. The Chinese model is actively implemented in many regions, with primary health physicians as gatekeepers for the population's health, a hierarchal referral system, and investments in primary health care facilities. Access to and equity of primary health care has since improved.

Strengthening health systems in the countries of the Eastern Mediterranean Region is based on and guided by the values and principles of primary health care, with the adoption of family practice as the approach for the delivery of essential health services. The establishment of the model is at a relatively early stage of development. In most countries the complete family practice model does not exist and in many only a few components are being implemented. Successful examples can be found throughout the region, with family health programs contributing to great improvements of health indicators. In Jordan, the United Nations Relief and Work Agency for Palestinian Refugees (UNRWA) succeeded in establishing a community-based family care program that is comprehensive in nature. In Iran, the foundation of the Primary Health Care Network System is the family practice team; the network is built around health houses responsible for a clearly defined population, a network of community health workers and a simple yet effective health information system. In Egypt, the Family Health Model was adopted as an integral part of health sector reform.

Thailand's health system, dating back to the 1880s, was traditionally anchored in hospital medicine. Thus when the family medicine concept was introduced in the 1980s, it was immediately perceived as relating to a hospital-based doctor without a specific specialization. When the push for universal health coverage gained political momentum in the 1990s, primary care reform then became necessary and urgent – it was within this context that family medicine and community-based care finally made headway in Thailand's hospital-centered medical culture. A strategy that proved instrumental in facilitating the reforms was that of "demonstration" and "diffusion." The idea behind the "demonstration health centers" was to develop and demonstrate the family practice concept in a few selected areas in order to stimulate interest and demand for primary health care. When the universal coverage policy was adopted some years later, family practice as a cornerstone for health sector development had already proven its worth and was therefore taken up as a tested model of care.

All of these case studies clearly bolster the fundamental concepts of family medicine as advocated by the World Organization of Family Doctors (WONCA): a comprehensive approach and individual care within the context of the family and community. In almost all of the countries studied, these concepts were embodied in health sector reform linked to the overall goal of universal health coverage. When these concepts are genuinely the basis for a new way of providing care, family medicine within a family- and community-oriented model of care has a real added value to demonstrate.

Several key lessons emerge from these case studies: first, family care-oriented reforms are not easy to implement and all of the studied countries went through an initial struggle before family practice eventually took root. It was only when the health policy objective was universal coverage and the operationalization of universal coverage included primary health care reform that the multidisciplinary family care approach made progress. But the interpretation and local adaptation of family practice varies considerable across these countries. In many of these countries family practice is not necessarily practiced by physicians specialized in family practice, and this is still an important shortcoming of the reforms undertaken.

Second, family medicine as a medical specialization can maximize its contribution to family and community models of care when family doctors are part of an interdisciplinary team. However, investments in training for family doctors and nurses, as well as supporting cadres, must coincide with the political will to implement reform. More important, they must be sustained over a long period of time to ensure a high-quality workforce trained within the values of primary health care and universal coverage.

Third, piloting of the family care approach can be an effective way to introduce primary health care to communities. In Thailand and several countries of the Eastern Mediterranean Region, it served both to test the approach and assess its repercussions as well as to popularize the concept and demonstrate to communities its benefits and the empowerment it can bring.

Fourth, family medicine, within a family- and community-oriented model of care, needs to establish strong coordination with other levels of specialized care in order to guarantee continuity of care across the different levels and settings of care. Even in successful cases of rapid primary health care expansion, this coordination has proven very difficult to implement in the majority of the case studies analyzed.

Last, we learn from these exemplary case studies that the core of primary health care and, indeed, universal coverage is really the community. Without community involvement in implementing family care teams as the basis for primary health care, universal coverage cannot be achieved. Regardless of setting, whether Brazil or China or the Eastern Mediterranean Region or Thailand, we see time and again that community involvement is no longer optional when designing health care strategies.

6.1 THE BRAZILIAN UNIFIED HEALTH SYSTEM: PRIMARY HEALTH CARE IN ACTION

Brazil is a federal republic made up of three categories of federal units with administrative autonomy: the federation, states, and municipalities. It has a total area of 8 511 996 km², five macro-regions (North, North East, South West, South and Central West), 26 states, one federal district and 5565 municipalities. With a total population of 190 755 799 (Brazilian Institute of Geography and Statistics 2010 census),[5] it is the fifth most populous country in the world. The population is distributed unevenly, concentrated in the South West (42%) and North East (28%).

Brazil is the sixth-largest economy in the world. Total spending on health in 2010 was approximately USD 161 billion, or the equivalent of 8.4% of Gross Domestic Product. Of this expenditure, 45% was on public health (US$76 billion) and 55% was in the private sector (US$85 billion) in the form of out-of-pocket expenses, health insurance and medicines.[4] The median life expectancy is 73.4 years and the infant mortality rate is 15.6 per 1000 live births.[5]

The Brazilian National Health System was the fruit of the 1998 Constitution, which consolidated significant social progress following a long period of military dictatorship. It is a health system based on universal and comprehensive access, monitored by the community and organized on a decentralized, line-managed and regionalized basis in which delivery of health services is primarily a municipal responsibility but is financed on a tripartite model.

Prior to the health reform that resulted in the institution of the Unified Health System pursuant to Act No. 8.080 of 1990,[6] health care was financed by the National Institute for Social Security and was limited to workers in formal employment. Brazilians who were unable to pay for health services relied on charity dispensed by denominational hospitals or certain units at health clinics focusing on communicable diseases or maternal and childhood illnesses.

The development of primary health care in Brazil

From a historical perspective, primary health care in Brazil began in the 1920s with health education centers that concentrated on disease prevention.[7] The Special Public Health Service model, which combined preventive and therapeutic approaches to communicable diseases only, was prevalent in the 1940s. State health clinics were established in the 1960s; these incorporated medical treatment into preventive programs, although once again this model applied only to vertical programs for maternal and childhood and communicable diseases. The network of health clinics was expanded in the 1970s, based on a simplified model and selective primary health care.

In some Brazilian cities, primary health care models linked to medical residency programs were developed, such as in Porto Alegre with the Murialdo Teaching, the Vitória de Santo Antão in Pernambuco, the Comprehensive Medical Service at Rio de Janeiro State University, Petropolis, Vitória, Natal, Cotia, Pelotas, Sete Lagoas, and Joinvile. However, these initiatives lacked the impetus to become institutionalized as public policy even within their own regions.

A process of health care decentralization began in the 1980s, when municipalities took over the responsibility for health centers. In parallel with this process, other municipality-based experiments were conducted, for example at the University of São Paulo Medical Faculty where gynecologists, pediatricians, and other clinicians followed a programmatic approach to child health, women's health, and adult health. Under the Cuban-inspired Family Doctor Program in Niterói, one general practitioner and a nursing auxiliary became responsible for approximately 250 families.

In the 1990s, municipalities delivered health care in accordance with the guidelines in the Federal Constitution on decentralization of health activities. Health centers became generalized nationwide, but were plagued by inadequate infrastructure, low case resolution rates, and a minimum level of health intervention and service delivery based around selective primary health care focusing on interventions typically found in poorer countries, such as growth monitoring, oral rehydration, breastfeeding, and immunization. Owing to poor signaling of the preferred points of entry into the Unified Health System and lack of universal accessibility, much of the population used specialized outpatient services in hospitals and emergency rooms as the source of routine medical services.[8]

An important impetus to the establishment of the Family Health Program in the 1990s was the success of the Community Health Worker Program. This was originally an emergency program to reduce infant mortality in Ceará State.

In view of the extremely low medical and health coverage in regions where the Community Health Worker Program was implemented initially, certain medical services were incorporated to extend the scope of health interventions both quantitatively and qualitatively. The result was the Family Health Program, the proposed replacement for all the existing models nationwide and preferred entry point into the Unified Health System.

Consolidating the Family Health Strategy

In 2006, this program was relaunched as the National Primary Health Care Policy, the stated goal of which is "to consolidate and present the Family Health Strategy as the principal primary health care model and the hub of the health care networks in the Unified Health System."[9]

Family health comprises health promotion and protection, diagnosis, prevention of complications, treatment, recovery, and maintenance of good health. It is the preferred point of contact between the health system and its users, and is informed by the principles of universality, accessibility and coordination, inter-relationships and continuity, integration, accountability, humanity, equity, and community participation.[9] This set of principles and guidelines reflects Brazil's desire to build a comprehensive primary health care system that is wide ranging and inclusive, in contrast to a selective primary health care system with basic packages for "poor people."

The institution of a form of per capita funding for family health – the Basic Care Fund – has enabled this model to expand rapidly, with many more municipalities signing up to the strategy. In addition, special incentives have been made available to provide medical services to communities of slave descendants (quilombolas), rural settlements, indigenous populations, and all municipalities in Brazil with a low Human Development Index.

Family health has three important characteristics that differentiate it from primary health care systems in other countries:

1. Multidisciplinary teams are responsible for geographical areas and their populations, with the task of identifying operational, organizational, or social problems in an appropriate manner.
2. The presence of community health workers.
3. The inclusion of oral health in the public health system.

The complexity of the triple burden of diseases in a developing country makes it imperative that multidisciplinary teams work in a coordinated manner to deliver effectively the services that people actually need. Family health teams need to be multidisciplinary and should comprise, as a bare minimum, a general practitioner, a nurse, a medical auxiliary or nursing technician, and community health workers. The team may also include oral health professionals such as a dental surgeon, a dental assistant, and/or an oral health technician.

Each family health team is responsible ideally for between 3000 and 4000 people, according to the socioeconomic profile of the population, or less where the population is more socially vulnerable. The maximum ratio of community health workers to the population should be 1:750.[9] Family support core units, made up of professionals with various areas of expertise, were established in 2008 to work together in a more integrated fashion. They are tasked with supporting family health teams in the health care network by extending the outreach and case resolution capacity of each team.[10]

The teams have the following mission:
- to be a part of the process of zoning and mapping the area of health intervention by identifying groups, families, and individuals at risk or in situations of vulnerability;
- to keep up-to-date records on families and individuals and to use these data for routine health monitoring;
- to provide health care to the population for which they are responsible, primarily in health facility settings, but also, where necessary, at home and in other community settings, thereby adopting a comprehensive approach through activities to promote, protect, and restore health and prevent complications;
- to guarantee access to treatment as and when the need arises;
- to carry out programmatic, collective, and health surveillance activities;
- to carry out active case-finding and reporting of compulsorily notifiable diseases and complications, and of other problems and situations of local importance;
- to be responsible for their assigned population, by ensuring coordination of care even when this requires treatment in other facilities of the health system;
- to provide family care and treatment in collective and community group settings with a view to carrying out interventions that impact on the health and disease processes of individuals, families, groups, and the whole community;
- to hold team meetings to jointly discuss, plan, and evaluate team-led actions based on available data;
- to routinely monitor and evaluate ongoing activities with a view to adapting the work processes;
- to ensure the quality of recording of activities in basic care information systems;
- to carry out health education activities with the assigned population;
- to identify partners and resources in the community that could strengthen intersectoral and community monitoring activities.

The mission of the physician members of the teams is:
- to provide health care to the individuals for whom they are responsible;
- to hold clinical consultations, carry out minor surgical interventions, participate in group activities at basic health facilities and, when indicated or necessary, at home and/or in other community settings such as schools;

> ➤ to carry out program activities and provide treatment as and when required;
> ➤ where necessary, to refer patients to other health facilities, taking account of local patient flows, while continuing to exercise responsibility through supervision of the patient's treatment plan;
> ➤ in consultation with other health facilities to recommend that a patient be admitted to hospital or be treated at home, all the while remaining responsible for supervising the care of the patient.

The Brazilian model, therefore, combines clinical aspects with public health interventions and delivers care based on health protection and promotion, community participation through health education and promotion, comprehensive and continuous care, coordination with the local health system, continuing education for health care staff, and competitive salaries for personnel and encouragement of community participation.[11]

Family Health is now public policy in Brazil and is high on the agenda of Unified Health System managers. There are 33 420 family health teams covering 55% of the population, 256 847 community health workers covering 65% of the population, 20 113 oral health teams and 1250 family support core units operating nationwide.[12]

Results achieved

The positive results noted in a number of studies on family health take into consideration a range of factors such as evaluations by patients, managers, and health professionals,[13–15] choice of health interventions offered, access to and use of health services,[16–20] reduction in infant mortality,[21–23] reduction in the number of hospital admissions for conditions treatable at the primary care level,[24–28] and improvement in the socioeconomic indicators of the population.[6]

Infant mortality

A study carried out in the period 1990–2002 indicated that a 10% increase in Family Health coverage had reduced infant mortality by 4.6%, thus having a greater impact during this period than improvement in access to drinking water (2.9%) and increase in the number of hospital beds (1.3%). The only factor that had a more significant impact on infant mortality was the level of education among mothers.[21]

Hospital morbidity

Between 1999 and 2006, hospital admission rates for conditions treatable at the primary care level fell by 20%, twice as fast as admissions for other reasons. For three categories of chronic treatable conditions, the decrease in the rate of admissions among women in municipalities that had expanded their Family Health coverage translated into savings of 120 million reais (about US$60 million).[27]

In one study of hospital admission rates for conditions treatable at the primary care level in adults over 20 years of age, more than 60 million hospital admissions between 1999 and 2007 were analyzed. These admission rates went down by 5% a year and, when controlling for factors such as per capita income, treated water, illiteracy, health plans, medical consultations per head, premature mortality, and age, Family Health coverage in municipalities was the most significant predictive factor in the reduction of hospital admission rates for conditions treatable at the primary care level in adults, together with the lack, or smaller number of, private hospital beds.[25]

A study carried out in Belo Horizonte municipality immediately after the establishment of more than 500 family health teams, found a reduction of 26.4% in hospital admission rates for conditions treatable at the primary care level over 4 years. The rate was higher for women with low incomes, and the presence of the same physician in a team over a longer period correlated with a reduction of 11 hospital admissions per 10 000 women per year.[28]

Reduction of inequalities

Data from the National Household Sampling Survey of 2008[30] shows that many of the most vulnerable members of the population had been included in the Unified Health System. 62% of families with no income or up to one minimum wage were registered with family health teams and 63.8% of households with a head of family having up to 1 year of formal education had been treated by family health teams.

For certain socioeconomic indicators, a recent study notes that the introduction of family health teams in poor regions of Brazil already correlates with an increase in adult employment, a reduction in fertility with longer intervals between pregnancies, and increased rates of school attendance among adolescents.[29]

According to a population-based survey conducted in 2008 on the basis of the historical studies by White et al. (1961)[31] and Green et al. (2001),[32] which aimed to evaluate access to and use of services in Brazil, the rate of home care for the elderly was higher than that indicated in studies of North American and British populations.[33] A study carried out in 2006 indicated that Family Health achieved better results than the traditional model of health care for the elderly, including better access, greater ability of the multidisciplinary team to meet demand, better delivery of medical consultations, medication provision, and involvement with groups of elderly persons suffering from chronic illnesses, and better access to home care, including for people with motor function disabilities.[19]

Population satisfaction

Research published by the Institute for Applied Economic Research in 2011[34] evaluated public perception of the services provided by the Unified Health System and by private health insurance plans and showed that treatment by family health teams was the health service most highly valued by respondents in all regions, with a "very good" or "good" satisfaction score almost double that recorded by users of conventional health centers. The proportion of dissatisfied users of family health teams was six times lower than the proportion of those dissatisfied with emergency services and conventional health facilities.

Some studies comparing the quality of care provided by family health teams with that provided by other primary health care models such as adult medicine clinics, gynecologists, and pediatricians have shown better results in terms of primary health care indicators. Harzheim et al.[18] verified that children associated with family health teams had a better chance of receiving high-quality primary care than children associated with conventional basic facilities, and that high-quality primary care is associated with higher satisfaction and better health, as perceived by the caregiver. This study compared the quality of care provided by physicians working in family health teams with pediatricians working in basic health facilities.

In the municipality of Curitiba, family health teams comprising family physicians conformed more closely to the primary health care paradigm than conventional facilities such as adult medicine clinics, pediatricians, and gynecologists.[35]

The provision of dental and oral health services through the dental and oral health teams integrated into Family Health has resulted in a 49% increase in the number of dentists working in the Unified Health System. Between 2003 and 2008, 17.5 million Brazilians went to see a dentist, and the impact was greatest in families with an income of up to two times the minimum wage. In 7 years, since the extension of the program to embed dental and oral health teams in 2003, the dental caries index in children aged 12 has fallen by 26%, thus placing Brazil in the group of low dental caries prevalence countries.[36]

In a survey of community health workers and their positive impact on the achievement of the Millennium Development Goals, the Brazilian experience of community health workers achieved the highest score in a comparison of eight countries across three regions.[37]

There has been significant progress in regulating the profession of community health workers, for example by raising their average level of training and putting their jobs on a less precarious footing. In 2001, 72.4% of community health workers had an insecure professional status compared with 31.8% in 2008; over the same period the number of community health workers increased by 34.7%. The challenge for the coming decade is to strengthen the role of community health workers by enabling them to "forge relationships based on solidarity and confidence, build support networks and strengthen the organisation and involvement of individuals and communities in collective initiatives to improve their health and well-being, especially of vulnerable social groups," which is one of the recommendations of the National Commission on the Social Determinants of Health.[38]

In 2010, the decline in the mortality rate among children under 5 in Brazil was acknowledged as being one of the steepest falls ever recorded in the world, and this result has been attributed in large measure to the Family Health Strategy.[39]

In a recent publication the Brazilian Family Health Program was referred to as probably the most impressive experiment worldwide in terms of rapid expansion of a comprehensive and cost-effective primary health system. The authors also suggest that "even the richest countries could learn something from the manner in which the Family Health Program has impacted on chronic diseases, the demand for tertiary-level health services and health promotion."[40]

Challenges

Financing

The challenge is to break with the logic of supply-side financing and to invest based on the needs of the population assigned to each family health team in the country. This means empowering the system of primary health care and ensuring that new resources for the Unified Health System, which are essential to achieve a comprehensive level of care, are invested in accordance with the needs identified in the primary health care/family health context.

In the 10 years from 2002 to 2012, basic care expenditure has increased by 84.07%. Investment in the National Plan for Construction and reforms of the Unified Health System involving family health teams was provided under the Accelerated Growth Program and allows for the construction of 8694 basic health facilities by 2015.

The future challenge in the area of funding of primary health care has to do with the effectiveness of allocations to the Unified Health System. New federal, state, and municipal resources for the Unified Health System should be allocated on the basis of the needs of the population assigned to the family health teams, thereby enabling Family Health to become the structural core of the whole health system.

Management

One of the most complex processes in the construction of health systems is the interrelationship between the different facilities providing treatment. The integration and coordination of the primary health care network requires management structures to enable Family Health to coordinate the treatment inside the network. It is imperative to professionalize management at the municipal level in order to organize health systems geared to Family Health, and also to install managers at basic health facilities who are able to implement mechanisms to ensure that the population assigned to the teams takes advantage of the four core attributes of primary health care, namely first contact access, a comprehensive approach, continuity of care over time, and coordination with the wider treatment network.

Management geared to primary health care should be based on a population-based project design with the following components:

➤ registration of the population in an electronic database
➤ physical infrastructure with adequate facilities
➤ adequate human resources
➤ clinical guidelines that take into account classification of risk and vulnerability
➤ regulated access by the population to consultant specialist consultations, examinations, diagnostic facilities and hospital beds on the basis of the needs of the population registered in primary care
➤ mechanisms to ensure that primary care becomes the communications hub of the network including use of electronic communications systems, electronic patient files, and smart waiting lists that include classification of risk and vulnerability. These mechanisms need to be established within the primary health care system itself, when patients are seen by different members of the team and when the information is generated in different places or with other specialists.

As to the management challenge, it should be stressed that 80% of Brazilian municipalities have a population of less than 20 000. For those municipalities, technical assistance is required from the state health authorities and their regional structures in order to manage the inflow of patients into the network of intermunicipal services.

In the bigger municipalities, the selective approach to delivering health services to the poor should be abandoned, and primary health care services should be extended to the entire population. Everyone should have access to excellent primary health care services irrespective of the individual patient's ability to pay through private health insurance schemes, and public resources for primary health care should account for no more than 45% of public health expenditure in Brazil.

Professional training geared to the needs of the population

Working in teams is necessary to address the complexity of primary health issues. This requires familiarity with the social determinants of health and the risks and vulnerability of families or individuals with a view to developing targeted interventions. Expertise and practices derived from the training given in hospitals and specialist outpatient clinics need to be transformed into training programs for primary health care specialists and ongoing in-service education.

The most common problem cited by managers is the lack of family and community physicians with technical training and expertise, in sufficient quantity to ensure the technical underpinning of the Family Health program now being implemented. In opting for a primary health care model based on family health, Brazil has not taken the parallel step of redesigning its specialist medical training arrangements to enable practitioners to exercise this function. The institution of medical and family physicians was not made compulsory only because there were not enough specialists in this field nationwide. Of the 204 563 medical specialists currently practicing, just 1.3% are family or community physicians.[41] The shortage of primary health care specialists has not diminished their importance; on the contrary, it is possible to say that the presence of family physicians and/or nursing staff specialising in family health and primary health care reinforces the presence and extension of the core components of primary health care.[35,42,43]

The challenge of defining whether family physicians are primary health care specialists should be addressed in conjunction with the other policy criteria of primary health care in the health system.

Although in recent years the number of vacancies for family and community physician residencies has increased nationally, in most cases these posts remain unfilled. Where vacancies are successfully filled, it is because the image of family medicine has been enhanced through incentives such as differentiated payments and in-service training arrangements in those municipalities where medical residencies are located, and by directly placing family and community medical residents in municipal services and increasing their remuneration progressively as their training advances. Basic health facilities and family health teams must be used as a tool to train and qualify health professionals in teaching hospitals whose clinical excellence confers the necessary social status to persuade others to choose primary health care as a worthwhile field of health activity.

Improving the social and political image of primary health care

Strong primary health care can help society to define its needs and rights by acting as a vehicle for the concepts of empowerment and social capital. Citizens who are satisfied with the services they receive will defend the public model and will approve the necessary funding to continue pursuing a policy of greater social inclusion, through the Unified Health System geared to family health.

6.2 PROMOTING UNIVERSAL PRIMARY HEALTH SERVICES IN CHINA THROUGH GENERAL PRACTICE REFORMS

In 2010, the total population of mainland China was 1.341 billion (669.78 million urban residents and 671.13 million rural residents)[44] with a per capita gross domestic product of US$4614.15.[45] The income gap between urban and rural residents was very large, as the average disposable income for the former was US$2939.85 while the average net income for the latter was only US$910.62.[44] The population aged 65 years or older accounted for 8.9% of the total population.[44,46]

In 2011, the average life expectancy at birth reached 74.83 years. The maternal mortality rate was 30/100 000 and the under-5 mortality rate was 16.4 per 1000 live births. The national total health expenditure was 19 921.35 billion RMB (US$306 billion), of which the government health spending was 5688.64 billion RMB (US$87.52 billion) (28.6%), social health spending was 7156.55 billion RMB (US$110.11 billion) (35.9%), and personal health spending was 7076 billion RMB (US$108.86 billion) (35.5%). Total health expenses accounted for 5.01% of gross domestic product.[47] Despite the significant achievements and advancements, several major challenges still exist in the area of health, which include insufficient financing, rapid population aging, and low efficiency of health resources utilization, poor public health security and protection systems, and lack of qualified health professionals.

The development of general practice

From the late 1960s to the 1980s, the county-township-village three-tier health care network was widely established and the cooperative medical care system covered more than 90% of residents in rural areas. The "barefoot doctors" provided daily health services for prevention and treatment of disease and family planning, with an average of two doctors per 1000 people. This was recognized as a good model of primary health care in the developing world. At the next level were the township health centers, which each functioned primarily as outpatient clinics for about 10 000–30 000 people. Only the most seriously ill patients were referred to the third and final level, the county hospitals, which each served 200 000–600 000 people and were staffed by senior doctors who held 5-year degrees from medical schools.

Economic reforms starting from 1978 led to a fundamental transformation of the health care system in both urban and rural areas. The decollectivization of agriculture resulted in a decreased desire on the part of the rural populations to support the collective welfare system, of which health care was a part. In 1984, surveys showed that only 40%–45% of the rural population was covered by an organized cooperative medical system, as compared with 80%–90% in 1979. Along with decreasing or ceasing financial support from government, primary health care facilities in urban areas were privatized and finally sank into atrophy, with significantly weakened service capacity in both urban and rural areas because of the aging workforce and staff turnover. In contrast, large hospitals were able to compensate their reduced income from government sources by increasing the quantity and range of clinical services provided, and therefore expanded very fast, which resulted in the seriously imbalanced allocation of health care resources between urban and rural areas, as well as between primary health care facilities and large hospitals. In addition, limited medical insurance coverage induced residents to seek medical service in large hospitals instead of primary health care facilities because the "family doctor as gatekeeper" system was not established. All of these points led to rapidly increased medical expenses, low equity of health service, and restricted access to medical services. Additionally, combating the threat from infectious diseases and the rapidly rising rates of chronic noncommunicable diseases[48] such as cardiovascular diseases, cancer, diabetes, and chronic respiratory diseases, as well as the reduction of maternal, infant, and child mortality rates were key tasks for public health.[49] After many nationwide consultations and debates, a consensus was achieved on strengthening the general practice discipline and reshaping the primary health care system in both urban and rural areas.

The discipline of general practice in China

General practice was introduced to China in 1988. The National Association of General Practice was formed in 1992, which indicated that general practice was officially recognized as a medical discipline within the Chinese Medical Association. As a first step toward promoting general practice in China, the Capital Medical University initiated the first courses on general practice and established a pilot class for medical undergraduates in 1992. However, the exploration at this stage only reached the level of a pilot study. General practice received little recognition from the society and its development was quite slow.

In 1999, the Ministry of Health brought the discipline of general practice into the discipline of Western clinical medicine alongside Western disciplines such as internal medicine, surgery, and pediatrics. However, its development remained very slow because of inadequate awareness of its importance. Until 2007, among 485 medical colleges in the whole country,[50] only 28 had established compulsory courses for general practice, and only four had postgraduate training. In 2010, the government implemented a new plan for gradually establishing a series of education programs at medical school, at postgraduate level, and through in-service training for general practitioners.

The increasing capacity of general practitioners

In 1997, the Chinese government launched a national strategic plan aimed at reforming health service systems and promoting community health services in urban areas.[51] One of the objectives was to accelerate the development of general practice and train general practitioners, which facilitated the synchronous development of general practice and community health services.

In 1999 and 2006, the central government issued instructions on the development of community health service in urban areas with supporting policies and actions.[52,53] The key policies included:

➤ to include general practice in the system of clinical professional and technical qualification examinations and assessment[54]
➤ to provide postgraduate training and standardized training of general practitioners[55,56]
➤ to offer graduate and continuing education in general practice[57]
➤ to establish the general practitioner qualification system[58] and the technical qualifications registration management system[59]
➤ to put forward related policies on attracting and retaining community health personnel.[60]

As a consequence of implementing those policies, the rapid development of general practice was achieved.

Though community health services and general practice were developed in many places across the country, the general practice team was still not mature due to insufficient financial investment from government, inadequate supporting policies, and lack of sufficient general practice education and training in place. The main causes of this situation included a lack of knowledge of the importance of the general practitioner, unfavorable remuneration and social status of general practitioners. and lacking social recognition of the career prospects of general practitioners. A research study in 2007[61] showed that only 19 of 32 provinces carried out the registration work of the professional practice of general practitioners, with only 6321 registrations. Though postgraduate training of general practitioners was carried out in all provinces, the effect was not obvious as it was a mere formality or superficial training in most cases. Only four provinces conducted standardized training programs on general practice for undergraduates, with a total of 368 health professionals trained. There were significant gaps between the eastern and western regions, as well as between urban and rural areas in terms of development of general practitioners. The main challenge was lack of qualified trainers.

In 2009, a new health care reform was launched by the central government based on the principles of "government-led" and "public welfare."[50] The main duty given to primary health workers was that of "gatekeeper" through promoting the transformation of the service model and continuously improving service capacity, providing active health service to patients at home as required. Furthermore, hospitals are now required to set up a general practice department if they are listed as training bases for general practitioners. In addition, the "project of free rural-oriented order medical training of medical personnel" and the "project on recruitment of general practitioners in township hospitals" were launched. A variety of channels including in-service training and standardized training for general practitioners were adopted to train primary care workers. The model of the interdisciplinary teams collaborating with each other and signing service contracts with patients was implemented while providing services. The long-term mechanism for establishing hierarchal referral systems, primary health physicians as gatekeepers and two-way referral systems was actively explored in many regions.[62]

The State Council issued instructions on the establishment of the General Practitioners System in 2011,[63] providing the overall structure for the general practitioner training system, working model, and incentive system.

The construction of primary health facilities

In order to reshape the primary health care system, the Chinese government decided to strengthen the construction of primary health facilities in 1997. However, the construction moved slowly because of government's insufficient investment. In some places like SuQian City, the government sold all the town hospitals but did not invest in primary health care. In 2006, the central government changed track to adhere to "public welfare" and government-orientation, with a requirement to increase investments to establish primary health facilities through construction of new centers or transforming street hospitals or privately owned facilities. Each neighborhood was required to own at least one community health service center. Since 2009, the central government has invested US$6.15 billion in total to support the construction of 1877 county hospitals, 5169 town hospitals, 2382 community health centers, and 11 000 village clinics.

So far, primary health care services have been provided in both urban and rural areas. The services include prevention of disease, diagnosis, and treatment of frequently occurring diseases, referral, rehabilitation, and chronic disease management. However, the essential medicine system implemented in government-run primary health facilities since 2009 permitted only about 500 types of essential medicine, which hindered the development of general practice and primary health service due to its ignorance of patients' actual demands, and thus patients lost trust in their doctors. Moreover, during the whole process of reform, China was facing challenges such as low qualifications among primary health care personnel, low training outcomes, and insufficient knowledge of the importance of general practice.

Lessons learned

Contributing factors

In October 2006 the central government made the commitment that all citizens should have access to affordable primary health services,[50] and this was reaffirmed in the new health care reform in 2009. Strong political commitment of governments at all levels is critical to achieving the objective of universal primary health services and to promoting the reform and development of general practice in China.

The national basic public health services program launched in July 2009[64] provided a total of 41 basic public health services in 11 categories.[65] The program facilitates responsibilities of the general practitioner to conform to the objectives of the National Health Service, which promoted investment from government at all levels in the reform and development of general practice.

Toward the end of 2011, the number of urban and rural residents who participated in the three basic health care insurance schemes exceeded 1.3 billion, constituting a coverage of over 95%[66] as the Chinese government promised to build a basic health care insurance system for all people. An increased subsidy proportion and reduced deductions for visiting primary health service facilities encouraged patients to utilize these services.[67] This greatly promoted the use of primary health care and the development of general practice.

Finally, experts, academics, and health workers played key roles in lobbying the public and policy makers by using successful experiences drawn from other countries and providing good options taking into consideration China's national conditions in order to develop and implement national policies and plans.

Myths and barriers

There was misunderstanding of general practice by society as many people believed that it was different from family medicine, resulting in varied paths of development, which hindered its real development. "General practitioner" was translated into "general doctor" in Chinese. However, people thought "general" in circumstance of Chinese traditional cultural and linguistic characteristics meant the physician was proficient in all clinical disciplines. The misconception led to the social bias of general practice: patients and specialists had reservations against general practitioners and even primary health workers themselves lacked in-depth understanding of general practice.

Also, the capacity of the primary health care teams to provide medical services was inadequate, and did not match patient expectations. In addition, generally there was no Division of General Practice in training sites for family medicine, and there was a severe shortage of qualified teachers. These factors prevented the smooth development of general practice in China.

Results and impact

By the end of 2010, 63 of the 128 medical colleges had established departments of general practice and offered relevant courses. There were 75 medical colleges carrying out postgraduate courses for students pursuing a master degree. The education system for general practice had been placed on a firmer foundation. By the end of 2011, 15 provinces conducted "5+3" standardized training, and all provinces provided training for job transfer. Gradually, the training for general practice has become standardized.

At the end of 2011, the number of primary care physicians reached 0.42 per 1000 residents, representing an increase of 0.08 compared with 2005. Although the number in urban areas was much less than in rural areas, because rural areas have a much lower population density and more general practitioners are needed, the number in urban areas increased threefold compared with 2005, basically achieving the objective of "two to three primary health care physicians per 10000 residents" (*see* Table 6.1). The total number of primary health care facilities reached 733004 nationwide with 37295 township hospitals and 7861 community health service centers,[68] basically realizing the objectives of "at least each neighbourhood has a community health service centre"[69] and "each township a hospital" (*see* Table 6.1).[70]

The number of outpatients who visited primary health care facilities accounted for 51.1% of the total who visited medical facilities at all levels across the country[69] constituting an increase of 18% compared with 33.1% in 2005.[71] The number of patients managed in various categories included 16 million pregnant women, 81 million children up to the age of 6 years, and 110 million old people. The initial effect on chronic disease management became evident as hypertension and diabetes control rates improved.[72] Primary health care services in China are playing an increasingly important role in the overall health system.

Access to and equity of primary health care services have been improved through the substantial increase in coverage of the three-tier health service network in rural areas and urban community health service facilities and the realization of universal health care insurance at a basic level.

China has set strategic goals for a rational National Health Service System by 2020, which includes establishment of a hierarchical referral system, primary health physicians as gatekeepers, and the formulation of a family doctor system. A standard mode of general practitioner training will be established, and general practitioners should be recognized as primary health service providers by urban and rural residents. There will be two to three qualified general practitioners per 10 000 residents in both urban and rural settings, and general practitioners will provide health services adequate to meet the basic needs of the people.

China is still facing a mammoth task in trying to provide medical and welfare services adequate to meet the basic needs of the immense number of citizens spread over a vast area. In doing so, the focus should be on improving health care service delivery and on the establishment of qualified and registered family doctors and general practitioners.

TABLE 6.1 The number of primary health care facilities, physicians, and outpatient visits in primary health care facilities in 2005 and 2011[68,71]

Variable	Area	2005	2011
Number of physicians in primary health care facilities (per 1000 residents)	Rural areas (excluding village physicians)	0.54	0.62
	Urban areas	0.07	0.23
	Total	0.34	0.42
Number of primary health care facilities	Rural areas	624 116	700 144
	Urban areas	17 128	32 860
	Total	641 244	733 004
Number of outpatient visits in primary health care facilities (in ten thousands)	Rural areas	191 335	265 856
	Urban areas	12 220	54 654
	Total	203 555	320 510

6.3 FAMILY PRACTICE PROGRESS AND PROSPECTS IN COUNTRIES OF THE EASTERN MEDITERRANEAN

Many countries of the Eastern Mediterranean Region are facing health system challenges that include inequities in health, rising exposure to health risks, increasing health care costs and unacceptably low levels of access to quality health care.[73] Despite the building of extensive modern networks of health infrastructure, increasing the skilled health workforce, and wide deployment of medical technologies over the last several decades, the gains are not shared evenly across the region. In addition, the recent sociopolitical movement for change underway in several countries of the region, popularly known as the "Arab Spring," is likely to influence population health. Among the several challenges facing countries in the region is the need for governments to develop a clear vision for health reform and build a sustainable health system and financing strategy that ensures equitable access to essential health services.

Strengthening health systems in the Eastern Mediterranean Region is based on and guided by the values and principles of primary health care,[74] the four reform areas outlined in the World Health Report 2008,[75] and the Qatar Declaration on Primary Health Care which was adopted by all Eastern Mediterranean Region countries in an international conference held in Doha in 2008. Underpinning these guiding documents and declarations is the adoption of family practice as the principal approach for the delivery of essential health services, thereby making progress toward the achievement of universal health coverage.

Family practice, sometimes also referred to in the Eastern Mediterranean Region as family medicine, is a specialty devoted to comprehensive health care for people of all ages. It is a component of primary care that provides continuing and comprehensive health care for the individual and family across all ages, genders, diseases, and parts of the body.[76] It is based on knowledge of the patient in the context of the family and the community, emphasizing disease prevention and health promotion.

What follows is a brief overview of family practice programs in Eastern Mediterranean Region countries, the current status of family practice programs including challenges and opportunities, and lessons learned about instituting family practice as the principal approach for the delivery of primary health care services in the Eastern Mediterranean Region.

Commitment to family practice in countries of the Eastern Mediterranean Region

The Eastern Mediterranean Region comprises 23 countries that span from Morocco to Pakistan and cover a population of 630 million people. The commitment of the countries in the Region to the adoption of family practice is variable and can be considered across the three subgroups of Eastern Mediterranean Region countries.

➤ The six oil-rich Gulf Cooperation Council Countries (Bahrain, Kuwait, Oman, Qatar, Saudi Arabia, United Arab Emirates) have expressed high levels of commitment to adopt family practice and are in the process of implementing different components of it as the fundamental approach to the delivery of primary health care services. These countries nevertheless face capacity challenges and rely on expertise and experience, especially from economically developed countries, for shaping their national family practice programs.

➤ Among the 10 middle-income countries in the Region (Egypt, Iran, Iraq, Jordan, Lebanon, Libya, Morocco, Palestine, Syria, Tunisia) most have expressed commitment to family practice, however, implementation is patchy and there are significant capacity challenges related to human resources, financing and organizational aspects of family practice programs. Countries that have demonstrated government-level commitments include Iran, Iraq, Bahrain, Egypt, and Jordan. The subsequent sections provide an update on progress made and the bottlenecks faced.

➤ There is insufficient commitment and capacity to establish widespread family practice programs in the seven low-income countries of the Eastern Mediterranean Region (Afghanistan, Djibouti, Pakistan, Somalia, South Sudan, Sudan, Yemen), most of which are also least developed, and which together account for more than 50% of the Region's population. Sudan stands out as a country that has demonstrable vision and commitment to establishing a family practice program in Gezira State. A further challenge in these countries is to determine whether the globally recognized model of family practice centered on a family physician will be realistic, or whether alternative models for family practice need to be considered in such settings.

➤ Finally, many Eastern Mediterranean Region countries continue to be in a state of conflict and protracted emergencies. This puts additional pressures on already stretched health systems. Establishing or strengthening family practice programs poses a much greater challenge in these situations than under normal circumstances.

Situation analysis of family practice in the Eastern Mediterranean Region: family practice – essential elements

A rapid assessment of the situation of family practice programs in selected countries of the Eastern Mediterranean Region was undertaken. This was based on two sets of criteria.

The first related to the broad and more strategic approach to family practice in countries and included:

➤ national policy and commitment
➤ community perception
➤ establishment and scaling-up of postgraduate training programs and on-the-job training
➤ existence of family practice accreditation
➤ financing schemes for family practice programs.

The second set of criteria, related to the operational aspects of family practice programs, focused on:

➤ implementation of a health service essential package, essential medicines list, standard equipment list, and existence of clinical guidelines and protocols
➤ staffing pattern
➤ existence of functioning referral systems
➤ extent of registration of the population and adoption of family folders
➤ a health information system geared to support family practice programs.

The countries that provided information were Bahrain, Egypt, Islamic Republic of Iran [referred to herein as Iran], Iraq, Jordan, Sudan, Tunisia, and the United Nations Relief and Work Agency for Palestinian Refugees (UNWRA), which is the United Nations Agency that provides services to five million Palestinian refugees living in Jordan, Lebanon, Syria, West Bank, and Gaza.

Strategic aspects of family practice programs
National policy and political commitment to family practice
Among the countries reviewed, Bahrain, Iran, and Egypt have incorporated family practice as the principal approach for the delivery of primary health care services. In Iran, family practice has been included in several 5-year development plans starting in 1995, and had been expanded to all provinces by 2012.[77] The national policy for family practice in Bahrain is supported by a strategic mission, guidelines, and well developed strategies. In Egypt, family practice is the principle that underpins the national policy for improving health care delivery.

Among the factors that have encouraged these countries to commit to establishing family practice programs are the changing epidemiologic and demographic profile in Eastern Mediterranean Region countries which has created demands for services that provide continuity of care. In these countries there is increasing emphasis on providing a package of services that meets health promotion and preventive aspects of care. Accumulating evidence from several countries in the Region, both developed and developing, has demonstrated the success of the family practice approach, and countries have heeded the message of the World Health Report 2008 that puts patients at the center of care.

The inclusion of family practice in a national policy or strategy document does not necessarily imply unequivocal commitment to its adoption and subsequent implementation. Although not part of their national health policy or strategic framework, Iraq, Jordan, and Sudan have shown an increasing commitment to family practice. The commitment of Bahrain and Iran has been translated into inclusion of family practice in national plans and allocation of resources for its implementation. Egypt committed to family practice as early as 1999, and this was supported by a health sector reform project funded by multiple donors. This commitment has not always translated into allocation of adequate funds from national sources. Although a framework for the development of family medicine was approved in 2008 in Tunisia, the family practice program is yet not functioning.

Community perception and acceptance of family practice programs

Given the different levels of development, the perception and acceptance of family practice programs varies among countries. There is greater community engagement in Bahrain, Iran, and Gezira State of Sudan. In Iran, community representatives (*Shura*) have a major role in the planning of these services, and households are free to register with any of the recognized family physicians within their area of residence. In Egypt, the Ministry of Health and Population has developed and implemented a marketing strategy to improve community perceptions of family practice. In Iraq, Jordan, and Tunisia, additional efforts are needed to raise the level of awareness and to better define the roles of communities.

Training programs for family physicians and practitioners

The duration of the training program for family practice in Iran is 6 years. There is also a continuing medical education program for family practitioners, with 5-year intervals between relicensing, and which represents an important step in maintaining standards of care provided by family practitioners. Many physicians from the Arab countries take the Arab Board in Family Medicine, which is a 4-year program. Others have developed their own national programs – for example, the Egyptian Fellowship Board is offered over 3 years. In Bahrain, almost 230 family physicians had graduated up to the year 2012 and there is also regular in-service training of family physicians working in health facilities. Jordan has a well-developed postgraduate training program in family medicine. In Gezira, Sudan, the University of Medical Sciences and Technology offers a 1-year diploma in family medicine. Tunisia has developed postgraduate and continuing service training courses for family practice and a specific curriculum for family medicine has been introduced.

Despite the existence of these and other family medicine training programs in the Eastern Mediterranean Region, their scope remains limited and the numbers of graduates produced are far less than the requirements of national programs. Underlying factors include a lack of effective coordination between ministries of health and higher education institutions, limited institutional capacity to provide large-scale training for family physicians and converting the existing cadre of general practitioners to family physicians through customized programs, and the inability to establish family medicine as an attractive career path for recent medical school graduates.[78,79] There is also a lack of uniformity in the curricula and duration of family practice training programs across the region.

Accreditation of family practice programs

Many schemes to accredit family practice programs exist and are described as primary health care accreditation programs in some countries. The family practice program in Bahrain has been accredited for some years by Accreditation Canada. Jordan has a similar program for primary health care facilities accredited by its own Health Care Accreditation Council. Accreditation programs in Iran and Egypt exist but need to be strengthened and institutionalized, as many of the requirements are only partially met, and they function under the administrative authority of the respective health ministries and lack the independence required of such programs. Iraq, Jordan, Sudan, and Tunisia are developing accreditation programs.

Financing of family practice programs

Family practice programs are generally financed along the same lines as the health sector. In Bahrain, the family practice program is entirely financed from public sector revenue and the expatriate population has to rely on private insurance schemes to access similar services. Similarly, in Iran the public sector is largely responsible for financing family practice programs. In Sudan, the Gezira

State program is jointly funded by the state ministry of health, a health insurance agency, and other partners. The national health sector strategy 2012–2016 of Sudan proposes to scale up family practice with financing from national resources and the support of partners.[80] In Egypt, the donor-financed Family Health Fund was the major source of financing for family practice programs, but since its abolition the sustainability of the program has been questioned due to low revenue and lack of funds from national resources. The government of Tunisia has not allocated special funding for its family practice program.

There is limited experience in the Eastern Mediterranean Region in strategic purchasing of services and adoption of different payment methods. In Egypt, the Family Health Fund introduced mechanisms for the purchase of health services from public or private health facilities based on capitation methods that met predefined service quality standards. In Iran, the Ministry of Welfare purchases the services of family physicians for the provision of a defined package of services by offering an annual contract.

Family practice components: operational aspects
Essential Health Services Package, Essential Drug List, treatment protocols, and essential technology

Most countries included in the review have an essential or a basic package of health services. The major challenge is the inclusion of health promotion and preventive interventions and the implementation of the Essential Health Services Package itself. Bahrain has developed and introduced the Essential Health Services Package and Essential Drug List, and treatment protocols for common chronic diseases are available in all health care facilities. In Iran a package of services for each level of care comprising preventive care, screening, diagnostic services, treatment, referrals, and rehabilitative health services has been developed. The Essential Drug List is accessible at all health facilities, as are treatment protocols for most prevalent diseases, and the guidelines and essential equipment are in line with the package of services to be delivered. In Egypt, the Essential Health Services Package includes preventive and curative health services that target the whole population while the program has been implemented with special emphasis on the poor. Treatment protocols are fully developed and standard equipment and furniture and building designs have been developed to upgrade facilities. In Iraq, the Essential Health Services Package and Essential Drug List have been developed since 2009 but not fully implemented. The treatment protocols in Iraq are only available for those problems that are covered under vertical programs such as diseases involving diarrhea, diabetes, and hypertension. The Essential Health Services Package and Essential Drug List are available in Sudan, but implemented only in Gezira State and the treatment protocols are developed for only some prevalent diseases. Jordan has developed an Essential Health Services Package and Essential Drug List but has not implemented these, and treatment protocols are available for some vertical program-related diseases. Tunisia has not yet implemented an Essential Health Services Package, but the terms of reference for family physicians have been defined.

Staffing pattern

Given the limited capacity of family practice training programs in the region, staffing of facilities by qualified family physicians, family practice nurses, and other health workers is the single most important challenge. Despite acceptable health worker to population ratios in many countries, these are by and large general physicians and general nurses and not qualified family health practitioners. Bahrain may be among the few countries in the Region where two-thirds of the primary care physicians in government health centers are trained family physicians, and the majority of these are Bahraini nationals. In Egypt, standardized staffing patterns exist and post descriptions for family physicians are available, but there is a shortage of available trained family practitioners. In Iraq, the number of qualified physicians is limited, and there is lack of a clear job description for family physicians along with the absence of trained paramedical staff in family medicine. Jordan has developed norms for family physicians but has not implemented these yet. The staffing pattern has not been identified in Sudan and Tunisia.

Referral system

The lack of a well-functioning referral system in support of family practice programs is a problem faced by most countries. With the exception of Bahrain, where a referral system is operational, Iran, Egypt, Jordan, and Sudan are all struggling to make this functional. In Iran, the weakness in the referral chain is less from the "health house," the most peripheral health facility in the rural setting providing primary health care services to a defined population of 1500 by trained community health workers, to the rural health centers than from the rural health centers to the hospitals. In Sudan and Tunisia, the referral system has yet to be properly designed.

Registration of catchment area population and development of family folders

Four elements are important: (1) the identified catchment population in the vicinity of the health facility, (2) registration of all members of households at the health facility with the choice of selection of a family physician in their area of residence, (3) development of the family physician roster (the number of families assigned to each family physician), and (4) the existence and use of a system of family folders to ensure continuity of care. These functions can be undertaken manually by staff, be semiautomated or be recorded electronically. Bahrain, Egypt, and Iran are the only countries that are more or less implementing all four elements. In Iran, women health volunteers function as a bridge between households and health facilities to follow up any defaulters. In Egypt, most of the health facilities register their catchment population and family folders exist but are implemented only partially. In the pilot area of Gezira State in Sudan, the catchment population for each facility is defined and is registered in an electronic database. Family registers have been designed and their completion is the responsibility of the family physician.

Family practice information system

The health information system in most countries is usually not geared to support a robust family practice program. Once again, it is functional and automated in Bahrain. In Iran and Egypt key health indicators related to the defined catchment area have to be reported on a regular basis to the higher level based on defined health information system tools and guidelines. The health information system for the family practice program in Egypt requires further strengthening. In Jordan, key information is collected and reported by health facilities on a manual basis.

Case studies on family practice from the Eastern Mediterranean Region

The following section presents three case studies that provide insight into the development of family practice programs in three different contexts. It highlights many challenges faced as well as achievements in reconfiguring existing primary health care delivery programs into family practice programs.

Establishing a family practice program in United Nations Relief and Work Agency for Palestinian Refugees (UNWRA) refugee camps in Jordan[81]

UNRWA, established in 1949, provides health and social services to five million Palestinian refugees living in camps in Jordan, Lebanon, Syria, West Bank, and Gaza Strip. In 2010, a study carried out by the WHO in Nuzha and Baqa'a camps in Jordan, with a population of 200 000 Palestinians, revealed that primary health care services delivered in these two camps focus on maternal and child health, including antenatal and postnatal care, family planning, immunization, growth monitoring, promotion of breastfeeding, oral rehydration, food supplementation, and iron supplementation, as well as family planning and communicable disease prevention according to defined standards and procedures. Subsequently, UNRWA made efforts to integrate management of noncommunicable diseases, introduce a screening program for detection of diabetes and hypertension in adults, and to prevent micronutrient deficiencies. Health centers located in the camp areas introduced a home visit system for high-risk clients. Outpatient medical care, dental care, rehabilitation of physically disabled persons, laboratory and radiological facilities, and provision of medical supplies were strengthened to deliver an expanded package of services in these camps. All registered Palestinian refugees, irrespective of their income, social status, or gender were considered eligible to receive UNRWA health services. "Healthy family" files were maintained in the health centers and contained the medical history of each family member, which ensures the UNRWA health programs are family focused.

The UNRWA health department has also adopted the integrated community-based action framework as a bottom-up approach to socioeconomic development. It aims to reduce poverty, improve health and environmental conditions, and achieve better quality of life through active community involvement. A camp health committee including representatives from the health center, community members, camp administration, local leaders, and police was established to ensure that community members are involved in the planning, monitoring, and evaluation of primary health care services. Monitoring of the implementation of primary health care services is carried out by a systematic assessment based on measurable indicators through regular visits to the camps.

The program has contributed to increasing immunization coverage among infants to 99.3%, deliveries assisted by skilled health personnel to 100%, contraceptive prevalence rate to 53%, and access to safe drinking water to 99.3%. The infant mortality rate has reduced to 22.6 per 1000 live births and the maternal mortality ratio to 22.4 per 100 000 live births.

Family practice in Iran: political commitment and intersectional action as a key to success[82]

During the past 2 decades, Iran has made significant improvements in health indices, which have been achieved mostly through the establishment of a Primary Health Care Network System. However, the need to concurrently establish family practice and universal health insurance programs as part of health sector reform has been recognized for some time. The family practice program aims to improve continuity of care, especially for noncommunicable diseases, in a way that reduces referrals to higher levels, and improves and sustains the quality of primary care services.

Family practice programs are embedded within the primary health care framework. Family practice teams are the first contact at the primary care level and cover a well-defined population. The teams are also involved in public health functions including screening, surveillance, health promotion, health education, and preventive measures. More than 5500 physicians and 2500 midwives and nurses provide primary health care services for almost 23 million rural dwellers. Primary health care in rural areas works more efficiently with higher coverage rates than service delivery in urban areas.

The Primary Health Care Network System in Iran has three major components:

1. health houses established in a village where a group of nearby villages with a defined population can be served;
2. local (one male and one female) community health workers (*Behvarz*) who are trained over 2 years on delivery of primary health care services and are recruited by the government to serve in the same community;
3. simple and effective health information systems.

Health houses serve approximately 1500 people living in the main and satellite villages no more than one hour walking distance away. *Behvarzes* are committed to stay in the same village for at least 4 years after "graduation" and they then become eligible for continuing their education as health technicians in the nation's universities. Health houses provide primary health care services to their defined catchment population, actively follow up any defaulters, collect health data, and produce monthly reports to the nearest health facilities that are run by family practice teams. *Behvarzes* are part of the family practice team in rural areas. Introduction of this system has helped to improve greatly national health indictors within a short period of 10 years.

The nation's current 5-year plan for economic, social, and cultural development obligates the Ministries of Health and Medical Education, Cooperatives, Labour, and Social Welfare to extend services providing universal health insurance and family physicians to urban areas. The necessary work to expand the programs to urban areas and establishment of an electronic health information system is being done and implementation has begun in all provinces. Due consideration is being given to human resources, financing, and payment mechanisms, capacity building, and health information systems, but at this early stage several implementation challenges are being faced for each of these components.

Family Health Model: Egyptian health sector reform program[83]

The aim of the Egyptian Health Sector Reform Program was twofold: first, to introduce a quality essential package of primary health care services, contribute to the establishment of a decentralized, district-level, service system and improve the availability and use of health services; and second, to introduce institutional reforms based on the concept of purchaser-provider split and strengthening the regulatory functions of the Ministry of Health and Population. Egypt has adopted the Family Health Model as its principal strategy for the promotion of primary health care services in the country. The Ministry emphasized five key interventions while implementing the Health Sector Reform Program and the Family Health Model: facility architectural design and equipment; basic benefits package; staff capacity building and continuing training; quality and accreditation; and establishment of a Family Health Fund.

A total of 2078 primary health care facilities have been upgraded to work as Family Health Units. The upgrading included physical infrastructure, development of family health folders, and updating family health operational manuals. In addition, health care providers at the primary health care level have been extensively trained to assume their new role as family health care providers. The ongoing plan is to accredit the upgraded primary health care facilities.[84]

A study comparing user satisfaction between accredited and nonaccredited Family Health Units was done in 2005 and showed high levels of satisfaction in accredited units due to positive attitudes of family physicians and community nurses, cleanliness, and short waiting lists.

The Family Health Fund was established in 2001 to act as a purchaser of health care services on behalf of the Egyptian population. It was intended to be a financially independent body established as an insurance unit to put into effect separation of service provision from financing. The role of the Family Health Fund was to purchase curative and preventive primary health care services, to be extended to secondary care in the future, by contracting health service providers in both government and nongovernment sectors, paving the way for competition and improved access and efficiency.

With the closure of the Health Sector Reform Program in 2005, it has been difficult to sustain the quality of health services. Lack of motivation of patients to use family practice services, weak referral systems, a high turnover rate among family physicians, and inadequate health system financing mechanisms are among the major challenges for sustainability of the family practice program in Egypt.

Integrated district health system based on the family practice approach: an Eastern Mediterranean Regional Office initiative

In 2011, the WHO Eastern Mediterranean Regional Office launched an initiative called the "Integrated District Health System based on the Family Practice Approach." The initiative has been launched in four districts of Iraq and one district of Jordan since 2011 and the assessment phase has been completed.

The project proposes the following interventions for the establishment of a family practice model:

➤ mapping of available health facilities at the district level
➤ development of an Essential Service Package and Essential Drug List
➤ financing modalities, including payment methods, to improve access at district level
➤ public-private partnership contractual and noncontractual arrangements
➤ decentralization of health service management
➤ enhanced health system monitoring and evaluation
➤ workforce capacity building and human resource management
➤ financial, administration, logistics, and maintenance management system
➤ improved information systems for information collection, processing, analysis, and use of information for health service planning and management
➤ community ownership in local health development
➤ sustained intersectoral collaboration.[85]

Conclusions and lessons learned

The establishment of family practice in Eastern Mediterranean Region countries is at a relatively early level of development. In most countries the complete family practice model does not exist and in many only a few components are being implemented. Despite these shortcomings a reasonable beginning has been made and this needs to be sustained over the next decade. Family practice programs, if implemented well, constitute an essential component to achieving universal health coverage in countries of the Eastern Mediterranean Region.

The lessons learned from these programs are not unique but, rather, reinforce the lessons learned from other regions of the world and are summarized here.

Sustained political commitment is critical for acquiring a vision, evolving strategies and implementing family practice programs. Political commitment should translate into provision of financial resources as well as organizational support to program implementers.

There is no perfect family practice model and every country has to come up with the model that best suits its requirements and resource availability.

Nevertheless every family practice model, sophisticated or otherwise, should adhere to the fundamental elements of family practice that include, among others, patient-centeredness, continuity of care, whole person orientation, and the promotion of equity, quality, and safety.

Developing a qualified and well-trained workforce of family physicians supported by well-trained family practice teams is critical to the success of any family practice program. This requires establishing and scaling up competency based long-term, as well as short-term, training programs, especially to convert the cadre of existing generalist medical practitioners into family physicians.

Family practice programs will be successful only when they gain the acceptance and active participation of the community. This is essential as communities will only register with and utilize family practice facilities if they are involved in their planning, appreciate the quality of services provided and trust the functionality of the referral system for more serious ailments.

Piloting of family practice programs may provide opportunities to adapt and refine a model of family practice that best suits the context. It can help minimize costly errors prior to pursuing the policy to scale up.

There is good rationale to explore the implementation of the family practice model through private sector facilities, for which there is limited experience in the Region. Engaging contractually with private providers that meet eligibility criteria to deliver an essential package of publicly financed services based on a specified payment method requires new sets of skills and capacities for the provider as well as the purchaser.

More research and, equally important, good quality documentation is needed among Eastern Mediterranean Region countries to share and disseminate positive as well as negative experiences on all aspects of family practice programs.

6.4 FAMILY MEDICINE AND COMMUNITY ORIENTATION AS A NEW APPROACH OF QUALITY PRIMARY CARE IN THAILAND

In Thailand, hospital medicine was introduced in 1888.[86] A pattern was set with subsequent influence of the Rockefeller Foundation,[87] which resulted in the introduction of technology and a proliferation of hospital-based specialties.[88] In less than four generations hospital-based medicine became the norm, conferring high social status and prestige on its practitioners. Whereas hospital-based medicine has flourished, family practice, as defined by WONCA,[89] has almost been absent, unknown in the field as well as in academia. The term "general practice" has been used restrictively in Thailand, indicating a hospital-based nonspecialist or a doctor who is not yet a specialist.

To maximize the competencies of individual hospital doctors, general practice has been set up as a specialty since 1969, requiring 3 additional years of post-graduate training with a strong biomedical orientation and a vision of a general practitioner as a "super-specialist." It has never been very attractive and only a minority of physicians are specialists in general practice. Doctors generally continue to be hospital doctors but most also provide ambulatory care outside a hospital setting in their after-hours private clinics. They do this mostly as specialists on the basis of their hospital reputations.

There is dissatisfaction with health care as it is provided, coming from different sides, each with distinct arguments for attempting to reorient the system toward family practice. These include the good care argument, maintaining that good care must be close to the population and focussing on responsiveness and patient-centeredness and functioning as a bridge between Western scientific logic and the patient's culture and nosology while providing coordination between diverse professionals and advocating for patients' rights in a continuous and integrated manner; and the sustainability argument emphasizing medicalization, cost-explosion, and iatrogenesis.[90]

A survey in 1931 underscored the problems and proposed the training of junior doctors to work at the health centers.[91] But the decision was taken to produce "junior sanitarians" instead responsible for communicable diseases control and preventive sanitation activities working in the health centers at the sub-district level. Since then the junior sanitarians have become the main staff working at the health centers. The district hospitals are under the administrative and technical health authority of the Provincial Health Officer, while the health centers are under the administrative and technical authority of the District Health Officer. There is no administrative integration between the district hospital and the health centers of the district.[92]

Within the private sector, private clinics provide curative ambulatory care, and private hospitals provide curative services for outpatients and inpatients. There is no coordination between public and private facilities and no referral mechanisms.[93] Private drug stores are available in every district. The traditional health sector remains present with different types of methods. To solve the problems of fragmentation and commercialization of health care, integration of health care systems at the district level is needed.[94]

In 2010, the life expectancy of Thai people at birth was 74.1 years, the maternal mortality ratio was 48 per 100 000 live births, and the under-5 mortality rate was 14 per 1000 live births.[95] The leading cause of death in 2005 was stroke.[96]

Primary care reform in Thailand

Demonstration Diffusion Strategy

The family medicine concept, as a new approach to the provision of quality primary care and community orientation were introduced through demonstration health centers from the 1990s in some provinces (Ayutthaya, Korat, Songkla, and KhonKhean), in what was called the "Demonstration Diffusion Strategy."[97]

The first step of this strategy was to multiply the number of demonstration health centers through field model development activities. By improving professional capacity and know-how, and by ensuring visibility of these models of primary care, it was hoped to stimulate supply and demand in the community for family practice. This in turn would help disseminate knowledge about this approach and shift the focus from hospitals and consultant specialists to family practice.

The main features of these demonstration health centers were a well-defined population, regular community meetings to listen to people's views, a strengthened use of home visits and home care, an information system built around the family folder, and financial accessibility and solidarity through a flat rate per illness episode. The flat rate was initially 70 Baht; it was later reduced to 30 Baht under the label of the "30 Baht Scheme," until the service was eventually provided free of charge. The range of services covered curative care, care and active follow-up of people with chronic health conditions, care and active follow-up of identified risk groups, and other services based on the needs of the individual community. Importantly, the model also introduced a new way of interacting with people during consultation by emphasizing privacy, listening, and negotiation, not prescription alone.[90] Visits were organized to these demonstration health centers by politicians, senior officials, representatives of civil society and consumer organizations, and students and health workers.[98]

Universal health coverage

Universal health coverage was achieved in 2002. This means that all Thai people (99.36% in 2009) have affordable access to a comprehensive package of health services through three complementary schemes: the Universal Coverage Scheme (75% of the total population), the Civil Servant Medical Benefit Scheme (15%), and the Social Security Scheme (10%). In 2009, Thai health spending was 4.3% of the gross domestic product. Government expenditure on health was 76% of the total health expenditure, with the remainder being private health expenditure.[99] Thailand had an extensive network of health facilities before achieving universal coverage: at least one referral hospital in each district (for 30 000–100 000 people) and one health center in each sub-district (for an average of 5000 people).[100] The experience of the demonstration health centers has been considered as the cornerstone of the Universal Coverage Policy in setting up criteria for Primary Care Units. Family medicine is considered as an academic breakthrough to support primary care or proximity care at the health center level.

Under the Universal Coverage Scheme, known as the "30 Baht Scheme," patients have to register with a contracted Primary Care Unit. They are then eligible to use the health center where they have registered, or the outpatient department of the hospital belonging to the same Contracting Unit for Primary Care. To access the service, people initially had to pay a flat rate of 30 Baht (about US$1) copayment for each episode of illness including hospitalization. Since 2007, to decrease financial barriers, especially for the poor, the service has become free at the point of service.

Contracting Units for Primary Care

In order to reinforce integrated health care systems, health care providers must be organized as a Contracting Unit for Primary Care to get funding. Health services providing primary care must fulfill criteria to be recognized as a Contracting Unit for Primary Care, particularly in relation to human resources: they must have a doctor (in favor of at least 1:10 000 population, flexibility is possible up to not more than 1:30 000 population; each Contracting Unit for Primary Care must have a doctor for at least one Primary Care Unit); a pharmacist (in favor of at least 1:20 000 population, flexibility is possible up to not more than 1:30 000 population); and a dentist (in favour of at least 1:20 000 population, flexibility is possible up to not more than 1:40 000 population). Personnel employed by a Contracting Unit for Primary Care must be present more than 75% of their working time, services have to be available at least 56 hours per week, and a laboratory system for investigations must be available as well as vehicles for transferring patients.

In rural areas, where the qualified staff members (i.e., doctor, pharmacist, and dentist) are only available in hospitals, the health centers must associate with the district hospital to constitute a Contracting Unit for Primary Care. In that case the Contracting Unit for Primary Care often consists of a network of public services in the district: one Contracting Unit for Primary Care is equivalent to one health district. In urban settings, where there is a higher number of health services, there may be several hospitals in the same administrative health area and there may be doctors working in health centers. Each Contracting Unit for Primary Care can consist as part of a network of several health centers plus one hospital, or as part of a network of health centers or even private clinics only if they can fulfill the human resources criteria. A Contracting Unit for Primary Care in the private sector is called a "warm community clinic."

Family medicine development

Family medicine is a relatively new concept in Thailand. The concept was marginally introduced through Chiang Mai University in 1986, as a hospital-based biomedicine discipline but with well-developed psychosocial and community-based programs.

All medical universities have now taken up the teaching of family medicine, at least at undergraduate medical student level; however, many have an exclusively theoretical approach. Since 1998 family medicine has been recognized as a specialization in its own right.[101]

A 3-year formal residency training program for family medicine was started in 1999 and, from 1999 to 2011, this program had produced 429 family doctors. Another three-year formal training program has been established in the workplaces of trainees, mainly in district hospitals, since 2009. In 2009, 2010, and 2011, the number of doctors who participated in this program was 11, 37, and 17, respectively.

In an effort to quickly provide a large number of family medicine physicians at the early stage of the Universal Coverage Policy, those doctors who showed interest and had experience in any branch of medicine of more than 5 years were offered conversion courses to familiarize them with the concepts of family medicine. These courses were planned on a twice-a-year basis only from 2001 to 2003. The number of participants in this "fast track" program was surprisingly high. Altogether 6127 doctors were able to pass the examinations. The majority of these doctors thought that a diploma in family medicine might be financially useful for them, in that their private clinics could be registered under the Universal Coverage scheme. In reality, this was not the case: private clinics approved as Primary Care Units under the scheme had no requirements that practicing doctors had a diploma in family medicine.

Since 2004, the fast track has become the informal track: with 5 years of professional experience, most often experience as a generalist medical practitioner in a hospital, and a few days of additional training, doctors have to pass examinations to be family doctors. These doctors sit the same tests as doctors who undergo 3 years of formal residency training. From 2004 to 2011, this informal track has produced 106 family doctors.

A new strategy for training family doctors was launched in 2012 called Family Practice Learning. Family doctors should be able to provide direct health care to individuals and families, and also to support health care provision by family health care teams. Four dimensions have been planned in this new scheme for postgraduate training in family medicine: primary care to individuals; community participation; technical support to first-line health services; and management of wards at the referral hospital. In its implementation, some "special" families, a first level health facility, a ward in the referral hospital and a community are assigned to each family practice trainee and these are considered as the learning units. The trainee is coached in his or her practice by one preceptor qualified in family medicine and a second preceptor qualified in health care systems. The family practice trainees benefit from complementary lectures on issues related to primary care and family medicine, and health system management. The trainees have to perform assignments for learning at least for 1 year. They will be eligible to take examinations to be family doctors after having professional experience of at least 5 years. In 2012, 88 doctors applied as the first batch of this new program.

To give more recognition and value to family medicine, new methods to measure the human dimensions of health care have been introduced to the training, such as simulated patient surveys to analyze responsiveness, patient-centeredness, therapeutic decision making, the cost of different facilities in private and public sectors[102] and in family practices and non-family practices,[103] and the measurement of responsiveness as part of person-centered care by using a set of questionnaires and vignettes to assess the experience at the intersection between the patient and the health system.[104]

Reinforcement of the workforce

In terms of human resource development and mobilization, to invest more in the development of human resources, the policy extends the 2-year training for health center nurses to a 4-year training track, and makes provision for sending some of the new nursing graduates with 4-year training, or existing hospital nurses, to work in health centers. Some of the new graduates are also trained for an additional four months to become nurse practitioners with the expectation that they will perform better in the provision of curative services at the health center level.

Recently, context-based learning has been introduced; it started in five districts in 2007, and was extended in 2011 to at least one district in every province. Context-based learning is a complementary strategy to formal training to improve the skills of existing health center staff to provide quality primary care within their integrated district health system. Context-based learning aims at acquiring and transferring knowledge and skills in one's own working environment. Context-based learning is much more than a training exercise to improve on skills of the staff; it is an organizational development process, based on team building and stimulating the development of integrated health care systems. Context-based learning utilizes family doctors in training the health center staff and is at the same time an opportunity for training doctors in the framework of Family Practice Learning.

Some challenges encountered during the reform process
Coexistence of different models
In Thailand, different people clearly have different models of family practice in mind. What mainly differs is the relative importance attached to medicine and public health, and the biomedical, psychosocial, individual, and collective aspects of care, taking into account the sociopolitical context, history, evolution of health care systems, and the needs of society. No explicit consensus has yet been found and so different models continue to coexist and generate confusion.

In terms of primary care at the health center level, on the one hand the prevailing model entails a clear separation between curative and preventive activities, with the essential responsibility of health centers being to develop health promotion and preventive activities. On the other hand, the model is promoted by the experiments as a new approach, where the system is organized around decentralized and versatile first-line services. The health center should be able to provide an answer to most of each patient's health problems through offering integrated curative and preventive services.

One of the main reasons for confusion is that almost all health professionals in Thailand come from a hospital-centered culture. Even if some health policy decision makers are familiar with the concepts of primary care, family medicine, and integrated health systems, and have a theoretical vision, they do not have practical experience and may sometimes feel torn between the theoretical vision they advocate and their own professional culture.

Confrontation of the hospital culture with primary care and family practice concepts
The Universal Coverage Policy aims at strengthening primary care. However, the main actors leading its implementation are hospital staff and hospital managers.

The vast majority of health professionals working in hospitals are not familiar with concepts of primary care, family medicine, and health systems. For many of them, their interpretation of the new policy is strongly biased within their own frame of reference, experience, and organizational culture. Not many health professionals seem to have a deep understanding of family medicine, in terms of having internalized the theoretical concepts through direct experience of the practice itself. The essential idea is that biomedical, psychosocial, individual, and collective aspects of care are not alternative options for care, but rather different dimensions of care, and that the point is not to make a choice between them but to articulate them in the consultation process and in service provision.

Continuously clarifying aims and strategies, making explicit the existing sources of confusion and clarifying them has been helpful. For that purpose, communication, discussion, and debate between policy makers and different participants in the process need to be sustained.

Impact and lessons learned

Massive bypassing of Primary Care Units by patients who directly access hospital outpatient departments has been decreasing. The proportion of patients of hospital outpatient departments/primary care units by numbers of all visits was 1.2 in 2003 and reduced to 0.7 in 2011. This includes numbers of visits of referred patients of hospital outpatient departments and number of visits of patients at the primary care units who were referred back from the hospitals to their primary care unit. This indicates an increase in the use of primary care units, a better pathway of patients from primary care units to referral hospitals and vice versa as a direction of the Universal Coverage Policy.[105]

In terms of patient experiences and patient satisfaction, family practice has been systematically rated better than non-family practice.[102,106,107] In simulated patient surveys, with standardized complaints of anxiety presenting as recurring stomachache responding well to self-administered antiacids, patients with an average 25 years of age were instructed to express fear of cancer, express anxiety, and request information and explanation through agreed-upon cue questions and statements. The studies revealed that family practices, especially outside hospital contexts, were significantly more patient-centered and responsive as well as cheaper and less inclined to overmedicalization.[102,103] There is a lower tendency to overinvestigate in responding to anxiety and fear of this kind of health problem in family practices (*see* Box 6.1).[103]

The positive impact of primary care reform as part of the Universal Coverage Policy is linked with a declining trend in the incidence of catastrophic health expenditure, defined as out-of-pocket payments for health care exceeding 10% of total household consumption expenditure; the incidence dropped from 6.8% in 1996 to 2.8% in 2008.[108] The province-specific incidence of household health impoverishment, measured by the additional number of nonpoor households falling below the national poverty line as a result of payment for medicines and outpatient and inpatient health services reduced significantly after 2002 in the poorest rural northeast region of Thailand, and the number of impoverished households dropped from 3.4% in 1996 to 2.3% in 2002 and to 0.8% in 2008.[99] There was still a degree of impoverishment, a main reason being that some

BOX 6.1 Tendency of overinvestigation comparing family practices and non-family practices in response to a patient presenting with minor stomachache, anxiety, and fear

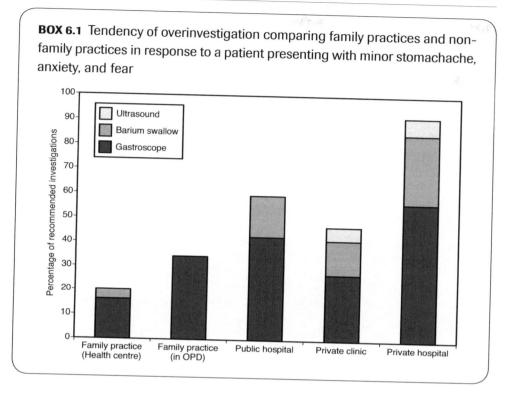

people chose to opt out of their scheme and pay out of their own pocket for outpatient and inpatient services especially in private hospitals, which were not yet covered by the Universal Health Coverage.[109]

A key lesson from the Thai experience is that both technical fieldwork and political pressure are important in facilitating change. When the political movement for universal coverage resulted in national reforms, the model of family practice health centers was already tried, tested, and known, and was therefore adopted as the means of delivering health care to all.

Having an adequate workforce is a crucial issue for the reform. This relates not only to the overall shortage of human resources but also to the skills of the staff required in each health setting. The question of human resources can only be tackled once there is an agreement on what is expected from first line health care services.

To increase the capacity of health center staff, to work along the lines of person-centered, continuous, integrated, and effective care,[110] and to gain the confidence of the whole population, calls for clearer support from the hospital and the Contracting Units for Primary Care. It is essential to support nurses and other health center staff as well as medical staff. Doctors, especially family physicians, can logically find their places in the system through support of primary care. Apart from working at health centers or district hospitals, the effective support of family physicians to health center staff is a key issue to gain the confidence of a population used to bypassing health centers.

REFERENCES

1. PAHO/WHO. *Renewing Primary Health Care in the Americas: a position paper of the Pan American Health Organization.* Washington DC: PAHO/WHO, 2007.
2. World Health Organization. *World Health Report 2008. Primary health care: now more than ever.* Geneva: WHO, 2008.
3. World Health Organization: Resolution WHA62.12. Primary health care, including health system strengthening. In: *Sixty-Second World Health Assembly, Geneva, 18–22 May 2009. Resolutions and Decisions.* Geneva, 2009 (WHA62-/2009/REC/1).
4. World Health Organization. Sustainable health financing structures and universal coverage. Sixty-fourth World Health Assembly Resolution, WHA64.9, Agenda item 13.4, 24 May 2011.
5. Brasil. Ministerio do Planejamento, Orçamento e Gestão. Instituto Brasileiro de Geografia e Estatística/IBGE. Rio de Janeiro: IBGE, 2010. Available at: www.ibge.gov.br/home/presidencia/noticias/noticia_visualiza.php?id_noticia=2170&id_pagina=1
6. Brazil. Presidência da Republica. Lei nº 8.080, de 19 de setembro de 1990. Dispõe sobre as condições para a promoção, proteção e recuperação da saúde, a organização e o funcionamento dos serviços correspondentes e dá outras providências.
7. Mendes, EV. *O cuidado das Condições Crônicas na atenção primária a saúde: o imperativo da consolidação da estratégia saúde da família.* Brasilia: Organização Panamericana da Saude 2012, 512.
8. Giovanella, L, Mendonça MH. *Atenção Primária à Saude. Em: Políticas e Sistema de Saúde no Brasil.* Rio de Janeiro: Editora Fiocruz 2008, 1112.
9. Brazil. Ministry of Health, Health Care Department, Basic Health Care Department. *National Basic Health Care Policy.* Brasília: Ministry of Health, 2007. (Series E. Health legislation) (Series Health Covenants 2006; 4). Directive No. 648, 28 March 2006. Official Gazette of the Union, Executive Power, Brasília, DF, 29 March 2006.
10. Brazil. Ministry of Health, Health Care Department, Basic Health Care Department. *Principles and Guidelines for Family Support Core Units.* Brasília: Ministry of Health, 2010; 152 p. (Series A. Technical Standards and Manuals) (Basic Health Care Handbook, No. 27).
11. Sampaio LFR. The Brazilian health system: highlighting the primary health care reform. *Italian Journal of Public Health.* 2010; **8**: 360–8.
12. National Register of Health Facilities. September 2012.
13. Macinko J, Almeida CSE, de Sa PK. Organization and delivery of primary health care services in Petrópolis, Brazil. *International Journal of Health Planning Management.* 2004; **19**: 303–17.
14. Harzheim E, Starfield B, Rajmil L, et al. Internal consistency and reliability of Primary Care Assessment Tool (PCATool-Brazil) for child health services. *Cad Saúde Pública.* 2006; **22**: 1649–59.
15. Zils AA, Castro RCL, Oliveira MMC, Harzheim E, Duncan BB. Satisfação dos usuários da rede de Atenção Primária de Porto Alegre. *Revista Brasileira Médica Famaceutica e Comunitaria.* 2009; **4**: 270–6.

16. Facchini LA, Piccin RX, Tomasi E, et al. Desempenho do PSF no Sul e no Nordeste: avaliação institucional e epidemiológica da Atenção Básica á Saúde. [Performance of the Family Health Programme in the South and North East: institutional and epidemiological assessment of Basic Health Care]. *Revista Ciência & Saúde Coletiva*. 2006; **11**: 669–81.

17. Elias PE, Ferreira CW, Alves MCG, et al. Atenção Básica em Saúde: comparação entre PSF e UBS por estrato de exclusão social no município de São Paulo. [Basic health care: comparison of the Family Health Programme and basic health care facilities by social exclusion stratum in São Paulo municipality]. *Revista Ciência & Saúde Coletiva*. 2006; **11**: 633–41.

18. Harzheim E, Duncan BB, Stein AT, et al. Quality and effectiveness of different approaches to primary care delivery in Brazil. *BMC Health Services Research*. 2006; **6**: 156.

19. Piccini RX, Facchini A, Tomasi E, Thumé E, Silveira DS, Siqueira FV, Rodrigues MA. Necessidades de saúde comuns aos idosos: efetividade na oferta e utilização em atenção básica à saúde. [Common health needs in the elderly: effectiveness of supply and use of basic health care]. *Ciência e Saúde Coletiva*. 2006; **11**: 657–67.

20. Viana AL, Rocha JSY, Elias PE, Ibañez N, Novaes MHD. Modelos de Atenção Básica nos grandes municípios paulistas: efetividade, eficácia, sustentabilidade e governabilidade. [Basic health care models in the urban municipalities of São Paulo: effectiveness, efficiency, sustainability and governance] *Rev Cienc Saude Coletiva*. 2006; **11**: 577–606.

21. Macinko J, Guanais FC, Souza MFM. An evaluation of the Family Health Programme on Infant Mortality in Brazil, 1990–2002. *Journal of Epidemiology Community Health*. 2006; **60**: 13–19.

22. Aquino R, de Oliveira NF, Barreto ML. Impact of the Family Health Programme on Infant Mortality in Brazilian Municipalities. *American Journal of Public Health*. 2009; **99**: 87–93.

23. Zanini RR, Moraes AB de, Giugliani ERJ, Riboldi J. Tendência da mortalidade infantil no Rio Grande do Sul, Brasil, 1994–2004: uma análise multinível de fatores de risco individuais e contextuais. [Infant mortality trends in Rio Grande do Sul, Brazil, 1994–2004: a multi-level study of individual and contextual risk factors]. *Cad Saúde Pública*. 2009; **25**: 1035–45.

24. Alfradique ME, Bonolo PF, Dourado I, et al. Internações por condições sensíveis à atenção primária: a construção da lista brasileira como ferramenta para medir o desempenho do sistema de saúde (ICSAP Project – Brazil). [Hospital admissions for conditions treatable at the primary health-care level: the construction of the Brazilian list as a tool for measuring health system performance]. *Cadernos de Saúde Pública. Rio de Janeiro*. 2009; **25**: 1337–49.

25. Guanais F, Macinko J. Primary care and avoidable hospitalisations: evidence from Brazil. *Journal of Ambulatory Care Management*. 2009; **32**: 115–22.

26. Macinko J, Dourado I, Aquino R, et al. Major Expansion of Primary Care in Brazil linked to Decline in Unnecessary Hospitalisations. *Health Affairs*. 2010; **29**: 2149–60.

27. Macinko J, de Oliveira VB, Turci MA, et al. The Influence of Primary Care and Hospital Supply on Ambulatory Care-Sensitive Hospitalisations Among Adults in Brazil, 1999–2007. *Am J Public Health*. 2011; **101**: 1963–70.

28. Mendonça CS, Harzheim E, Duncan BB, et al. Trends in hospitalisations for primary care sensitive conditions following the implementation of Family Health Teams in Belo Horizonte, Brazil. *Health Policy and Planning*. 2011: 1–8.

29. Rocha R, Soares RR. *Evaluating the Impact of Community Based Health Interventions: evidence from Brazil's Family Health Programme*. Forschungsinstitut zur Zukunft der Arbeit – Institute for the Study of the Future of Labour. IZA Discussion Paper No. 4119. April 2009.

30. Instituto Brasileiro de Geografia e Estatística (IBGE). *Pesquisa Nacional por Amostra de*

Domicílios, PNAD, 2008: um panorama da saúde no Brasil – acesso e utilização dos serviços, condições de saúde e fatores de risco e proteção à saúde. Rio de Janeiro: IBGE, 2010.

31. White KL, Williams TF, Greenberg BG. The Ecology of Medical Care. *New England Journal of Medicine.* 1961; **265**: 885–92.

32. Green LA, Fryer GE, Jr, Yawn BP, et al. The ecology of medical care revisited. *N Engl J Med.* 2001; **344**: 2021–5.

33. Facchini LA, Piccini RX, Tomasi E, et al. Grupo de Pesquisa AQUARES, Avaliação em Saúde. Relatórios, em: dms.ufpel.edu.br/aquares/

34. IPEA, System of Indicators of Public Perception (SIPS – Health). Brasília, 2011. Available at: www.ipea.gov.br/portal/images/stories/PDFs/SIPS/110207_sipssaude.pdf

35. Chomatas ER da V. Avaliação da presença e extensão dos atributos da atenção primária na rede básica de saúde no município de Curitiba, no ano de 2008. [Evaluation of the presence and extension of the core components of primary health care in the basic health care network in Curitiba, 2008]. Available at: www.lume.ufrgs.br/bitstream/handle/10183/24606/000747716.pdf

36. Brazil. Ministerio da Saude. Departamento de Atenção Básica. Coordenação Nacional de Saúde Bucal. SB 2010. Pesquisa Nacional de Saúde Bucal. Relatório Final. Brasilia: 2011. Em: dab.saude.gov.br/CNSB/sbbrasil/arqivos/projeto_sb2010_relatorio_final.pdf

37. Bhutta ZA, Lassi ZS, Pariyo G, et al. Global Experience of Community Health Workers for Delivery of Health Related Millennium Development Goals: A Systematic Review, Country Case Studies, and Recommendations for Scaling Up. Global Health Workforce Alliance (GHWA), Switzerland, April, 2010. Available at: www.who.int/workforcealliance/knowledge/publications/alliance/Global_CHW_web.pdf

38. Available at: determinantes.saúde.bvs.br/docs/relatorio_cndss.pdf

39. World Health Organization. *The World Health Report 2008. Primary health care, now more than ever.* Geneva: WHO, 2008.

40. Harris M, Haines A. Brazil's Family Health Programme. *British Medical Journal Editorial.* 2010; **341**: c4945.

41. CFM/AMB/CNRM. Pesquisa Demografia Médica no Brasil [Demographic and Medical Research in Brazil] 2011.

42. Leão CDA, Caldeira AP. Assessment of the association between the qualification of physicians and nurses in primary healthcare and the quality of care. *Revista Ciência & Saúde Coletiva.* 2011;**16**: 4415–23.

43. Castro RCL de. Percepção dos profissionais médicos e enfermeiros sobre a qualidade da atenção à saúde do adulto: comparação entre os serviços de atenção primária de Porto Alegre. [Perception by medical professionals and nurses of the quality of adult health care: comparison between primary health care services in Porto Alegre]. Available at: hdl.handle.net/10183/18766

44. National Bureau of Statistics of China. Statistical Communiqué of the People's Republic of China on the Sixth National Population Census (2010). Available at: www.stats.gov.cn/

45. National Bureau of Statistics of China. Statistical Communiqué of the People's Republic of China on the 2010 National Economic and Social Development. Available at: www.stats.gov.cn/

46. Wang Weixia. Situation, Problems and Countermeasures of the Aging Population in China. 2011; **8**: 315.

47. Chinese Ministry of Health. *Chinese Health Statistical Yearbook 2011.* Chinese Peking Union Medical College Press.

48. Guiding opinions of the CPC Central Committee and the State Council on Deepening the Reform of the Medical and Health Care System, 2009. Available at: www.gov.cn

49. Guiding Opinion of the Ministry of Health on Further Strengthening the Work of Maternal and Child Health, 2007. Available at: www.gov.cn

50. Li Yan, Wen Liyang. Studies on the structure of higher medical education in China. *China Higher Medical Education*. 2012; **1**: 1–5.

51. Decision of the Central Committee of the Communist Party of China and the State Council Concerning Public Health Reform and Development, 1997. Available at: www.gov.cn

52. Notice about Several Opinions on the Development of City Community Health Service, 1999. Available at: www.moh.gov.cn

53. Guiding Opinion on Developing Urban Community Health Service by State Council, 2006. Available at: www.gov.cn

54. Ministry of Personnel and Ministry of Health Issuing the Intermediate and Advanced Technological Accreditation Conditions for Clinical Professions (trial), 1999. Available at: www.gov.cn

55. Notice of the Ministry of Health Issuing the General Practitioner Standardised Training Pilot Scheme 1999. Available at: www.moh.gov.cn

56. Notice of the Department of Medical Science, Technology and Education, MOH, Issuing the General Practitioner Standardised Training Outline (trial), 1999. Available at: www.moh.gov.cn

57. Notice of the Ministry of Health Issuing Opinions on Developing General Practice Education, 2000. Available at: www.moh.gov.cn

58. Notice of the Ministry of Health Issuing Implementation Measures of Clinical Medicine, Preventive Medicine, General Practice, Pharmacy, Nursing and Other Health Professional and Technical Qualification Examinations, 2000. Available at: www.moh.gov.cn

59. Notice of Interim Provisions of Practice Scope in General Practitioner's Registration by the Ministry of Health, 2001. Available at: www.moh.gov.cn

60. Guiding Opinion on Strengthening the Urban Community Health Personnel Team Building by the Ministry of Personnel and Four Other Ministries, 2006. Available at: www.moh.gov.cn

61. Dong Yanmin. Status of General Practitioners in China and the Strategy for Development. *Chinese General Practice*. 2009; **2**: 529–31.

62. Zhang Ling, Zhu Yuewei. Discussing the service model of general practitioners teams in the community. *Chinese Health Service Management*. 2008; **24**: 327–9.

63. State Council's Guiding Opinion on Establishing the General Practitioner System, 2011. Available at: www.gov.cn

64. Ministry of Health, Ministry of Finance and National Population and Family Planning Commission Jointly Issuing the Opinion on Promoting the Equalisation of Basic Public Health Service, 2009. Available at: www.moh.gov.cn

65. Ministry of Health. 100 Frequently Asked Questions about National Basic Public Health Services, 2011. Available at: www.moh.gov.cn

66. Health Care Reform Office of State Council. Summary Report on Three Years Deepening the Health Career Reform, 2011.

67. Ministry of Labour and Social Security. Guiding Opinion on Encouraging Patients with Health Care Insurance to Take Full Advantage of Community Health Care Service, 2006. Available at: www.moh.gov.cn

68. Chinese Ministry of Health. *Chinese Health Statistical Yearbook 2011*. Chinese Peking Union Medical College Press.

69. Notice on Issuing Guiding Opinions on Setting and Staffing Standards of Urban Community Health Care Service Institutions, 2006. Available at: www.gov.cn

70. Notice of State Commission Office for Public Sector Reform, Ministry of Health and Ministry of Finance on Issuing the Guiding Opinion on the Staffing Standard of Township Hospitals, 2011. Available at: www.gov.cn

71. Chinese Ministry of Health. *Chinese Health Statistical Yearbook 2005*. Chinese Peking Union Medical College Press.

72. LuZuXun, LiYongbin, WangFang, et al. The development, effect and concerned issues of pilot work of national community health service system building in key contact cities – based on the comprehensive analysis of the baseline survey and routine monitoring data. *Chinese Journal of Social Medicine*. 2009; **26**: 321–5.

73. World Health Organization, Eastern Mediterranean Regional Office. Health systems strengthening in countries of the Eastern Mediterranean Region: challenges, priorities and options for future action. EM/RC59/TechnicalDiscussion. September 1, 2012.

74. *Primary Health Care: report of the International Conference on Primary Health Care; 1978 Sep 6–12; Alma-Ata, USSR*. Geneva: World Health Organization, 1978.

75. *The World Health Report 2008: Primary health care: now more than ever*. Geneva: World Health Organization, 2008.

76. American Board of Family Medicine. *Definitions and Policies*. Available at: www.theabfm. org/about/policy.aspx

77. Ministry of Health and Medical Education. *Family Physician Guide*. In: I.R of Iran, MoH &ME 2012 (published in Persian).

78. Abdulrazak A, Al-Baho AK, Unluoglu I, et al. Development of family medicine in the Middle East. *Family Medicine*. 2007; **39**: 736–41.

79. Hamad B. Community-based education in Gezira, Sudan. Paper commissioned by WHO for the international meeting on community-based education. Geneva: November 1986.

80. World Health Organization, Eastern Mediterranean Regional Office. Report on the Regional Consultation on Family Practice: assessing the current situation and paving the way forward. WHO/EMRO, December 2011.

81. World Health Organization, Eastern Mediterranean Regional Office. Good practices in delivery of PHC in urban areas. WHO/EMRO, 2012.

82. World Health Organization, Eastern Mediterranean Regional Office. An overview on FP. In: I.R of Iran, WHO/EMRO, December 2012.

83. Ministry of Health and Population. Egypt Health Sector Reform Programme. Central Administration for Technical Support and Projects, 2005.

84. World Health Organization, Eastern Mediterranean Regional Office. Report on the Regional Consultation on Family Practice: assessing the current situation and paving the way forward. WHO/EMRO, December 2011.

85. Integrated district health system based on family practice approach; assessment tool and guidelines. WHO/EMRO, July 2010.

86. Sangvichean S. Siriraj Hospital, The first hospital in Thailand. In: Sangvichean S (ed). *100 years of Siriraj Hospital, History and Evolution*. Bangkok: Faculty of Medicine of Siriraj Hospital, Mahidol University 1998: 1–14.

87. Pearce RM. Letter from The Director of Medical Education of The Rockefeller Foundation to The Minister of Education of Siam. Archive of the Thai National Library, 1922.

88. Donaldson PJ. Foreign intervention in medical education: a case study of the Rockefeller Foundation's involvement in a Thai medical school. *International Journal of Health Services*. 1976; **6**: 251–70.

89. WONCA. Statement issued at 13th WONCA Conference. Vancouver, 1991.

90. Pongsupap Y. *Introducing a Human Dimension to Thai Health Care: the case for family practice.* Brussels: VUB Press, 2007.

91. Zimmerman CC. *Siam Rural Economic Survey 1930–31.* London & New York: GP Putnam's, 1931. 2nd ed. Bangkok: White Lotus, 1999.

92. Nitayarumphong S, Srivanichakorn S, Pongsupap Y. Strategies to respond to health manpower needs in rural Thailand. In: Ferrinho P, Van Lerberghe W (eds). *Providing Health Care under Adverse Circumstances: health personnel performance & individual coping strategies.* Antwerp: ITG-Press 2000; 16: 55–72.

93. Nittayaramphong S, Pannarunothai S. Thailand at the crossroads, challenges for health care reform. In: *Proceedings of the 5th WONCA Asia Pacific Regional Conference on Family Medicine Education "Learning and Teaching Family Medicine", 1998 Feb 8–10*; Bangkok.

94. Nittayaramphong S, Tangcharoensathien V. Thailand: private health care out of control? *Health Policy and Planning.* 1994: 31–40.

95. World Bank. *Thailand Overviews and Key Indicators, 2011.*

96. Rao C, Porapakkham Y, Pattaraarchachai J, et al. Verifying causes of death in Thailand: rationale and methods for empirical investigation. *Population Health Metrics.* 2010; **8**: 11.

97. Health Care Reform Project Team. *Final Report, Thailand's Health Care Reform Project, 1996–2001, Annex 2: Strategy for developing family practice.* Bangkok: Health Care Reform Project, 2001.

98. Pongsupap Y, Vatcharasil P, Suksom J. *Analysis of Visitors of Ayutthaya Urban Health Centres.* Bangkok: Health Care Reform Project, 2002.

99. McManus J. *Thailand's Universal Coverage Scheme: achievement and challenges, an independent assessment of the first 10 years (2001–2010), a synthesis report.* Bangkok: Health Insurance System Research Office, 2012.

100. Pacharanrumol W, Tangcharoensathien V, Limwattananon S, et al. Why and how did Thailand achieve good health at low cost? In: Balabanova D, Mackee M, Mills A (eds). *'Good Health at Low Cost' 25 Years On: what makes a successful health system?* London: London School of Hygiene and Tropical Medicine, 2011: 193–234.

101. Prueksaritanond S, Tuchinda P. General practice residency training program in Thailand: past, present, and future. *Journal of the Medical Association of Thailand.* 2001; **84**: 1153–7.

102. Pongsupap Y, Van Lerberghe W. Choosing between public and private or between hospital and primary care: responsiveness, patient-centredness and prescribing patterns in outpatient consultations. *Tropical Medicine & International Health.* 2006; **11**: 81–9.

103. Pongsupap Y, Van Lerberghe W. Is motivation enough? Responsiveness, patient-centredness, medicalization and cost in family practice and conventional care settings in Thailand. *Human Resources for Health.* 2006; **4**: 19–28.

104. Polpak A, Pongsupap Y, Aekplakorn W, et al. Responsiveness under different health insurance schemes and hospital types of the Thai health care system. *Journal of Health Systems Research.* 2012; **6**: 207–21.

105. National Health Security Office. *Annual Report of the National Health Security Office.* Bangkok: NHSO, 2011.

106. Pongsupap Y, Van Lerberghe W. Patient experience with self-styled family practices and conventional primary care in Thailand. *Asia Pacific Family Medicine.* 2006; **5**: 4–12.

107. Pongsupap Y, Boonyapaisarncharoen T, Van Lerberghe W. The perception of patients using primary care units in comparison with conventional public hospital outpatient departments and "prime mover family practices": an exit survey. *Journal of Health Sciences.* 2006; **14**: 475–83.

108. Prakongsai P, Limwattananon S, Tangcharoensathien V. The equity impact of the universal coverage policy: lessons from Thailand. *Advances in Health Economics and Health Services Research.* 2009; **21**: 57–81.

109. Limwattananon S, Tangcharoensathien V, Prakongsai P. Catastrophic and poverty impacts of health payments: results from national household surveys in Thailand. *Bulletin of the World Health Organization.* 2007; **85**: 600–6.

110. World Health Organization. *World health report: Primary health care – now more than ever.* Geneva: World Health Organization, 2008.

CHAPTER 7

"The African family physician": development of family medicine in Africa in the twenty-first century

Compared with the rest of the world, health care in Africa is characterized by a huge discrepancy between the high burden of disease and the scarcity of health care workers to carry this burden, particularly doctors.[1] This chapter describes the specific health status of Africa and the different problems that the continent is facing in health and health care and provides an overview of the development of family medicine in Africa, with the support of Flemish universities, from South Africa to East Africa and the rest of the continent. The way forward in strengthening family medicine in the health systems of Africa is described.

In Africa, doctors have been working as generalists in primary care and rural hospitals without any further training since the start of the nineteenth century. In the twentieth century, the development of family medicine in Africa was mainly restricted to initiatives taken in two countries: South Africa and Nigeria. Although the first academic department of family medicine was started in the 1960s at the University of Pretoria in South Africa, the South African government officially recognized family medicine as a specialty only in 2007.[2] In Nigeria, family medicine training started in 1980,[3] but the first World Organization of Family Doctors (WONCA) Regional Africa Conference only took place in Nigeria in 2000. In 2012 fewer than 10 countries were represented in the Africa Region of WONCA.

The discipline of family medicine adopts the biopsychosocial model as one of its fundamental principles, although this still challenges the status quo of health care where the biomedical model dominates. This ideological struggle is evident in the history of family medicine in South Africa[4] and other African countries. Recently graduated African family physicians are beginning to find their place in the health systems of the different countries of the continent. Academic departments of family medicine are struggling for recognition and the health systems are still dominated by a reliance on centralized consultant specialist services and vertical, disease-oriented approaches. The World Health Organization's (WHO) World Health Report 2006, *Working Together for Health*, emphasized the need for primary health care training in the local community in order to deal with the "brain drain" from countries in the African, Caribbean, and Pacific regions.[5] Training medical doctors in the field of family medicine to provide health care at the district level can be seen as a response to this call.

The health status of Africa

Lower-resource countries in sub-Saharan Africa face enormous challenges including high rates of infant and maternal mortality, HIV/AIDS, tuberculosis, endemic malaria, noncommunicable diseases, violence, trauma, and pervasive poverty. According to the World Health Report 2006, sub-Saharan Africa had 11% of the global population and 25% of the global disease burden. Only 3% of the world's health care workers were based in this region, and the region accounted for less than 1% of global health expenditure.[1] With the continuous growth of the population and underdeveloped economies, the number of people living in poverty in sub-Saharan Africa continues to increase, with 20.6% living on less than US$1.25 a day in 2008.[6]

Despite the work of governments and nongovernmental organizations in local, national, and international programs, the majority of people in Africa still do not have easy access to affordable quality health care. And even though a growing urban middle class is able and willing to pay for quality health care, the majority of the community is still unable to afford better treatment.[7] The richest 20% of the population receive over twice as much financial benefit from government health service expenditures than the poorest 20%. Wealthier population groups have a higher probability of obtaining health care when they need it, though they use less of their total expenditure on health care than the poor, and are more likely to be seen by a doctor and receive medicines when they are ill.[8] The "inverse care law,"[9] noting that the fewest health care professionals are found where they are most needed and vice versa, is still very much applicable in most African countries. For example, in Ghana in 2008 the two most urban regions had 75.2% of all medical doctors, while the three most deprived rural regions only had 3.8% to provide care to the community.[8] Similar inequity exists in Rwanda with women in urban areas much more likely to be attended by a skilled birth attendant during labour than women in rural areas. Poverty also predicts inequity in Rwanda, with the wealthiest 20% having more than double the chance of being attended by a skilled birth attendant than the poorest 20% of Rwandan women.[10]

The unbalanced distribution of human resources creates highly inequitable health care provision.[11] Not only are the poor more prone to illnesses but also they are unable to cope with diseases, as health care is often hard to access.

BOX 7.1 Poverty is the world's biggest killer

The World Health Organization acknowledges that poverty is the world's biggest killer:[4]

Poverty wields its destructive influence at every stage of human life, from the moment of conception to the grave. It conspires with the most deadly and painful diseases to bring a wretched existence to all those who suffer from it.

In addition to poverty, "brain drain," or human capital flight, is a major contributor to the problems in health care in Africa. Research shows that approximately 65 000 African-born physicians and 70 000 African-born professional nurses were working outside Africa in high-income countries in the year 2000. This represents about one-fifth of African-born physicians in the world, and about one-tenth of African-born professional nurses.[12]

Brain drain is not only international and external to Africa, but also happens within the African continent with health workers relocating to countries with higher salaries or more stable environments. For example, many doctors from Nigeria and the Democratic Republic of the Congo have relocated to Namibia, South Africa, and Botswana. Within countries, internal brain drain leaves large parts of the community deprived of adequate numbers of health care personnel. This most often affects groups in the population who are already underprivileged, with lower socioeconomic status and a higher need for health care. Brain drain happens from rural to urban areas, from public to private care or well-funded nongovernmental organizations, from primary care to tertiary care, and from clinical care to health management or public health. Most countries in sub-Saharan Africa have more specialist doctors working in the tertiary hospital in the capital city than generalist doctors working in the district hospitals or health centers, despite the higher need of care closer to the community.

BOX 7.2 "I dream of the day when these doctors will return"

I dream of the day when these … doctors … will return from London and Manchester and Paris and Brussels to add to the African pool of brain power, to enquire into and find solutions to Africa's problems and challenges.

—Thabo Mbeki, former president of South Africa,
on "the African Renaissance"[13]

There are many reasons why people leave, not only for a higher salary, but also for better working conditions, higher living standards, more opportunities for family members, job satisfaction, or career opportunities. Another very important reason is personal safety to avoid political instability, war, or threat of violence in the workplace or community.

Family medicine, starting in South Africa

In 1968, the University of Pretoria in South Africa developed the first academic department of family medicine to train specialized primary health care physicians, what we now call family physicians. All seven Health Science faculties at the other universities in South Africa followed this initiative, which led to the development of the discipline of family medicine in South Africa.

In 1997, a workshop involving the academic departments of family medicine of all the eight medical schools in South Africa, and staff from the Ghent University in Belgium, took place in Durban on "Training in Family Medicine and Primary Health Care in South Africa and Flanders." At the end of the workshop, the "Durban Declaration" was formulated, in which the departments of family medicine agreed to form a network for communication and consultation. The Family Medicine Educational Consortium (FaMEC) was established to share and exchange expertise, to support each other's development, to standardize training outcomes and underlying core curricula, and to develop appropriate assessment and examinations.[14,15]

In the years following the establishment of FaMEC, the partnering departments developed and organized regular interuniversity meetings.[16] From 2003, this development was financed by a grant from the Flemish interuniversity development cooperation (VLIR-UOS).[17] An overall coordinator was appointed, yearly training workshops were organized and two groups of South African teachers in family medicine visited the Flemish University Departments of Family Medicine to exchange experiences on training family physicians. Gradually curricula were revised to be more socially accountable and to reflect national training outcomes.

Some programs, such as at Stellenbosch University, developed Internet-based modules with the potential to reach a wider population, including doctors in other African countries. National consensus was reached on the clinical procedural skills outcomes that should be expected of training programs.[18] In August 2007, the South African government officially recognized family medicine as a specialty.[19] Following this recognition more training was organized in primary health care centers and district hospitals, with formal training posts and direct supervision established. More training complexes, consisting of primary health care facilities, district hospitals, and regional hospitals, were developed in all the provinces of South Africa.

From South Africa to East Africa

In 2005, FaMEC made contact with universities and family medicine departments outside South Africa, including Tanzania, Uganda, Mozambique, and the Democratic Republic of the Congo. The positive experience of the collaboration in South Africa led to the development of a new project "Development of training in family medicine/primary health care in Southern and Eastern Africa: a contribution to the realisation of quality and equitable healthcare through a South-South Network."[20]

In this project a strategy of South-South cooperation was developed. The eight South African departments of family medicine that were working together in FaMEC created a link with emerging departments of family medicine in East Africa, including Tanzania (Aga Khan University), Kenya (Moi University – Eldoret), Democratic Republic of the Congo (Goma), Rwanda (National University – Butare) and Uganda (Mbarara University of Science and Technology and Makerere University). Two part-time coordinators were appointed, one for South Africa and one for East Africa. It was obvious that as far as the content of the training programs was concerned, all the expertise required was within the South-South collaboration. It was essential to find strategies to share the information, and to translate it into an appropriate educational context in the different settings. The South-South cooperation catalyzed developmental progress, as models that were developed in one site could be implemented in other places. Yearly workshops were an important platform for the exchange of experiences and although the context was quite different in the different countries, similar strategies were used, with an emphasis on social accountability, practice-based learning, and the creation of training complexes closer to the community.

Within this project a literature review on South-South cooperation was conducted.[21] Since colonial times African universities have had many links with universities in their colonizing countries in Europe (the "North"), for support, research and development of human resources. For many decades connecting with the North was the norm, while there were often very little linkages and cooperation between universities in the same geographical area. From the 1960s, when African countries became independent, there have been movements to focus on networking between countries in the "South," starting with the Bandung conference in 1955 where African and Asian country leaders came together to create links in cultural and economic areas by and for the global South.[21] In 2006, UNESCO (the United Nations Educational, Scientific and Cultural Organization) defined South-South cooperation as a process whereby two or more developing countries pursue their individual or collective development through cooperative exchanges of knowledge, skills, resources, and technical know-how. Linked by socioeconomic and political commonalities the countries of the South have many important lessons to share.[22]

BOX 7.3 "One can easily break one twig, but a bundle of twigs is unbreakable"

One can easily break one twig, but a bundle of twigs is unbreakable – together we may achieve more than one single institution.

—Professor Nelson Sewankambo, dean of the faculty of medicine at
Makerere University, Uganda (one of the oldest and most prestigious
universities in Africa, established in 1922)

As funding in many cases comes from the North, this often leads to North-South-South cooperation, with the North partner funding the Southern partners in their cooperation and sharing of resources and joined research.

Expanding from East Africa to the rest of Anglophone Africa

In 2007, a successful application was made to Edulink, which implements European Commission-funded programs in African, Caribbean, and Pacific regions, to form the Primafamed Network, the "Primary care/family medicine education network."[23] The aim of the Primafamed Network was to establish an institutional network between both emerging and established academic departments and units of family medicine in universities in sub-Saharan Africa.

The objectives of the Primafamed Network were to contribute to the health of communities through accessible, responsive, and quality health systems in sub-Saharan African countries by:

➤ educating and training family physicians to provide interdisciplinary, primary care services, oriented toward the needs of individuals, their families and the communities in which they live;

➤ planning, developing and strengthening academic departments or units of family medicine that offer family medicine training at undergraduate and postgraduate levels;

➤ developing a comprehensive vision and strategy, within the specific context of sub-Saharan countries, that delineates the integral contribution of family medicine and the primary care team to an equitable and quality primary health care system;

➤ establishing a specific institutional network between departments and units of family medicine and primary care.

Once the Primafamed Network started, the geographical scale of the network increased considerably. The eight academic departments of family medicine in South Africa were associates in the project and further departments participated in Tanzania, Kenya, Uganda, the Democratic Republic of the Congo, Rwanda, Sudan, Ghana, and Nigeria. In each of the 10 participating departments, a local coordinator was appointed to support the development of the department and training complexes were established with financial support from the project. Moreover, there was an opportunity for staff mobility, where departments could invite teachers from other African partners or associates to enhance local training capacity. In Kampala in 2008, at the first Primafamed Network conference on "Improving the quality of family medicine training in Sub-Saharan Africa," representatives from over 20 countries made a commitment to advocate for reform of their undergraduate medical school curricula, with increased exposure of students to primary health care, to develop and scale up the training of sufficient numbers of family physicians, to contribute to the scientific development of family medicine and primary health care, to interact with governments to develop and strengthen primary health care partnerships in the health system, and to create attractive and sustainable career paths in family medicine and primary health care.[24]

A major achievement during the conference was the launch of the *African Journal of Primary Health Care and Family Medicine*.[25] This open-access, online journal gives researchers the opportunity to publish articles on research in the African context and aims to document the development of the discipline of family medicine and of primary health care in Africa. The journal has stimulated a lot of African authors to publish their first articles and to document important aspects of the epidemiology of primary health care, primary health care processes, community-oriented primary health care, and the implementation of evidence-based medicine in the African context. In 2010, this journal became a bilingual French-English journal, which has opened the family medicine network toward nations in Central and West Africa.

In 2009, a new project to expand family medicine even further was started, called "Strengthening developmental capacity for family medicine training in Africa: the Southern Africa Family Medicine Twinning project."[26] In this project, each of the university departments of family medicine in South Africa "twinned" with a country elsewhere in Southern Africa to train family physicians. This includes countries without a university medical school department of family medicine:[27]

➤ University of Limpopo twinned with Rwanda
➤ University of Pretoria twinned with Swaziland
➤ Witwatersrand University twinned with Malawi
➤ University of the Free State twinned with Lesotho
➤ University of KwaZulu-Natal twinned with Mozambique
➤ Walter Sisulu University twinned with Zimbabwe
➤ University of Cape Town twinned with Namibia
➤ Stellenbosch University twinned with Botswana.

The twinning consisted of an exchange of learning programs, and support for the establishment and functioning of local training complexes in the "twinning" partners. One of the objectives of this project was to develop a strategy to stop the internal brain drain in the African continent, since very often students living in countries where there is no medical school leave their country to study medicine and never return to their country of origin. For example, Botswana has funded many students to go abroad for medical training but less than 20% of these students have returned to Botswana after graduation and in 2012 only 10% of the doctors in that country were local.[27] By establishing training complexes in each of these countries, and by stimulating the development of academic departments of family medicine, chances increase that after graduation medical doctors and family physicians will stay in their country of origin.

Despite some difficulties this project has further improved and expanded family medicine in sub-Saharan Africa. For example, at the University of Namibia a new medical school started in 2009 and incorporated family medicine training in 2010. The new medical school in Botswana incorporated family medicine training at both undergraduate medical student and postgraduate level and established training complexes in Maun and Mahalapye. Faculty support, training of trainers, and opportunities for student exchange are some of the other results of the project.

Family medicine in West Africa: the situation in Nigeria and Ghana

At the same time as the development of family medicine in South Africa occurred, one other country in Anglophone Africa had family medicine emerging. At the inception of the Postgraduate Medical College of Nigeria in the 1970s, general medical practice (now called family medicine) was listed as a specialty requiring postgraduate training. Private medical practitioners asked for and were saddled with the responsibility to develop this specialty; however, postgraduate training in family medicine did not start until about 10 years later. With the support of the Royal College of General Practitioners in the United Kingdom, working closely with the Association of General Medical Practitioners of Nigeria and missionaries based in Nigeria, the National Postgraduate Medical College of Nigeria accredited three faith-based mission hospitals to start family medicine training in 1981. The University of Calabar at its inception in 1990 started the first family medicine undergraduate department in Nigeria. A Family Medicine Unit in the Department of Community Health and Primary Care at the College of Medicine of the University of Lagos came on stream in 2010 with the support of the Primafamed Network.

Nomenclature of generalist medical practitioners in Nigeria is unique. General practitioners are the doctors working in private practice. Family physicians are doctors who have undergone 4 years residency training but most of these doctors work not in private practice but as consultants in public institutions like teaching hospitals, federal medical centers and general hospitals. Because of their broad training, they fill in for surgeons, obstetricians, internal medicine specialists, and pediatricians when there are shortages in general hospitals and federal medical centers, as well as fulfilling their generalist roles. There is a diploma-level training course to train general practitioners in private practice to become recognized as family physicians.

Nigeria has a strong culture of medical research. The specialties of family medicine, community health and public health are strong, both in academia and in clinical service. Publications by Nigerian family doctors in journals such as the *African Journal of Primary Health Care and Family Medicine* are common.

Family medicine extended to the West African subregion outside Nigeria in 1991 through the West African College of Physicians.[50] Postgraduate training began in 1999 in Ghana with only three residents. Like the Nigeria experience, the program was hospital-based and the initial trainers were private general practitioners who had been elected as fellows of the College. The first graduate fellows completed their training and assessment in 2005. That same year, the Ghana College of Physicians and Surgeons started another program in family medicine to run alongside the program of the West African College of

Physicians. Sponsorship for training in Ghana is provided by the Ministry of Health and family medicine graduates are given equal status and remuneration as graduates from other specialty training programs.[51]

What is family medicine in the African context?

In order to appropriately develop family medicine in Africa it was necessary to explore the crucial question "what is family medicine in Africa" and examine how family medicine can contribute to improving African health care and reducing the burden of disease. The first step in answering this question was an exploration of the key principles of family medicine in sub-Saharan Africa, using an international Delphi-consensus process.[28] This study revealed that core values and characteristics, such as being holistic, longitudinal, comprehensive, and family- and community-oriented, were recognized as relevant, with differences from more developed settings in terms of emphasis. Several key organizational principles of family medicine, such as first-contact care and home visiting, were seen differently in developed countries. Principles related to the scope of practice showed the greatest difference, with the need for family physicians to be competent in the clinical skills required in district hospitals and able to perform relevant procedural and surgical skills, and to act as consultants and teachers to members of the first-contact primary care team. This study invited further reflection on the role of family physicians in the African context and made clear that there is a specific role for such a medical clinical discipline in the primary health care team, working in both the district hospital and in primary health care, with different roles in different contexts, as care provider, consultant, capacity builder, supervisor, manager, and community leader.[29]

Participants at the 2009 WONCA Africa regional conference defined a consensus statement on family medicine in Africa describing the role of the family physician in Africa as "a clinical leader and consultant in the primary health care team, ensuring primary, continuing, comprehensive, holistic and personalized care of high quality to individuals, families and communities."[30] This document now serves as the core of understanding and the basis for further development of family medicine in Africa.

To analyze the progress that family medicine training had been making, the partners in the Primafamed Network developed a scale to assess the functioning of the various departments or units of family medicine. This scale examined important achievements such as structural implementation of the department, development of a curriculum, existence of training complexes, start of postgraduate training, and acceptance of family medicine as an area of medical specialization by the national Ministry of Health or Education. This study revealed progress made during the period 2008–2010, showed there are numerous factors influencing the development of family medicine training and the development of academic departments, and demonstrated how the Primafamed Network project was a catalyst in this process. At the start of the Primafamed Network project all partners had a unit or department of family medicine in place or under development, however only three had officially started postgraduate training. At the end of the project eight out of ten partners had started postgraduate training.

In 2013 a study was published on the views of key leaders on family medicine. Government and academic leaders were interviewed on their perspectives of family medicine in the African context. Benefits that leaders reported from family medicine included having clinically skilled "all-rounders" practicing holistic care in district hospitals, with a strong role in leadership and management in district health care and who can mentor primary health care teams in the community. There were also concerns expressed, specifically that family medicine is still unknown or poorly understood and therefore poorly recognised by many officials. Strong advocacy is needed from within the discipline to overcome struggles with policy ambivalence.[31]

Constraints

Despite the gradual expansion of family medicine in Africa, it is not an easy path and many obstacles continue to be faced by family medicine programs and family physicians. The integration of family medicine in local health systems is a slow process. In many countries policy makers remain very conservative, health systems are still oriented toward referral hospitals, hospital specialists, and vertical disease-specific programs, and this is often driven by donor funding.[32] Family medicine emphasizes the importance of generalist clinicians and health care systems based on primary health care. A critical mass of well-trained family physicians is needed to demonstrate the contribution of family medicine to effective primary health care in Africa. Most universities only train a few family medicine residents simultaneously because of limited capacity and it takes time to reach the critical "turning point." Gezira University in Sudan has shown that it is possible to create a large pool of well-trained family physicians who can make a difference in a short time. This was possible because of the synergy between policy makers, local authorities, and Gezira University to respond to the vital health needs of their population in a cost-effective way.

Experience has shown that it is difficult to find money to support family medicine and networks such as the Primafamed Network. Most international donors, including the Bill and Melinda Gates Foundation, the World Bank, the

International Monetary Fund, and the Clinton Foundation have been focusing most of their efforts on vertical, disease-oriented programs based in specific hospitals or districts as opposed to strengthening of nationwide, comprehensive, community-based primary health care and family medicine.

The Millennium Development Goals set targets to be achieved by 2015. It is a tragedy that in 2012 sub-Saharan Africa remains off track on all of the targets. Many African countries have not made sufficient progress in reducing rates of child and maternal mortality and the number of people with HIV/AIDS continues to increase. In many countries much more effort must be exerted to ensure universal coverage for all people, especially the poor.[33] It is clear that Africa has been most adversely affected by the widening global inequality in mortality rates, often as a result of the HIV/AIDS pandemic, and this has been exacerbated by prevailing economic inequities. For the two continents with the most extreme disparities in the distribution of wealth, North America and Africa, the gap in life expectancy fell from 30.6 years in the period 1950–1955 to less than 24 years in the period 1985–1990. However, the gap has since risen again, and in 2012 was again almost the same level as in the 1950s.[34] Worldwide, access to health care has become problematic for an increasing number of people, especially in developing countries. As a consequence of globalization, mobility and migration has increased significantly, leading to brain drain taking well-trained health professionals away from the places where they are most needed.

Family medicine in Africa and health systems development

In most developing countries, the majority of resources go to secondary and tertiary care hospitals that provide care for only a small percentage of the population. The attractiveness and the "power" of hospitals in the health care system are strong. A hospital is more visible, while primary health care is much more dispersed in the community, in the form of clinics, community health centers, and district hospitals. The 2008 World Health Report, *Primary Health Care, Now More Than Ever*, emphasized the need to move away from hospital-centrism and to focus on providing care closer to the community as one of the crucial steps to improve health care and to achieve universal access and equitable care.[35]

In recent years, another tension has become increasingly important. This is the antagonism between horizontal (person- and community-oriented care) and vertical (disease-oriented) care. Shortly after the Declaration of Alma-Ata of 1978, where the importance of comprehensive primary health care was emphasized so strongly,[36] the concept of selective primary health care has reinforced vertical "disease-oriented" programs. The HIV/AIDS epidemic in the 1980s gave a strong impetus to this development of vertical programs. Many international nongovernmental organizations have also concentrated on vertical programs. Although enormous amounts of money are invested in those vertical programs, the overall performance of many disease control programs remains poor[37] and in Africa most of the Millennium Development Goals for 2015 will not be met. A big problem of vertical programs is that they address only a fraction of the community's demand or need for health care. A report prepared for the Swiss Agency for Development and Cooperation identifies other disadvantages of vertical programs, including the creation of duplication as each single disease control program requires its own bureaucracy; inefficient facility utilization by the population, which may lead to gaps in care; incompatibility with quality health care delivery; and, where funded externally, such programs may undermine government capacity by reducing the responsibility of the state to improve health care through its own services.[38,39] Perhaps what is needed is a diagonal approach to decrease the polarization in the discussion between horizontal versus vertical care programs with programs gradually and carefully being transformed into a diagonal, and ultimately perhaps a horizontal, financing approach.

In March 2008, the 15by2015 campaign[40,41] was launched by WONCA in collaboration with Global Health through Education, Training and Service (GHETS),[42] the Network: Towards Unity for Health,[43] and the European Forum for Primary Care.[44] The 15by2015 campaign calls upon funding organizations to assign primary health care a pivotal role by investing, by 2015, 15% of the budget of vertical disease oriented programs in strengthening well-coordinated, integrated local health care systems and asking that this percentage further increase overtime. The campaign called for ministries of health to monitor the accessibility and quality of care in a transparent way to ensure that the 15by2015 initiative leads to the most effective improvements in the health of the community.

Scaling up capacity of family medicine in Africa
In 2012, the third WONCA African regional conference was held in Zimbabwe. In the days following the conference, participants from 20 countries convened for a Primafamed Network conference where the participants formulated the Primafamed Statement on "Scaling up family medicine and primary health care."[45] In line with Resolution 62.12 of the 2009 World Health Assembly (*see* Box 7.4),[46] the WHO Global Health Workforce Strategy,[47] and Resolution 59.23 of the 2006 World Health Assembly on "Rapid Scaling Up of Health Workforce,"[48] participants stressed the need for an integrated approach to comprehensive primary health care in order to address the fragmentation of care and health systems seen as a consequence of too great a focus on vertical disease-oriented programs.

BOX 7.4 Resolution 62.12 of the World Health Assembly on primary health care, including health system strengthening, 2009[48]

Train and retain adequate numbers of health workers, with appropriate skill-mix, including primary health care nurses, midwives, allied health professionals and family physicians, able to work in a multidisciplinary context, in cooperation with non-professional community health workers in order to respond effectively to people's health needs.

Encourage that vertical programmes, including disease-specific programmes, are developed, integrated and implemented in the context of integrated primary health care.

Family physicians fully support the work of African governments to implement universal health coverage that is oriented toward guaranteeing the right to health for all, including implementing the 2001 Abuja Declaration to increase government funding for health to at least 15% of each nation's budget,[49] developing national socially oriented health insurance systems to provide universal access, developing strong decentralized district health systems responsive to local communities, and implementing innovative payment systems to drive improvement of quality in integrated primary health care teamwork to achieve "Health for All."

The future of family medicine will be in the framework of the primary health care system and family physicians need to be trained accordingly in a community-based team approach in the district health system that focuses on accessibility, connectedness, health promotion and disease prevention, comprehensiveness, continuity, and coordination of care, in the context of families and communities, addressing the problems arising in the context of multimorbidity, and providing appropriate person- and people-centered care. All departments and training institutions for family medicine need to commit to a socially accountable approach in order to respond to workforce needs and to the requirements of the health care system. Training in family medicine must be based on the acquisition of appropriate knowledge, skills, and attitudes in the context of the community, with dominance of community-based training in the programs.

The 2012 Primafamed Statement on "Scaling up family medicine and primary health care" provides a list of concrete strategic actions that should be developed for scaling up, including:

➤ convince Ministers of Health and Education, and the leadership of medical schools, that a significant proportion of medical school graduates (between 40% and 60%) should be trained in family medicine;

➤ integrate the existing community service periods after undergraduate medical training into the training program of family medicine, in order to fast track scaling up at a lower cost;

➤ define appropriate content and duration of the training program in family medicine in each country;

➤ prepare family doctors for lifelong learning and develop appropriate continuous professional development.

Essential conditions to make this happen include:

➤ ensuring that all countries have training in family medicine and establish networks, synergies and collaborations to provide support through South-South cooperation;

➤ integrating exposure to primary health care and family medicine in each undergraduate medical school curriculum;

➤ establishing well-equipped training complexes for primary health care teams and create an environment for transformative learning;

➤ offering a sufficient number of funded posts for family medicine trainees;

➤ providing appropriate remuneration for family physicians and the other members of primary health care teams and attractive career paths;

➤ developing training the trainer programs, taking advantage of South-South cooperation;

➤ increasing the budget for primary health care and encouraging nongovernmental organizations and donors to invest in strengthening local primary health care systems;

➤ implementing population-oriented campaigns to promote family medicine and primary health care and stimulate cost-effective use of health care services by the population.

Discussion is ongoing on the optimal duration of postgraduate training in family medicine which will vary in relation to the relevance of undergraduate training opportunities and contextual factors such as the need to work in district and community hospitals following graduation.

Appropriate research in family medicine and primary health care in Africa is essential and requires building research capacity in academic departments of family medicine and developing an African family medicine and primary health care research network to support researchers and promote cross-country collaboration.

The development of family medicine in Africa will benefit from current strategic choices to focus on increasing access by means of universal coverage, supported by public insurance, social security systems, and community-based health insurance programs, among others. The reorientation of the health system from hospital-centrism to a focus on primary health care and the training of both undergraduate medical students and postgraduate medical doctors in programs with higher social accountability, closer to the community, are essential to create a large enough pool of African family physicians who are responsive to the needs of their communities in a comprehensive, accessible, affordable, equitable, quality, and continuous manner. By doing this, we are convinced that family medicine can make a difference where it really matters, to contribute to a healthier future for Africa.

Refocusing on primary health care should bring into practice the "message of hope" proposed by Archbishop Emeritus Desmond Tutu (*see* Box 7.5).[4]

BOX 7.5 "Message of hope" from Archbishop Emeritus Desmond Tutu

Doctors in family medicine are aware of the challenges, attempt to understand them better and work to address them … The issues of principles and values, relationships and meaning are not left to chance, but become an important element of service, systems, training and research.

This gives me hope of a transformation in the health service that can take care of our people, which can guide us through this difficult time. This hope is not only for South Africa, but also for our brothers and sisters in the rest of the continent and the rest of the world.

If the family medicine movement can play that role, let us join hands and realise that dream.

ACKNOWLEDGMENTS

The authors of this chapter thank the donors who provided funding for the different projects mentioned in this chapter, including VLIR-UOS, the European Union in the Edulink program, and GHETS for continuous financial support, and the members of the WONCA Africa Region for their contribution to the development of family medicine and primary health care in Africa. They thank all their colleagues in Africa and the rest of the world who provided inspiration through continuous and never-ending commitment, motivation, and creativity in the development of family medicine and family medicine training in sub-Saharan Africa.

REFERENCES

1. *World Health Report 2006. Working together for health*. World Health Organization, 2006. Available at: www.who.int/whr/2006/en/
2. Hellenberg D, Gibbs T. Developing family medicine in South Africa: A new and important step for medical education. *Medical Teacher*. 2007; **29**: 897–900.

3. Pearson A. *Training for General Practice in Nigeria.* University of Ibadan Press, 1980.
4. Hugo J, Allan L. *Doctors for Tomorrow.* NISC South Africa, 2008.
5. *World Health Report 2006. Working together for health.* World Health Organization, 2006. Available at: www.who.int/whr/2006/en/
6. World Databank. *World Development Indicators & Global Development Finance.* Available at: databank.worldbank.org/ddp/home.do?Step=3&id=4
7. The Economist. *The Future of Health Care in Africa.* A report from the Economist Intelligence Unit. Sponsored by Janssen 2012.
8. Discussion paper. International conference on Primary Health Care and health care systems in Africa: Ouagadougou 2008. Available at: www.afro.who.int/index.php?option=com_content&view=article&id=2034&Itemid=830
9. Hart JT. The Inverse Care Law. *Lancet.* 1971; **1**: 405–12.
10. www.who.int/gho/countries/rwa.pdf
11. Summaries of country experiences on Primary Health Care revitalization. International conference on Primary Health Care and health care systems in Africa: Towards the Achievement of the Health Millennium Development Goals. Ouagadougou 2008. Available at: www.afro.who.int/index.php?option=com_content&view=article&id=2034&Itemid=830
12. Clemens M, Petterson G. New data on African health professionals abroad. *Human Resources for Health.* 2008; **6**: 1.
13. The African Renaissance Statement of Deputy President, Thabo Mbeki. August 13, 1998. Available at: www.dfa.gov.za/docs/speeches/1998/mbek0813.htm
14. Supported by Ministry of Education of Flemish Community.
15. Training in Family Medicine and Primary Health Care in South Africa and Flanders: report of a study visit (16–25/09/97). Projectnr. ZA.96.11, Ministerie van de Vlaamse Gemeenschap, Departement Onderwijs.
16. Williams RL, Reid S. Family practice in the new South Africa. *Family Medicine.* 1998; **30**(8): 574–8.
17. The VLIR-ZEIN2003 PR290 project financed by VLIR UOS.
18. Mash B, Couper I, Hugo J. Building consensus on clinical procedural skills for South African family medicine training using the Delphi technique. *South African Family Practice.* 2006; **48**(10): 14.
19. Hellenberg D, Gibbs T. Developing family medicine in South Africa: A new and important step for medical education. *Medical Teacher.* 2007; **29**: 897–900.
20. The VLIR-ZEIN 2006 PR320-project financed by VLIR UOS.
21. Du Toit L. *South-South Cooperation in Health Science Education: a literature review.* Johannesburg: Wits Centre for Rural Health, 2011.
22. UNESCO Executive Board 2006. Report by the director-general on the financial implications of creating and implementing a South-South cooperation programme in education. Paris: UNESCO. Available at: www.unesco.org
23. EuropeAid/124308/D/ACT/ACP. Available at: www.primafamed-ugent.be
24. The Kampala commitment. Primafamed conference. 17–21 November 2008, Kampala, Uganda. Available at: www.nivel.nl/sites/default/files/bestanden/KAMPALA_DECLARATION.pdf
25. African Journal of Primary Health Care and Family Medicine www.phcfm.org
26. The VLIR ZEIN 2009 PR360 project funded by the VLIR UOS.
27. www.aho.afro.who.int/profiles_information/index.php/Botswana:Analytical_summary_-_Health_workforce

28. Mash R, Downing R, Moosa S, et al. Exploring the key principles of Family Medicine in sub-Saharan Africa: international Delphi consensus process. *South African Family Practice.* 2008; **50**(3): 60–5.

29. Mash B. Reflections on the development of family medicine in the Western Cape: A 15-year review. *South African Family Practice.* 2011; **53**(6): 557–62.

30. Mash R, Reid S. Statement of consensus of family medicine in Africa. *African Journal of Primary Health Care and Family Medicine.* Available at: www.phcfm.org/index.php/phcfm/article/view/151/50

31. Moosa S, Downing R, Mash B, et al. Understanding of Family Medicine in Africa: a qualitative study of leaders' views. *British Journal of General Practice.* 2013; **63**(608): 209–16.

32. Reid S, Mash R, Downing R, et al. Perspectives on key principles of generalist medical practice in public service in sub-Saharan Africa: a qualitative study. *BMC Family Practice* 2011; **12**: 1–9.

33. International Bank for Reconstruction and Development/World Bank. *Global Monitoring Report 2006: Millennium Development Goals: strengthening mutual accountability, aid, trade and governance.* Washington: IBRD 2006.

34. Dorling D, Shaw M, Smith GD. Global inequality of life expectancy due to AIDS. *British Medical Journal.* 2006; **332**: 662–4.

35. World Health Report 2008. *Primary Health Care, Now More Than Ever.* World Health Organization, 2008.

36. International Conference on Primary Health Care. Declaration of Alma-Ata; USSR. World Health Organization, September 1978 (*see* Annex A).

37. Unger JP, De Paepe P, Ghilbert P, et al. Disintegrated care: the Achilles heel of international health policies in low and middle-income countries. *International Journal of Integrated Care.* 2006; **6**: 1–13.

38. Brown A. *Integrating Vertical Health Programmes into Sector Wide Approaches – experiences and lessons. Swiss Agency for Development and Cooperation.* London: Institute for Health Sector Development, 2001.

39. Ooms G, Van Damme W, Baker B, et al. The 'diagonal' approach to Global Fund financing: a cure for the broader malaise of health systems? *Globalization and Health.* 2008, **4**: 6.

40. De Maeseneer J, van Weel C, Egilman D, et al. Strengthening Primary Care: addressing the disparity between vertical and horizontal investment. *British Journal of General Practice.* 2008; **58**: 3–4.

41. De Maeseneer J, van Weel C, Egilman D, et al. Funding for primary health care in developing countries: money from disease specific projects could be used to strengthen primary care. *British Medical Journal.* 2008; **336**: 518–19.

42. www.ghets.org

43. www.the-networktufh.org

44. www.euprimarycare.org

45. Scaling up Family Medicine and Primary Health Care in Africa: Statement of the Primafamed Network. 23 November 2012, Victoria Falls, Zimbabwe.

46. www.who.int/hrh/resources/A62_12_EN.pdf

47. www.who.int/hrh/documents/en/workforce_strategy.pdf

48. www.who.int/workforcealliance/knowledge/resources/wha_scalingup/en/index.html

49. World Health Organization. *The Abuja declaration. Ten years on.* 2011. www.who.int/healthsystems/publications/abuja_report_aug_2011.pdf

50. *Faculty of Family Medicine curriculum.* West African College of Physicians, 2008.

51. Essuman A, Anthony-Krueger C, Ndanu TA. Perceptions of medical students about family médicine in Ghana. *Ghana Medical Journal.* 2012; 7: 148.

Annex A

DECLARATION OF ALMA-ATA[1]

The International Conference on Primary Health Care, meeting in Alma-Ata this twelfth day of September in the year Nineteen hundred and seventy eight, expressing the need for urgent action by all governments, all health and development workers, and the world community to protect and promote the health of all the people of the world, hereby makes the following Declaration:

I

The Conference strongly reaffirms that health, which is a state of complete physical, mental and social well-being, and not merely the absence of disease or infirmity, is a fundamental human right and that the attainment of the highest possible level of health is a most important world-wide social goal whose realization requires the action of many other social and economic sectors in addition to the health sector.

II

The existing gross inequality in the health status of the people particularly between developed and developing countries as well as within countries is politically, socially and economically unacceptable and is, therefore, of common concern to all countries.

III

Economic and social development, based on a New International Economic Order, is of basic importance to the fullest attainment of health for all and to the reduction of the gap between the health status of the developing and developed countries. The promotion and protection of the health of the people is essential to sustained economic and social development and contributes to a better quality of life and to world peace.

IV

The people have the right and duty to participate individually and collectively in the planning and implementation of their health care.

V

Governments have a responsibility for the health of their people which can be fulfilled only by the provision of adequate health and social measures. A main social target of governments, international organizations and the whole world community in the coming decades should be the attainment by all peoples of the world by the year 2000 of a level of health that will permit them to lead a socially and economically productive life. Primary health care is the key to attaining this target as part of development in the spirit of social justice.

VI

Primary health care is essential health care based on practical, scientifically sound and socially acceptable methods and technology made universally accessible to individuals and families in the community through their full participation and at a cost that the community and country can afford to maintain at every stage of their development in the spirit of self-reliance and self-determination. It forms an integral part both of the country's health system, of which it is the central function and main focus, and of the overall social and economic development of the community. It is the first level of contact of individuals, the family and community with the national health system bringing health care as close as possible to where people live and work, and constitutes the first element of a continuing health care process.

VII

Primary health care:
1. reflects and evolves from the economic conditions and sociocultural and political characteristics of the country and its communities and is based on the application of the relevant results of social, biomedical and health services research and public health experience;
2. addresses the main health problems in the community, providing promotive, preventive, curative and rehabilitative services accordingly;
3. includes at least: education concerning prevailing health problems and the methods of preventing and controlling them; promotion of food supply and proper nutrition; an adequate supply of safe water and basic sanitation; maternal and child health care, 'Including family planning; immunization against the major infectious diseases; prevention and control of locally endemic

diseases; appropriate treatment of common diseases and injuries; and provision of essential drugs;

4. involves, in addition to the health sector, all related sectors and aspects of national and community development, in particular agriculture, animal husbandry, food, industry, education, housing, public works, communications and other sectors; and demands the coordinated efforts of all those sectors;

5. requires and promotes maximum community and individual self-reliance and participation in the planning, organization, operation and control of primary health care, making fullest use of local, national and other available resources; and to this end develops through appropriate education the ability of communities to participate;

6. should be sustained by integrated, functional and mutually supportive referral systems, leading to the progressive improvement of comprehensive health care for all, and giving priority to those most in need;

7. relies, at local and referral levels, on health workers, including physicians, nurses, midwives, auxiliaries and community workers as applicable, as well as traditional practitioners as needed, suitably trained socially and technically to work as a health team and to respond to the expressed health needs of the community.

VIII

All governments should formulate national policies, strategies and plans of action to launch and sustain primary health care as part of a comprehensive national health system and in coordination with other sectors. To this end, it will be necessary to exercise political will, to mobilize the country's resources and to use available external resources rationally.

IX

All countries should cooperate in a spirit of partnership and service to ensure primary health care for all people since the attainment of health by people in any one country directly concerns and benefits every other country. In this context the joint WHO/UNICEF report on primary health care constitutes a solid basis for the further development and operation of primary health care throughout the world.

X

An acceptable level of health for all the people of the world by the year 2000 can be attained through a fuller and better use of the world's resources, a considerable part of which is now spent on armaments and military conflicts. A genuine policy of independence, peace, detente and disarmament could and should release additional resources that could well be devoted to peaceful aims and in particular to the acceleration of social and economic development of which primary health care, as an essential part, should be allotted its proper share.

The International Conference on Primary Health Care calls for urgent and effective national and international action to develop and implement primary health care throughout the world and particularly in developing countries in a spirit of technical cooperation and in keeping with a New International Economic Order. It urges governments, WHO and UNICEF, and other international organizations, as well as multilateral and bilateral agencies, nongovernmental organizations, funding agencies, all health workers and the whole world community to support national and international commitment to primary health care and to channel increased technical and financial support to it, particularly in developing countries. The Conference calls on all the aforementioned to collaborate in introducing, developing and maintaining primary health care in accordance with the spirit and content of this Declaration.

REFERENCE

1. World Health Organization (WHO)/UNICEF. *Primary Health Care: Report of the International Conference on Primary Health Care, Alma-Ata, USSR, 6–12 September 1978.* Health for All Series, No.1. Geneva: WHO, 1978.

Annex B

REORIENTATION OF MEDICAL EDUCATION AND MEDICAL PRACTICE FOR HEALTH FOR ALL[1]

WHA48.8 *The Forty-eighth World Health Assembly*

Considering the need to achieve relevance, quality, cost-effectiveness and equity in health care throughout the world;

Mindful of the importance of an adequate number and mix of health care providers to achieve optimal health care delivery, of the reorientation of the education and practice of all health care providers for health for all, and of the need to begin systematic consideration of each;

Recognizing that it is important to place medical education in the context of multidisciplinary education and to provide primary health care in a multidisciplinary way;

Recognizing the important influence of medical practitioners on health care expenditure and in decisions to change the manner of health care delivery;

Aware that medical practitioners can play a pivotal role in improving the relevance, quality and cost-effectiveness of health care delivery and in attaining health for all;

Concerned that current medical practices should be adapted in order to respond better to health care needs of both individuals and communities, using existing resources;

Acknowledging the need for medical schools to improve their contribution to changes in the manner of health care delivery through more appropriate education, research and service delivery, including preventive and promotional activities, in order to respond better to people's needs and improve health status;

Recognizing that reforms in medical practice and medical education must be coordinated, relevant and acceptable;

Recognizing the important contribution that women make to the medical workforce;

Considering WHO's privileged position in facilitating working relations between health authorities, professional associations and medical schools throughout the world,

1. URGES Member States:
    (1) to review, within the context of their needs for human resources for health, the special contribution of medical practitioners and medical schools in attaining health for all;
    (2) to collaborate with all bodies concerned, including professional associations, in defining the desired profile of the future medical practitioner and, where appropriate, the respective and complementary roles of generalists and specialists and their relations with other primary health care providers, in order to respond better to people's needs and improve health status;
    (3) to promote and support health systems research to define optimal numbers, mix, deployment, infrastructure and working conditions to improve the medical practitioner's relevance and cost-effectiveness in health care delivery;
    (4) to support efforts to improve the relevance of medical educational programmes and the contribution of medical schools to the implementation of changes in health care delivery, and to reform basic education to take account of the contributions made by general practitioners to primary health care-oriented services;

2. REQUESTS the Director-General:
    (1) to promote coordinated efforts by health authorities, professional associations and medical schools to study and implement new patterns of practice and working conditions that would better enable general practitioners to identify, and to respond to, the health needs of the people they serve in order to enhance the quality, relevance, cost-effectiveness and equity of health care;
    (2) to support the development of guidelines and models that enable medical schools and other educational institutions to enhance their capacity for initial and continuing training of the medical workforce and reorient their research, clinical and community health activities in order to make an optimal contribution to changes in the manner of health care delivery;
    (3) to respond to requests from Member States for technical cooperation in the implementation of reforms in medical education and medical

practice by involving networks of WHO collaborating centres and non-governmental organizations and by using available resources within WHO;

(4) to encourage and facilitate coordination of worldwide efforts to reform medical education and medical practice in line with the principles of health for all, by cosponsoring consultative meetings and regional initiatives to put forward appropriate policies, strategies and guidelines for undergraduates and postgraduates, by collecting and disseminating relevant information and monitoring progress in the reform process;

(5) to pay particular attention to the needs of many countries that do not have facilities to train their own medical practitioners;

(6) to present to the Executive Board at its ninety-seventh session a report on the reorientation of education and practice of nurses and midwives, and at its ninety-ninth session a similar report relating to other health care providers for health for all, complementary to the reorientation of medical education and practice in this resolution, and to request the Executive Board to present its recommendations on the reorientation of nurses and midwives and other health care providers to the Forty-ninth and Fiftieth World Health Assemblies, respectively.

May 1995

REFERENCE

1. World Health Organization (WHO). *Proceedings of the 48th World Health Assembly.* WHA48/1995/REC/1; 8–10. Geneva: WHO, 1995.

Annex C

EXTRACT FROM WORLD HEALTH REPORT 2008: *PRIMARY HEALTH CARE – NOW MORE THAN EVER* [1]

What has been considered primary care in well-resourced contexts has been dangerously oversimplified in resource-constrained settings

Primary care has been defined, described and studied extensively in well-resourced contexts, often with reference to physicians with a specialization in family medicine or general practice. These descriptions provide a far more ambitious agenda than the unacceptably restrictive and off-putting primary-care recipes that have been touted for low-income countries:[2,3]

➤ Primary care provides a place to which people can bring a wide range of health problems – it is not acceptable that in low-income countries primary care would only deal with a few "priority diseases";

➤ Primary care is a hub from which patients are guided through the health system – it is not acceptable that, in low-income countries, primary care would be reduced to a stand-alone health post or isolated community-health worker;

➤ Primary care facilitates ongoing relationships between patients and clinicians, within which patients participate in decision-making about their health and health care; it builds bridges between personal health care and patients' families and communities – it is not acceptable that, in low-income countries, primary care would be restricted to a one-way delivery channel for priority health interventions;

➤ Primary care opens opportunities for disease prevention and health promotion as well as early detection of disease – it is not acceptable that, in low-income countries, primary care would just be about treating common ailments;

➤ Primary care requires teams of health professionals: physicians, nurse practitioners, and assistants with specific and sophisticated biomedical and social skills – it is not acceptable that, in low-income countries, primary care would be synonymous with low-tech, non-professional care for the rural poor who cannot afford any better;

➤ Primary care requires adequate resources and investment, and can then provide much better value for money than its alternatives – it is not acceptable that, in low-income countries, primary care would have to be financed through out-of-pocket payments on the erroneous assumption that it is cheap and the poor should be able to afford it.

REFERENCES

1. *The World Health Report 2008: Primary health care – now more than ever.* Geneva: World Health Organization, 2008. Available at: www.who.int/whr/2008/whr08_en.pdf
2. *Primary Care. America's health in a new era.* Washington DC: National Academy Press, Institute of Medicine, 1996.
3. Starfield B. *Primary Care: balancing health needs, services, and technology.* New York: Oxford University Press, 1998.

Annex D

WHO-WONCA COLLABORATION

One of the central goals of both the World Health Organization (WHO) and the World Organization of Family Doctors (WONCA) is the attainment of health for all of the world's population. This common cause has led these two organizations to communicate and collaborate on projects of mutual interest over the past 2 decades.

This collaboration was foreshadowed in 1963 by an Expert Committee of WHO in its report entitled *The Training of the Physician for Family Practice*, which stressed the need for family doctors in every country in the world, regardless of its state of economic development. In 1973 a working group of WHO emphasized the importance of primary care and defined the primary health care unit as the general medical practitioner, the nurse, and the social worker. Five years later, WHO and the United Nations International Children's Fund (UNICEF) sponsored an International Conference on Primary Health Care at Alma-Ata in the former USSR (now Almaty, Kazakstan). The historic declaration that ensued from this conference called upon the WHO, UNICEF, and other international organizations, governments, the private sector, and the public to improve the length of productive life of the population and reduce disparities in health status among population subgroups. The Alma-Ata conference acknowledged the need for countries to provide essential health services to their entire population and to have an appropriate health care workforce, and recommended "that health workers, especially physicians and nurses, should be socially and technically trained and motivated to serve the community."

As the WHO was articulating a vision of health for all in the 1970s, a significant evolution in the training of generalist physicians was occurring in countries around the world. Instead of being educated in an undifferentiated manner as in the past, generalist physicians, termed family doctors, were provided with postgraduate training specifically designed to prepare them to diagnose and treat the majority of people's health problems within the context of the people's families and communities. These efforts received substantial reinforcement at the 5th World Conference on General/Family Practice, in Melbourne, Australia in 1972, when representatives of 23 countries established the World Organization of National Colleges, Academies, and Academic Associations of General Practitioners/Family Physicians (WONCA). Today, known as the World Organization of Family Doctors, WONCA has over 100 member organizations representing family doctors from over 130 countries in all regions of the world. WONCA has expanded rapidly in recent years and now represents more than 300 000 family doctors worldwide.

Embracing the concept of health for all, this growing global community of family doctors opened a dialogue with the WHO in the early 1980s that subsequently led to WONCA being recognized as a nongovernmental organization in official relations with the WHO. In October 1993, representatives of WONCA and WHO met during an international conference, held at the National Institutes of Health in Bethesda, Maryland, the United States, that explored the means by which consultants can provide effective assistance to countries and institutions desiring to train family doctors. At this time, a global working meeting was planned to develop a common vision and action plan for improving the health of individuals and communities that would be consistent with the goals of health for all. This meeting was held in November 1994 when the two organizations convened a strategic action forum in London, Ontario, Canada, involving 60 government health officials, medical educators, family doctors and public representatives from around the world. Participants examined the roles of physicians in the health system with special emphasis on family doctors. They analyzed the obstacles nations encounter when striving to develop publicly responsive systems of health care and medical education, and recommended 21 specific actions to address these challenges. The deliberations of this strategic action forum contributed to the publication of a WHO-WONCA working paper in January 1995, *Making Medical Practice and Education More Relevant to People's Needs: the contribution of the family doctor*. The vision guiding this partnership was captured in the following joint statement from this document:

> To meet people's needs, fundamental changes must occur in the health care system, in the medical profession, and in medical schools and other educational institutions. The family doctor (general practitioner family physician) should have a central role in the achievement of quality, cost effectiveness, and equity in health care systems. To fulfill this responsibility, the family doctor must be highly competent in patient care and must integrate individual and community health care. The cooperation between

the World Health Organization (WHO) and the World Organization of
Family Doctors (WONCA) towards this vision is historic.

The document ensuing from this conference provided the foundation for an
influential resolution adopted by the World Health Assembly in May 1995, on
the reorientation of medical education and medical practice for health for all
(*see* Annex B). This resolution recognized "the important influence of medical
practitioners on health care expenditure and in decisions to change the manner
of health care delivery." It requested the WHO Director-General to encourage
and facilitate coordination of worldwide efforts to reform medical education and
practice in line with the principles of health for all.

Subsequently, WONCA and the WHO published a progress report on activities undertaken, between 1995 and 1998, to implement the recommendations
made in Ontario. This report included cases from 31 countries that described
their progress toward making medical practice and education more relevant to
people's needs. This goal was further enhanced when 57 delegates representing
56 countries met in the United Kingdom to explore the relationship between
funding systems and health care on a worldwide basis. The participants examined the fundamental concern of how payment systems relate to quality of care,
cost-effective delivery, and equity of access to health services in both rich and
poor countries.

An action plan based on a WHO-WONCA Memorandum of Understanding
for Collaborative Activities for 1998–2001 gave impetus to the development of
this guidebook by calling for joint efforts to assist nations in making appropriate
decisions regarding the development of family practice and education in support
of their primary health care–oriented systems.

This new edition of this guidebook represents one of many current cooperative efforts between WONCA and the WHO. Current joint initiatives include
work in many areas such as strengthening primary health care, mental health,
noncommunicable disease prevention and management, primary care classification, health workforce training and support, rural health, occupational health,
environmental health, social determinants of health, social accountability of
medical training, people-centered health care, communicable diseases, and
tobacco cessation. The strong association between the WHO and WONCA
continues with the two organizations united by the goals of quality, relevance,
equity, and cost-effectiveness in health services and reduction of fragmentation
through greater integration of public and personal health.

Acknowledgments

CONTRIBUTORS TO THIS SECOND EDITION

Editor: Michael Kidd

Chapter 1: Cynthia Haq (lead), Liliana Arias-Castillo, Mary Kay Hunt, Vincent Hunt, Janko Kersnik, Donald Li, Khaya Mfenyana, Dan Ostergaard, Jinan Usta, Preethi Wijegoonewardene

Chapter 2: Igor Svab (lead), Charles Boelen, Jan De Maeseneer, Alex Warner

Chapter 3: Tiago Villanueva (lead), Bruce Arroll, Luís Filipe Cavadas, Gustavo Gusso, Juan Gérvas, Kim Griswold, Lawrence Loh, Luisa Pettigrew

Chapter 4: Jeffrey Markuns (lead), Marcelo Marcos Piva Demarzo, Nandani de Silva, Ilse Hellemann-Geschwinder, Inderjit Singh Ludher, Roar Maagaard, Allyn Walsh

Chapter 5: Waris Qidwai (lead), Samia Almusallam, William E Cayley Jr, Felicity Goodyear-Smith, Gustavo Gusso, Victor Inem, Tawfik AM Khoja, Meng-Chih Lee, Lesley Pocock

Chapter 6: Wim Van Lerberghe, Hernan Montenegro (leads), Dheepa Rajan, Mart Leys, Yun Yu (introduction), Claunara Schilling Mendonça (Brazil), Chen Bowen, Dong Yanmin, Guo Aimin, Yin Delu (China), Sameen Siddiqi, Hassan Salah, Mohammad Assai (Eastern Mediterranean), Yongyuth Pongsupap (Thailand)

Chapter 7: Maaike Flinkenflögel (Rwanda), Bob Mash (South Africa), Olayinka O Ayankogbe (Nigeria), Steve Reid (South Africa), Akye Essuman (Ghana), Jan De Maeseneer (Belgium)

Reviewers: Iona Heath, Jan De Maeseneer, Hernan Montenegro, Marc Rivo, Edward Shahady

Technical support: Alfred Loh, Garth Manning, Rachel Cork, Julie-Anne Burton

CONTRIBUTORS TO THE FIRST EDITION

The original edition of this guidebook was prepared by coauthors: Charles Boelen, Cynthia Haq, Vincent Hunt, Marc Rivo and Edward Shahady. Marc Rivo and Edward Shahady developed the concept and first draft with the guidance of a steering committee sponsored by the World Health Organization (WHO) and the World Organization of Family Doctors (WONCA). Working with Charles Boelen in Geneva, Cynthia Haq and Vincent Hunt amplified and revised the guidebook with valuable input from WHO staff. The coauthors prepared a final draft that was reviewed by WHO staff and members of WONCA. The final version was completed based upon reviewers' helpful feedback.

Overall direction was provided by the joint WHO-WONCA steering committee, which was composed of Dan Baden, Charles Boelen, Michael Boland, Wes Fabb, Alan Fatayi-Williams, Robert W Higgins, Vincent Hunt, Daniel J Ostergaard, Reg Perkin, Marc Rivo, Robert Schwartz, Edward Shahady, and Adam Windak. Oversight was provided by Ilse Hellemann, the WONCA liaison person to the WHO.

Many others contributed to the guidebook. Authors who provided specific sections include Marjukka Makela, Barbara Booth, and Richard Roberts (Enhancing quality of care and outcomes), John Beasley (Supporting primary care research), Denis Pereira Gray, Philip H Evans, Russell Steele, Adrian Freeman (Establishing professional organizations for family doctors), Scott Brown (Financing primary health care services and family doctors), and Wes Fabb (Promoting positive relationships, Resource Directory). Barbara Starfield contributed advice and critique of selected chapters and Mary Kay Hunt provided assistance throughout.

Others who assisted with specific aspects of the report, case studies, or feedback were Ian Couper, Javier Dominguez del Olmo, Pham Huy Dung, Sam Fehrsen, Abra Fransch, Adrian Freeman, Craig Gjerde, Jamie Gofan, Shatendra Gupta, Marc Hansen, Warren Heffron, Per Hjortdahl, Abraham Joseph, Zorayda Leopando, Alain Montegut, Marconi Monteiro, Faisal Al Naser, Robert Parkerson, Perry Pugno, Winnie Siao, Stephen Spann, Renato Torres, Chris van Weel, and Taiwoo Yoo. Many others contributed to this guidebook through their invaluable work, which has been incorporated into this publication and gratefully referenced. Valuable input was received from WHO staff including Orvill Adams, Ala Alwan, Raphael Bengoa, Philip Musgrove, Mario Dal Poz, Naeema AI-Gasseer, Alexandre Goubarev, Haile Kahssay, Kimmo Leppo, and Jorn Heldrup. Funding to support the project was provided through a contract from the WHO to WONCA.

The original version of this guidebook was published under the direction of

Alfred WT Loh, Chief Executive Officer, and Yvonne Chung, Administrative Manager, of WONCA. Administrative and technical support was provided by Nadine Buzzetti, Janet Clevenstine, Amel Chaouachi, and Aaron Lawrence, with editorial assistance from Angela Haden.

CHAPTER 6 OF THE SECOND EDITION

Index

Pages in *italics* refer to boxes; pages in **bold** refer to tables.

CPD with Radcliffe

You can now use a selection of our books to achieve CPD (Continuing Professional Development) points through directed reading.

We provide a free online form and downloadable certificate for your appraisal portfolio. Look for the CPD logo and register with us at: www.radcliffehealth.com/cpd